LONDON B(

CEN   `ARY`

In th
the

ULSTER 1969: THE FIGHT FOR CIVIL RIGHTS IN NORTHERN IRELAND

ULSTER 1969

The Fight for Civil Rights in Northern Ireland

by

MAX HASTINGS

LONDON
VICTOR GOLLANCZ LTD
1970

© Max Hastings 1970

ISBN 0 575 00482 7

PRINTED AND BOUND IN GREAT BRITAIN BY

THE GARDEN CITY PRESS LIMITED

LETCHWORTH, HERTFORDSHIRE

For Françoise

CONTENTS

LIST OF ILLUSTRATIONS

ACKNOWLEDGEMENTS

The high moments of 1968 and 1969 were spread over many months and many miles. For those I did not cover myself, I have drawn heavily on the help of other reporters and witnesses. Gerry Brown, who reported Ulster for the *Sun* until October 1969, has provided me with much essential information and guidance. Indirectly, anyone who covered Northern Ireland in 1969 would hand an outstanding bouquet to Harold Jackson of the *Guardian*, whose reporting of the main events showed many of us which way we should be looking. Fergus Pyle of the *Irish Times* probably knows Ulster politics better than any other permanent correspondent in Belfast, and once again almost every reporter in Ulster drew heavily on him for help and assistance. I owe much to Miss Carol Flynn, who has researched most of the basic information material and typed the manuscript. Also, there are the long-suffering Information Officers of the Ulster Government both in Belfast and in London, who from the beginning did their best to see that we knew their side of it. Tom McCaffery and Steve Andrews of the Home Office in London provided invaluable guidance. The judgements and the errors, however, belong to no one but myself.

I covered Ulster for the London *Evening Standard*, to whom I owe a special debt—for making up my mind for me. From the beginning of the year, whenever warned to stand by for Ulster, I couldn't decide between a groan at the prospect of more weeks in Belfast, and a magnetic fascination for the events unfolding there. The *Standard*, I'm delighted to say in retrospect, just told me which plane I'd be catching. . . .

For additional information on the crisis, the Report of Lord Cameron's Commission on the Disturbances in Northern Ireland is the invaluable work of reference from October 1968 to April 1969. Andrew Boyd's *Holy War In Belfast* offers a fascinating insight into the roots of sectarian unrest in the nineteenth century. Bowes Egan and Andrew McCormick's *Burntollet*, while written from an unashamedly Catholic standpoint, is a very useful guide to the events of January 4th 1969 and those which preceded them. Terence O'Neill has collected many of his own major speeches in *Ulster At The Crossroads*, with an introduction by John Cole. And Bernadette Devlin has given her impressions of some of the events in which she participated in *The Price Of My Soul*. For reminders on many of the names, dates and places, I have relied on the files of the London *Times* and the *Belfast Telegraph*.

London, February 1970   MAX HASTINGS

PREFACE

On the night of Thursday, August 14th 1969, this reporter was crouching beneath a Catholic block of flats in the Falls Road, Belfast, as a police armoured car roared past, turret traversing. Suddenly it screeched to a halt, and a long burst of fire from its heavy machine gun echoed the length of the street. Behind the corners half the way down the road lay police whose sub-machine guns and revolvers had been blazing intermittently for more than an hour. Two policemen wounded by snipers were being tended in the shelter of an armoured personnel carrier; flames were pouring from burning buildings higher up the street. A few minutes later, I was watching a nine-year-old Catholic boy dying where he lay, half his head blown away by a burst of automatic fire. Behind the police line, groups of Protestants armed with petrol bombs, dust-bin lids and staves wandered with impunity.

Had this been Chicago, Washington or Detroit, the scene might have been made almost bearable by its awful familiarity. But Belfast is part of Northern Ireland, Northern Ireland is part of Britain, and these were British policemen in a British city engaged in full-scale battle with British citizens. This melodrama had been played here before, it was to be played here again before 1969 was out, and New Year brought little guarantee against repetition. In London and Manchester, Plymouth and Hull—every city in England—people read their newspapers, were appalled, and yet totally bewildered.

I sat one day with a group of reporters in the lounge of our hotel in Belfast, all of us filled with despair and gloom after the slaughter and destruction of the previous weeks. By chance a leading English Catholic came in. He was in Belfast on a brief visit to look at the latest developments, and joined us for a chat. Why were we so miserable? Why were we so pessimistic? he asked. Was it not much better to look at all that was happening not as a meaningless tragedy, but as a very positive revolution? He felt

13

that however unhappy the death and devastation, the great victories Catholics were reaping more than justified them, in the long span of history. Perhaps his historical judgement will prove correct. But for anyone who knows Northern Ireland, whatever their religion, it is a difficult view to live with now. It may be argued that the Protestants and Unionists have done much to create the situation in which Ulster finds itself. But the Catholics are paying a bitter price for their prizes, however thoroughly justified.

For a "foreign" reporter covering Northern Ireland in 1969, it was weeks if not months before any shadow of understanding dawned. Well into 1969, it was very easy to treat Ulster with a kind of horrified disdain. But gradually also, fascination crept in. In England, we are indifferent to religion and thus tolerant about it. But in Ireland, the Fear of God allied to other, more mundane prejudices, is still real enough to drive men to violent battle.

Before the crises of 1968 and 1969 burst upon us, we might have heard of Terence O'Neill, possibly even of Cardinal Conway; but certainly not of Bernadette Devlin, John Hume, Ian Paisley, William Craig. Yet by the end of 1969, these names were almost household words. We felt we knew the streets of Belfast and Londonderry almost as well as those of London. We had seen the British Army engaged in shooting battles on British soil. We had 8,000 troops defending British citizens from each other. In 1969, we had an Irish problem once more. Kings and Queens have come and gone, the motor car is on our streets, men travel to the moon— but the Irish are always with us. And one of the earliest casualties of 1969 was the English privilege of speaking of Ireland facetiously.

This book is an attempt to fill in some of the gaps and to suggest some reasons for the events of 1968 and 1969 at a length the racing pace of the time made impossible. The Irish, no doubt, will merely add it to the long list of injustices perpetrated against them by the uncomprehending English. And it would be impossible to try to look at Northern Ireland embattled as we saw it, without considering first something of what has gone before. For this latest Irish crisis has very little to do with the twentieth century. It is the face of the ghost of history, four hundred years of insoluble hopelessness risen to haunt a new generation of politicians and priests.

I

WITHIN THE ENGLISH PALE

Like France and Germany; Greece and Turkey; Athens and
Sparta, England and Ireland have never been good neighbours.
For more than four hundred years, we have made a thorough job
of despising the Irish, and in return, they don't much like us. We
regard them as feckless and over-romantic, disorganised and above
all, belligerent. Certainly we love James Joyce and Brendan Behan
(now that they are dead). We delight in the Dublin Horse Show
or an invitation to Donegal. But historically, successive generations
of Englishmen have mistrusted, misunderstood and misgoverned
Ireland since time immemorial.

Most of our ancestors regarded the Irish with utter contempt:
Lancaster, in Marlowe's *Edward II*, recalled how "The wild
Oneyl with swarms of Irish kerns lives uncontrolled within the
English pale". Sidney Smith wrote, at the beginning of the
nineteenth century: "The moment the very name of Ireland is
mentioned, the English seem to bid adieu to common feeling,
common prudence and common sense, and to act with the bar-
barity of tyrants and the fatuity of idiots."* A few years later, the
Hare brothers added: "Every Irishman, the saying goes, has a
potato in his head. . . ."†

In modern times, the invective and the suspicion have merely
become better directed, while the sentiment remains little changed.
We have always liked to feel that Ireland is our national cross, a
burden to be borne with reluctant generosity. We hate to be reminded that the English presence in Ireland was one the Irish
themselves never sought, and indeed struggled for much of their
history to be rid of.

From the time of the first English essays into Ireland, the natives
faced them with fierce resistance. As early as the mid-twelfth
century, Anglo-Norman raiders and settlers had begun to descend
on the island, to be followed by English kings and expeditionary

---

* *Peter Plymley's Letters.*   † *Guesses at Truth*, series I.

forces in a long series of half-hearted attempts at conquest. They found an anarchic wilderness, but a resilient one. Their ventures left little impact, and it was not until the sixteenth century that the Tudor rulers of England embarked on and accomplished the total subjugation of the Irish. They succeeded only after a prolonged struggle, and although by the beginning of the seventeenth century Ireland was in English hands, the north was still very uncertainly held.

It was in 1609, with James I on the throne of England, that the Ulster of 1969 found its roots. James, himself a Scot, established a new colony of Scots and northern Englishmen in the north of Ireland in an attempt to create a power base for English rule. The north had been the most hostile corner of the country, and it was James' clear intention to ensure that it should be a threat no longer. The men who came to the north in "The Plantation of Ulster" were utterly different from the native Irish in character and outlook: mostly of Calvinistic faith and passionately British in their allegiance. Across the rest of Ireland, the Protestant landlords were thinly scattered and varied in their fortunes. But the Protestant settlement in Ulster grew, prospered, and became a dominant economic influence across the country. These new Irishmen tilled their farms, built up towns, raised cattle and cherished their religion. Such native Irish as were left became their servants or tenants.

Protestant domination, the introduction of English law and the ruination of the old Irish aristocracy drove the native Catholics to revolt in 1641. They retook much of the country and could not be suppressed while the English Civil War ran its own unhappy course across the Irish Sea. Finally, however, the victorious Cromwell brought his Ironsides to Ireland to smash the rebels. The Catholic Irish were broken, most of their leaders killed, and a new influx of English landlords brought in to bolster the victors' grasp once more.

But Cromwell's merciless battery had left a new residue of Catholic bitterness. Forty years later, the coming of William and Mary to the English throne in 1688 sent the evicted James II to Ireland, rallying support among his Catholic co-religionists to regain his kingdom. Once again, the English lost almost the entire province; only in the north did the Protestants show their mettle for the first time and hold Londonderry and Enniskillen against desperate Catholic siege until Protestant William of Orange relieved them with his armies. He defeated the rebels at the Battle of the Boyne in 1690. The Derrymen, loyal to England when all Ireland was in rebellion, had established a pride in their Protestantism against all comers that was to survive the span of three hundred years.

But in the eighteenth century, the non-conformist Protestants in Ireland found themselves in little better case than the Catholics. Both sects were ruthlessly persecuted, and the province faced a succession of disastrous famines and ever tighter English rule. When another abortive rising occurred in 1798, many of the rebels were Irish Protestants who were foremost in seeking revolution. In its wake, several Presbyterian leaders were hanged, and while restrictions on Catholicism had been eased a little, those on Protestant non-conformism to the Established Church remained severe for some time.

In 1801, England's relations with Ireland entered a new phase when the London Government determined to silence the Irish once and for all by uniting them totally with England. But the Act of Union achieved little. Periodic famine, the appalling abuses of English absentee landlords, and increasing Irish nationalism kept the province in a state of miserable unrest and growing tension throughout the nineteenth century.

From the early nineteenth century onwards, the Irish tragedy gained momentum rapidly. In the north especially, the situation worsened. As early as 1795, a Protestant society known as the Orange Order, founded allegedly to commemorate William of Orange's links with Ulster, had been created. Its purpose, it was announced, was "to maintain the laws and peace of the country and the Protestant constitution". Its membership soared to 200,000 in 1797. A few years later it was banned as a secret society, and suffered a considerable decline. But then came the development of political and religious thought which, within less than forty years, created the seeds of Northern Ireland as it is today, and boosted the fortunes of the Orange Order to new heights.

Even as late as the 1820's, relations between Catholics and Protestants in the north were relatively cordial. But as the boom in industry and the growth of the north gained speed, so the gulf between Catholic and Protestant communities widened. The Catholic Irish were experiencing a dramatic growth in nationalist feeling, and as their clamour for independence from England became louder across Ireland, so the Protestants' attachment to

England, most of all in the north where they were most concentrated, became more pronounced.

Allied to this came a sudden religious upsurge of militant Protestantism which drove an even more violent wedge between Protestants and Catholics. In the 1830's, Henry Cooke, a leader of the Presbyterian Church in Belfast, began to make a strong impact on local Protestants with a gospel of hatred and fear of Catholicism. Protestants—always in a numerical majority in the north—tightened their grip on civic power, while street preachers, lesser Cookes, roused the Protestant poor to fury. Rioting became an almost annual occurrence in July and August when the Protestants celebrated the anniversaries of the Battle of the Boyne and the Siege of Londonderry. The same words and the same people in the same streets as those of 1969 turned Belfast in the nineteenth century into a city of terror and loathing: "Your blood-bought and cherished rights have been imperilled by the audacious and savage outrages of a Romish mob", wrote one Protestant preacher addressing his flock. ". . . But you are not to be bullied or cajoled out of your rights. They are not to be surrendered, and they are to be strenuously maintained. . . ."

It was no easier then to ask how such words found their echo in gun battles and destruction than it is now. The results were the same:

"On Sunday morning, 17 August, the streets around Millfield, the Pound, Shankill Road and Falls Road were in a state of utter desolation . . . everywhere pavements were torn up. In some streets barricades were erected and shops boarded up against attack. In every street which bordered on the Catholic and Protestant districts, pickets of armed police and soldiers stood guard. . . ."*

Not yet 1969, this was Belfast in 1872. Government Commissions of Inquiry came, inquired, confirmed allegations of police partiality for the Protestants and unjustified aggression, but could do little. One such body reported after the 1857 riots, considering the role of the Orange Order:

"The Orange system seems to us to have no other practical result than as a means of keeping up the Orange festivals, and celebrating them, leading as they do to violence, outrage, religious animosities, hatred between classes, and too often,

* *Holy War in Belfast*, Andrew Boyd, Anvil Books 1969.

18

NORTHERN IRELAND

Scale of Miles

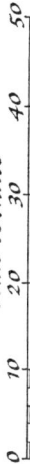

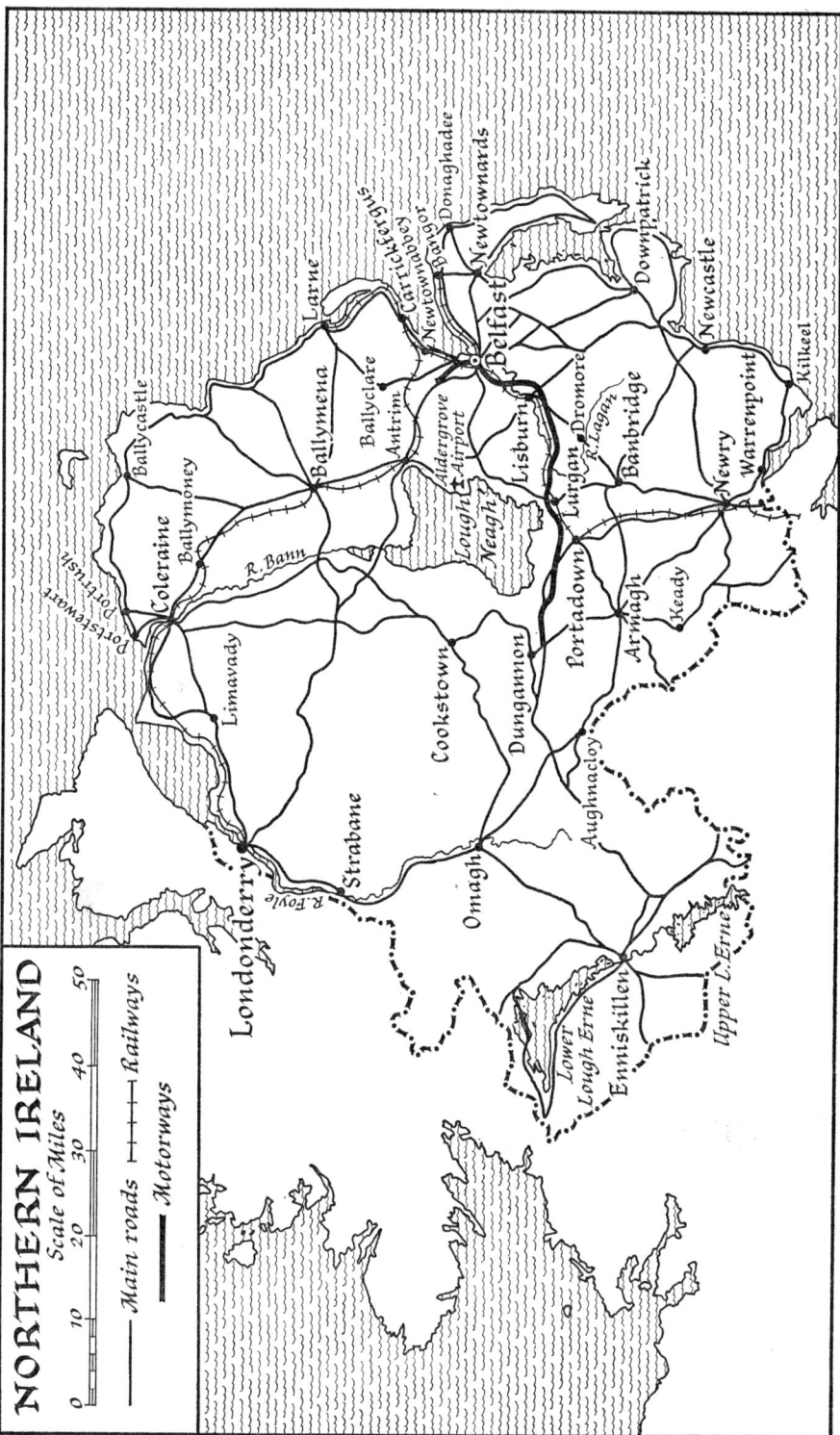

0 10 20 30 40 50

—— Main roads   +++ Railways
——— Motorways

Londonderry
Portstewart
Portrush
Coleraine
Ballycastle
Ballymoney
Ballymena
Larne
Ballyclare
Antrim
Carrickfergus
Newtownabbey
Bangor
Donaghadee
Newtownards
Belfast
Aldergrove Airport
Lisburn
Lough Neagh
Lurgan
Dromore
R. Lagan
Banbridge
Downpatrick
Newcastle
Warrenpoint
Kilkeel
Newry
Keady
Armagh
Portadown
Dungannon
Aughnacloy
Cookstown
Limavady
R. Bann
Strabane
R. Foyle
Omagh
Enniskillen
Lower Lough Erne
Upper L. Erne

bloodshed and loss of life. These opinions have been forced upon us, and, in giving them, we feel a hope that when the kind and generous minds belonging to the Orange Society see the results attending this organisation—so different from what they intended—they will think that it is well to consider whether there is any controlling necessity to keep it alive, notwithstanding the evils that, unfortunately, attend its existence."

Such words fell then, as they fall now, on deaf ears. The Protestants continued to beat their drums, parade their religion and fall to immediate battle when the Catholic nationalists of Belfast displayed their own colours in the streets. The more violent became the demands for independence from the nationalists in Dublin, the more sectarian, fanatical and anti-Catholic became the Protestants of north-east Ireland. As feeling rose, each riot raised the temper for the next. Catholics were being driven from factories, even from their homes, and forced further and further into a segregated existence.

The full consequence of northern Protestant militance became violently apparent as the final act in the nationalists' struggle for Irish independence began in the last quarter of the nineteenth century. Gladstone, as Prime Minister at Westminster, was making a series of determined attempts to persuade England that Ireland must be granted Home Rule. His efforts both united and enraged the Protestants of the north, so desperate to remain British. Gladstone being a Liberal, they became Tories—and "Unionists"—almost to a man. Membership of the Orange Order and a belief in Unionism became virtually synonymous. Despite the failure of Gladstone's own efforts, as Ireland moved into the twentieth century a new generation of English politicians pressed the Home Rule issue yet again, and the Ulster Protestants prepared to fight by force of arms, if need be. They signed a Covenant declaring their absolute commitment to remaining a part of Britain, and they began to run in guns to resist the creation of an independent Ireland. The outbreak of the First World War temporarily defused the situation as the Irish issue was forgotten. But the Dublin Easter Rising of 1916 by the Irish nationalists, although smashed, impressed on the British Government that Home Rule must come. In its aftermath, they set about the immensely complex task of attempting to settle Ireland once and for all.

In this, they appeared to be faced with a complete impasse. The nationalists in the South—a firm majority of all Irishmen—wanted total independence for the whole of Ireland. The northern Protestants—nearly a million of them—were still utterly determined to remain a part of Britain. The nationalists themselves misunderstood, as many still misunderstand, the attitude of the British Government to their demands. Most Englishmen would have been more than happy to dispose of Ireland lock, stock and barrel. But the certainty that to do so would provoke devastating civil war made compromise the only possibility.

The British Government's initial attempt to achieve this was the 1920 Government of Ireland Act. Under its terms, the six north-eastern counties (known as Ulster, although Ulster technically comprises nine counties) were separated from the other twenty-six counties of Ireland. Both North and South were to have their own Parliaments, with the framework of a Common Council to administer all Ireland as and when the two fragments could settle their differences. The whole structure was to remain self-governing within the British Empire—government to be administered, thus, in the King's name, as a sop to the northern Protestants, who would have much preferred to remain absolutely a part of Britain.

In the event, however, much of this arrangement collapsed in ruins. Civil War broke out in the South between those who were prepared to accept the Act and those who were not, and the struggle spilled over into the North. It had been agreed that it would be impossible to transfer all Catholics to the South and all Protestants to the North,* and many Catholics on both sides of the new Border were outraged at the Partition settlement. Those in the North were unwilling to be left to the mercies of Protestants who outnumbered them by two to one, and those in the South came North to join battle with the Protestants to prove their point.

In the end, although Catholic extremists continued sporadic guerilla warfare in the north for many years, something like peace was re-established, but on new terms. The South embarked on complete self-government in 1925, finally separating from the British Commonwealth in name as well as in fact in 1949. The plan for the "Common Council" was forgotten, and the Northern Parliament which had been established in 1921 went on its way

* In 1969, there were only 5 per cent Protestants among the 3 million population of the Irish Republic.

governing Ulster's internal affairs without co-operation or consultation with the South. The British Government at Westminster retained power over taxation, foreign affairs, defence and other supra-provincial matters, but was only too happy to leave Northern Ireland to run itself as best it might. It can be powerfully argued that had England been less hasty in shrugging off all real interest in the North at this stage, had Westminster returned to ruling Ulster like any other part of the United Kingdom, the events of 1969 would never have taken place. The Protestant majority in Ulster had not sought internal self-government, and they were acutely aware that they gained it only because the English regarded it as a stepping stone to getting rid of them altogether.

But at least they had gained an enclave—after a desperate struggle. And having done so, they set out to fortify it from threats from Dublin or from within Ulster with a determination and thoroughness Cromwell himself would have respected.

Understanding the Northern Ireland of 1969 becomes much easier for an outsider if he sees the Northern Ireland of the 1920's as the Protestants themselves saw it: a fortress, whose establishment and survival had been desperately threatened for years by politicians, Catholics and Irish nationalists: the Protestant peoples within it passionately attached to Britain, yet not to the reality of Britain, but to an ideal that barely existed then and certainly does no longer. There are significant numbers of them left today in Ulster—extremists, but men of whom much more will be heard later.

"Caricatures of Ulster Protestants," one Catholic calls them, "out-Britishing the British by a long shot. They are mad keen on the Union Jack . . . and they'll swear blind that Harold Wilson isn't British. Only the Tories are British, and the further they move from fascism, the more they are declining from British standards. The Paisleyites don't really want to have anything to do with England, because England has forgotten it's British. At one point they were talking about UDI—a Unilateral Declaration of Independence, on the model of Ian Smith and Rhodesia—which would leave Ulster the only unsullied little corner of the British Isles. . . ."*

But in 1969 as in 1921, the Protestants cling to Britain because they need her so desperately. Without her, as most of them

* *The Price of My Soul,* Bernadette Devlin, André Deutsch 1969.

were and are convinced, Ulster would be swallowed up by the dreaded Republic to the South.

The story of Ulster since it became a self-governing province has been entirely dominated by this pathological dread of absorption by the South. "The Border" has been the magic phrase in Ulster politics since 1920. Even now, it is impossible to discuss Ulster's future with many Northern Ireland Protestants without pre-assuring them in every sentence that there is no question of abandoning them to the Republic. They know very well, as they have always known, that the English care not at all for them, nor whether they belong to Ulster, the Republic, or Siberia. They have always had good reason to feel that if their interests are to be safeguarded, they must look to them themselves.

The facts of history had contributed much to creating the gulf between the Irish, Protestant and Catholic. Allied to this, among the Protestants, was a religious fervour uncommon in 1920 and unheard of anywhere else in Britain today. There are also some notable differences in character between Ulster Protestants and Ulster Catholics. It is broadly true that the Protestants have a more organised attitude to life, which can verge on dourness, and an industry and thoroughness that many Catholics lack. They are dogged, determined, and commercially orientated—in short, they like making money and are better at it than the Catholics. Frequently, they lack the gaiety and charm which many Catholics possess and which make them seem so much more forgivable even when they are at their worst. But the Protestants consider that they created Ulster, built it into what it is by their own blood and sweat, while the Catholics "played their harps, got drunk and worshipped Popery". It is a conviction which has governed the Protestant philosophy in Ulster for more than a hundred years, and like most such beliefs has just the element of truth in it which makes it appear a viable arguing base.

Beyond this, too, is an even deeper uneasiness which has lasted since the creation of Ulster as a province, about the basic loyalty of the Catholic minority within the state. In July 1933 Sir Basil Brooke—later Lord Brookeborough, Prime Minister of Ulster 1943–1963—told an Orange Assembly that "Catholics were out to destroy Ulster with all their might and power". In a sense, he was right. There can have been few Catholics in Ulster who had wished to become a sectarian minority in a Protestant state. Yet before Partition, as the Irish nationalists struggled for their right

23

to total Irish independence, the Ulster Protestants too had felt that they had their right: that of a choice of continuing their tie with Britain. Even this, it seemed, the Catholics sought to deny them. Throughout the 1920's, as Ulster's police battled with the guerillas of the Irish Republican Army, the Protestants could not withstand a feeling that the Ulster Catholics within their community were at best neutral, at worst determined enemy sympathisers. Even today, in Protestant terms, Catholic loyalty to the conception of Ulster—which several hundred Northern Irish Protestants have died to defend over the last fifty-odd years—is a frail thing. Economic standards in the Republic are notably lower than in the North, and Welfare benefits are far inferior. Northern Ireland itself is scarcely more viable economically than the South, but massive aid from England raises the standard of living, and unemployment benefits and pension rights are far above those Dublin can afford. Every Catholic as well as every Protestant is well aware of these facts. If only because of them, the vast majority of Ulster Catholics have no immediate wish to be part of a United Ireland separated from England. But were these economic differences removed, there can be no doubt that emotionally, many Catholics would dearly love to be part of the Republic. In their terms, they can have no real loyalty to a Northern Ireland run by the Protestants. They could hope for much more from the South in terms of a say in their own lives.

The Protestants, meanwhile, maintain their leech-like attachment to Britain. Perhaps above all, they have not forgotten the Second World War, when Britain's survival depended on the Battle of the Atlantic. The vital bases of the Irish Republic were denied to us, and Catholic Ireland remained a hostile neutral. Protestant Ulster, on the other hand, fighting with Britain and the Allies, made a critical difference in turning the tide towards us. They had held Londonderry for England in the seventeenth century, they held Ulster for us in the twentieth. The Catholics, they would argue, have brought us only grief.

In the light of all this, an outsider may feel tempted to share the view of some Northern Irishmen that democracy, as we understand it, is an almost unattainable prize for Ulster. For in a successful democracy, the extremes of left and right wings, of government and of opposition, must somehow be contained within a framework of consensus, of consent and agreement between the governed and the governing. This consent between the million

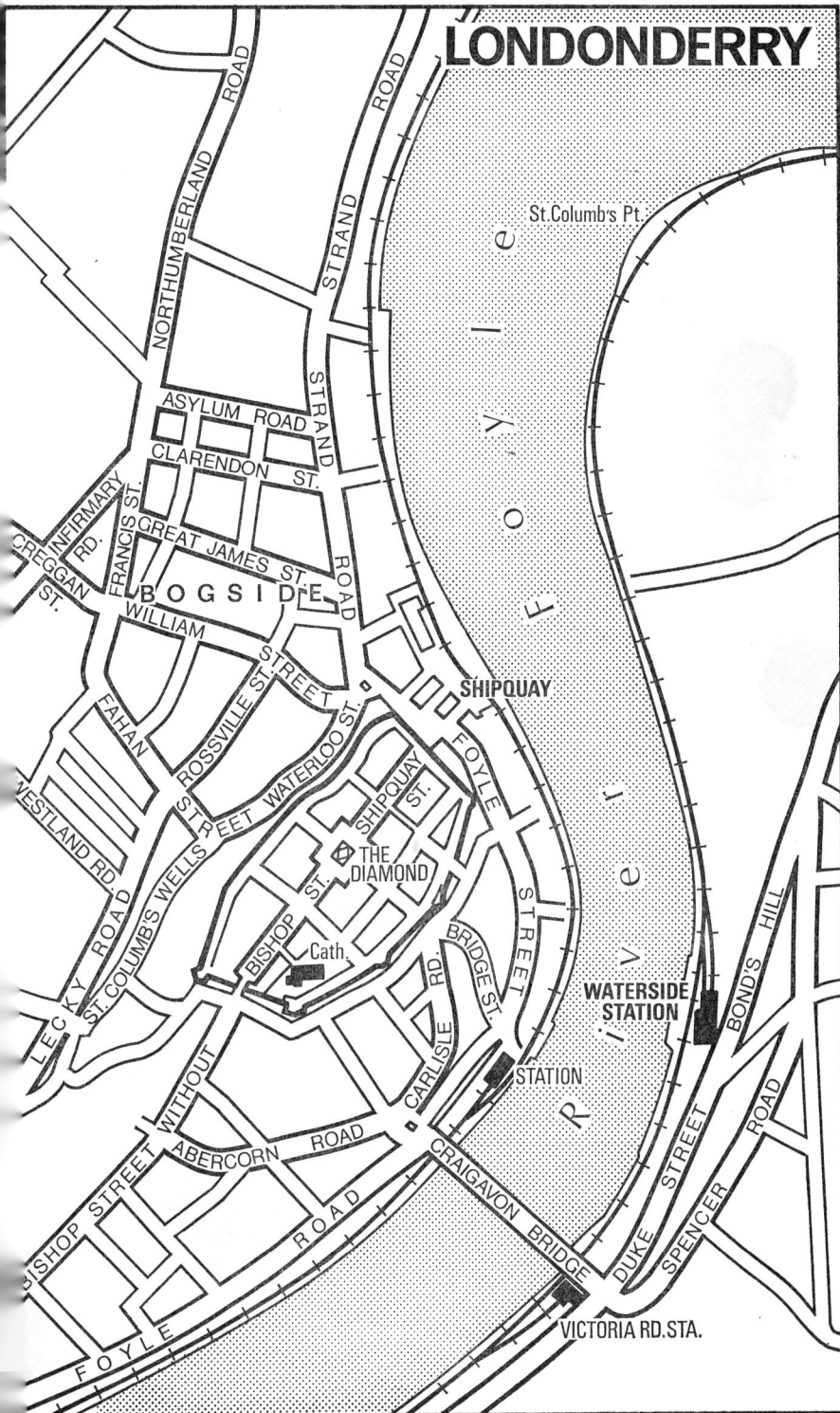

LONDONDERRY

St.Columb's Pt.

NORTHUMBERLAND ROAD

STRAND ROAD

ASYLUM ROAD

CLARENDON ST.

INFIRMARY RD.

FRANCIS ST.

CREGGAN ST.

GREAT JAMES ST.

STRAND ROAD

B O G S I D E

WILLIAM STREET

FAHAN STREET

ROSSVILLE ST.

WATERLOO ST.

WESTLAND RD.

ST COLUMB'S WELLS

LECKY ROAD

SHIPQUAY ST.

THE DIAMOND

BISHOP ST.

Cath.

SHIPQUAY

FOYLE STREET

BRIDGE ST.

CARLISLE RD.

F o y l e

R i v e r

WATERSIDE STATION

BOND'S HILL

STATION

BISHOP STREET WITHOUT

ABERCORN ROAD

ROAD

CRAIGAVON BRIDGE

DUKE STREET

SPENCER ROAD

F O Y L E

VICTORIA RD.STA.

Protestants and the half-million Catholics in Ulster has proved a desperately elusive goal. Since 1921, many Catholics have been very reluctant to offer more than a grudging lip-service to Ulster's Constitution—it is the only part of the United Kingdom to have such a document, written and specified, guaranteeing its continuing links with England.

When the self-governing Province of Northern Ireland was established, the Protestant leadership, on the other hand, had the very clearest ideas of how the machinery of democracy was to be adapted to ensure absolute and irrevocable Protestant supremacy. Under the terms of the settlement with the British Government at Westminster, power in Ulster was to rest nominally in the hands of a Governor (in 1969, Lord Grey of Naunton) in the name of the Crown. Below him, the province's internal affairs were to be governed by a Northern Ireland Parliament in Belfast. This Parliament comprised a House of Commons of fifty-two members and a Senate of twenty-six (the latter held little effective power). Northern Ireland had its own Prime Minister and Cabinet. The province passed its own domestic legislation, and within certain limits could choose which laws enacted by the British Government came into force in Northern Ireland.*

Ulster Protestants understood, even before the end of the nineteenth century, the importance of presenting a united front to the London Government, and against the Irish nationalists. When Northern Ireland's first Parliament met in 1921, the Protestant standard bearer was the Unionist Party. From that moment on, for more than forty years, the Unionists have fought with each other within the party, but only a tiny minority of Protestants have ever dared part company altogether with the body that represents the basis of their creed. The Unionists have always enjoyed an unshakeable majority in the Ulster House of Commons. In the handful of constituencies where Catholics can vote in sufficient numbers, Opposition M.P.s have been elected, but they are few in number, and almost invariably divided among themselves. After the 1969 election, there were still only thirteen Opposition members against thirty-nine Unionists. When Sir James Craig, Ulster's first Prime Minister, spoke gleefully of a "Protestant Government for a Protestant people", he could do so with assurance. In Ulster politics, there are no nation-wide swings at elections such

---

* Westminster's recent reforms of the laws on homosexuality, abortion, and divorce have not been introduced in Ulster for example.

as ring the changes on Governments and Presidents in England and America. When the chips are down, Protestants and Unionists become one at the ballot box. In effect, Ulster politics are Unionist politics. In most Ulster parliamentary constituencies, the election result is a foregone conclusion—a Unionist victory.

This means that the selection of the candidate is the really critical point in the democratic process. He is chosen by vote of the local Unionist association and that association has immense power to discomfit him if, as an M.P., he displeases it. A Unionist M.P. must prove that he is more Unionist than any other Unionist. He must bend his ear sharply when a senior member of the Orange Order indicates that he has something to say to him. And he must never forget that blackmail and intimidation, sometimes of a terrifyingly crude nature, are never far below the surface of Ulster politics. It is a style more familiar in Chicago than in London, and more easily understood if one conceives of Ulster not as a country nor even as a province, but as a village, where all is known and much is used. And since politics tend to become more extreme the further they are removed from the centre of power, so at grass roots level the local Unionists of the constituency associations are the greatest hard-liners of all. The full part the local associations played in influencing the actions and attitudes of M.P.s in 1969 will never be known, but that which is known is alarming enough. The machinery of the Unionist party is rusty, and until the crises of 1968 and 1969 it had been unchallenged for more than forty years. In many places it was grossly corrupt, and because of the self-perpetuating nature of the system, immensely difficult to reform. What has been surprising is not how many knaves and fools it produced, but that it brought forth at least a small core of decent, reasonably competent and honourable men. Since Ulster's beginnings, the size of the Protestant majority in the population guaranteed the safety of Unionism.

In addition to electing M.P.s to its own House of Commons, Ulster also returns twelve M.P.s to the Westminster Parliament. At the end of 1968, of these ten were Unionists, one was Labour and one seat was vacant. There had never been the slightest difficulty about ensuring supremacy when in the great majority of parliamentary constituencies in Ulster, the Protestants were in a very safe majority. There being no call for gerrymandering or serious meddling to achieve the desired result, full adult suffrage had been in force at parliamentary elections for many years.

But despite this happy state of affairs for the Unionists at a provincial level, Ulster Protestants had faced the harch reality that in certain of the areas controlled by Ulster's seventy-one local authorities, the Catholics were in a regional majority sufficient to dominate some councils. The Protestant answer to this was a system of ward-rigging which, together with a voting qualification which disenfranchised many Catholics in local elections, contributed greatly to the bitterness which erupted in 1968 and 1969. In Londonderry, where Catholics outnumber Protestants by around 36,000 to 18,000, the Unionists still managed to hold twelve out of twenty seats on the City Council until December 1968, when the Council was replaced by a statutory Development Commission after massive protests. Similar inequities prevailed in Armagh, Dungannon, Fermanagh, Newry, Omagh and other towns. Until 1969, housing in Ulster was largely in the hands of local councils, and there was the clearest evidence that in many areas Protestant-dominated councils had used their powers to discriminate against Catholics in the distribution of accommodation. They also pursued a firm policy of giving jobs in local government bureaucracy to Protestants wherever possible. With political power of such an invincible kind, the Unionists could leave the Catholic minority to beg in vain for crumbs from the Protestant table. Since the political structure they had established in 1921 was exactly that with which the Catholics found themselves embattled in 1969, its provisions had shown a lasting, if not an edifying character.

The Protestants of the 1920's had thus secured total effective political, economic and legislative control of Northern Ireland. Behind this power, they were able to establish a police force to guard their society that remained in 1968 one of the most formidable in the Western world. The Royal Ulster Constabulary was set up in 1922. At intervals for much of its early life, its prime function was to join battle with and to defeat the terrorists of the illegal Southern Irish Republican Army. It was trained and equipped to do this on para-military lines. By the 1960's times had changed, but the R.U.C. had not.

In 1968, it had an establishment of 3,200 men, under the command of an Inspector-General. Every man, together with his dark green uniform, boasted a revolver as a personal weapon, unlike any other police force in the United Kingdom. The Force's senior officers wore Sam Browne belts and shoulder straps with military badges of rank. "The Force," said a Government of Northern Ireland information leaflet, "has modern equipment for the detection of crime and the maintenance of law and order. . . ." To amplify these bland words a little: in October 1968, the R.U.C. included in its standard armoury water cannon, Sterling sub-machine guns, armoured cars mounted with heavy machine guns, and gas projectors. It was indeed a formidably trained force—but trained to what end? Some outside observers coming to Northern Ireland found themselves watching a force in action that at times looked to be—as certain persons undoubtedly intended—neither more nor less than the military arm of the Unionist Party.

It would be grossly unfair to the police to suggest that through-out every disturbance, they acted as a Protestant Gestapo. But their training, their history and their composition made it in-evitable that the R.U.C. should be a force ill-fitted to deal equit-ably with a Catholic minority. In 1968, a mere 11 per cent of the force were Catholics. At the time the force was originated, pro-vision had been made for a one-third Catholic membership. But somehow, this never happened. In the beginning, Catholics were reluctant to volunteer—and were discouraged by the authorities—when they knew that fighting their co-religionists from across the Border would be among their vital tasks. By the time the security situation had changed, the R.U.C. was too Protestant a body for a Catholic to feel easy in. There was indeed the Catholic 11 per cent, but in spirit this was a Protestant orientated force. In the Catholic strongholds in Belfast and Londonderry, the police had for years been unwelcome—indeed knew they put themselves at risk patrolling there. Ulster's history since Partition suggested to every Catholic, rightly or wrongly, that he could expect no love from the R.U.C.

But if the regular police force was regarded by the Catholics with suspicion, the police reserve body enjoyed a reputation in Catholic Ulster that induced paranoid terror and hatred. During the serious emergencies of the 1920's, a number of volunteer citizens' forces had been created to support the R.U.C. These bodies, the divisions of Special Constabulary, were again in-evitably of an almost exclusively Protestant character. They were remembered among Catholics for outrages and atrocities at the height of the Troubles that could never be forgotten. Over the years, their numbers had been run down, but in 1968, there were left some 8,000 part-time volunteers, available for call-up in

2—U1969 * *

emergency, known as the 'B' Specials. They underwent periodic training, kept a uniform and a personal weapon—which might be a sub-machine gun—in their homes, and cared enough for their province and its concept to take to the streets to defend it for nights on end if necessary. They were characterised, still, by at best a distaste for and a mistrust of Catholics. At worst, this could spill over into vicious hatred. Determined yet half-trained and little-disciplined, the threat of their mobilisation was the ultimate horror to Catholic peace of mind. They resembled in many respects America's National Guard, and were even less real use in a sensitive situation.

Perhaps the most powerful weapon of all in the hands of the Government, however, was the legislative statute of 1922 known as the Special Powers Act.* This document, passed in the stress of desperate crisis and still in force in 1968, gave the Government's forces powers of search, arrest, and detention without trial almost unheard of outside a police state. Its existence was one of the bitterest of all Catholic grievances. It had been kept in force year after year on the grounds that recurring outbreaks of terrorism demanded it. It had been used to detain suspected members of the illegal I.R.A. for periods of years. It offered blanket clearance to the Government for almost any action they should see fit to take. Normally, it lay dormant. But it was always there, supported by other legislation such as the Public Order Act, which gave powers unknown in England. All this, it was argued, was made necessary by the special conditions prevailing in Northern Ireland.

From a Protestant standpoint, perhaps it was true. But it might be imagined that the least an Irish Catholic could expect from being a part of Great Britain would be the rights that other English citizens enjoy. These the Special Powers Act threatened directly. At a political level, it may be argued that Protestants who believe in Unionism cannot be blamed for voting Unionist, nor can the Unionists be "blamed" for holding power for forty-eight years. But the climate which the Unionists created and maintained by such legislation as the Special Powers Act had nothing to do with politics in a democracy. And the province over which they presided would have driven less confident men to despair.

The Six Counties of Northern Ireland—Fermanagh, Tyrone, Antrim, Derry, Down and Armagh—comprise some 5,000 square miles, an area the size of Yorkshire or Connecticut. With the highest

* Civil Authorities Act (Special Powers).

The RIOT Areas of BELFAST

Scale of Miles

0   ¼   ½   ¾   1

——— Roads   +++++ Railways

Parks, etc.   Reservoirs, etc.

CRUMLIN RD.

BALLYSILLAN ROAD

OLD PARK RD.

CRUMLIN

ARDOYNE ROAD

ALLIANCE RD.

BERWICK RD.

ALLIANCE AV.

ETNA DRIVE

CLIFTONVILLE ROAD

CAVEHILL RD.

ALEXANDRA PARK AV.

ANTRIM ROAD

LIMESTONE RD.

BROMPTON PK.

TWADDELL AV.

WOODVALE AV.

N

FLAX ST.

OLD PARK ROAD

MANOR ST.

CLIFTONVILLE

GLENCAIRN RD.

MARTIN RD.

WOODVALE

BALLYGOMARTIN ROAD

WOODVALE ROAD

BRAY ST.

DISRAELI ST.

LEOPOLD ST.

CAMBRAI ST.

SYDNEY ST. W.

SILVIO ST.

BERLIN ST.

SNUGVILLE ST.

CRIMEA ST.

AGNES ST.

OLD LODGE RD.

CLIFTON ST.

N. QUEEN ST.

DONEGALL ST.

Forth R.

SHANKILL

TENNENT ST.

SHANKILL ROAD

PETERS HILL

NORTH ST.

ROYAL AV.

WEST CIRCULAR ROAD

AINSWORTH AV.

CUPAR STREET

LAWNBROOK AV.

CANMORE ST.

CONWAY ST.

N. HOWARD ST.

NORTHUMBERLAND ST.

PERCY ST.

DOVER ST.

MILLFIELD

CASTLE ST.

SPRINGFIELD

FORFAR ST.

CAVENDISH ST.

CLONARD ST.

LEESON ST.

FALLS RD.

ALBERT ST.

CULLINGTREE RD.

DIVIS STREET

DURHAM ST.

City Hall

DONEGALL SQUARE

SPRINGFIELD ROAD

GROSVENOR ROAD

HOWARD ST.

BEDFORD ST.

Royal
Victoria
Hospital

River

RODEN ST.

SANDY ROW

GT. VICTORIA ST.

DUBLIN RD.

DONEGALL P.

WHITEROCK RD.

ST. JAMES'S RD.

FALLS ROAD

DONEGALL AV.

BROADWAY

M1 MOTORWAY

Blackstaff

DONEGALL ROAD

LISBURN RD.

UNIVERSITY RD.

UNIVERSITY ST.

BOTANIC AV.

birth rate and the lowest death rate in the United Kingdom, Ulster's population of 1½ million—one-third Catholic—is expanding fast; so fast, in fact, that some Protestants are genuinely terrified that the disproportionately high Catholic birth rate will drive them all into the Republic by force of votes if they can't promote birth control in a hurry.

Yet Ulster faces economic and industrial problems that classify it in English terms as a depressed area, irrespective of all difficulties of politics and religion. Unemployment rarely drops below 7 per cent, and in Londonderry, the most desperate city, it attained a staggering 20 per cent at one point in 1967, and usually hovers above a minimum 11 per cent. The Gross Domestic Product—£615 million in 1967—has been rising steadily, but nowhere near fast enough. Twelve thousand houses a year are being built, but acres of slums still deface Belfast, Derry and almost every other major town. Shipbuilding, farming, textiles and fishing have been the major industries for many years, and although successive Governments have made strenuous efforts for years to bring in new industry, still they are not keeping pace. As new employment is created, redundancy in old industries reduces the rate of progress. The province has suffered a long series of setbacks since its earliest days. Between the two world wars, 50,000 houses were built—but the Germans destroyed the same number in the Blitz. The tourist industry had been painfully pushed forward until by 1968 it was worth £30 million a year: but progress could have been much faster had tourist policy been planned in direct cooperation with that of the Irish Republic. Wages are still notably lower than in most parts of Britain, and it has been a hard struggle to find the firms to set up new factories.

Nevertheless, by 1968 there were certain hopeful signs. Some able work on the part of the Ministry of Commerce, aided by generous investment grants, was speeding up the growth of new industry, while Government Training Centres had been established to prepare men for the jobs. A new city was being created at Craigavon, an industrial complex was coming into being around Ballymena. Ulster's two universities, Queen's in Belfast and the new University of Coleraine, were increasing their intake of students, and a series of top economic planners had been brought in to blueprint Ulster's development. The tragedy, of course, was that so much of what was coming about was still too little, too late. Over a very long period, far too many of Ulster's ablest young men and women had acquired the habit of migrating to England in search of success, almost as a matter of course. This is a trend inevitable in all provincial areas, but Ulster's special position is such that she desperately needs everyone of ability she can find. Geographically, Northern Ireland is dominated by Belfast: 400,000 people live within the city limits and half the population of the whole province lives within twenty-five miles of its grimy, industrial sprawl. It is a largely Victorian creation that grew up around the huge shipyards and factories that came in the wake of the Industrial Revolution. On the fringes of the city, new housing developments and suburban villas mingle into a hinterland like that of any other British industrial centre. The main shopping streets at the centre are unprepossessing, but wide and spacious. It is in the areas between the centre and the suburbs, in the core of mean streets and terraced houses built in their thousands a hundred years ago, that violence and strife breed. Catholics and Protestants live in their enclaves, each recognised as the territory of one sect or the other, in houses indistinguishable in their gloominess. Warehouses, mills and factories add to the smoky pallor. Long before the spotlight of world attention was focused on Ulster, sectarian feuds, violence and occasional murder were an accepted part of the way of life. The last major clashes were in 1935, but there have been many unreported fracas, less serious perhaps, since then.

A few miles outside Belfast, however, reaching the Stormont—the Parliament Building—one seems to be in another world. It is a classic symbol of the Imperialist ideal, a huge Palladian structure standing atop a long grassy hill. A statue of Carson, the Protestant idol of the Partition struggle, dominates the entrance drive; sweeping lawns and tall trees undulate gently into the distance. Hidden behind a wood at one side stands a preposterous mock-medieval castle—the headquarters of Government, the Cabinet Offices. Here the Prime Minister and his ministers administer an annual provincial budget which presently totals £338 million. The Prime Minister draws £7,550 a year in salary and allowances for his efforts, his senior Cabinet colleagues £4,550. It is accepted practice to keep private business interests in being while in office, if these do not clash directly with an official post. Rank and file Stormont M.P.s are paid a small salary for their attendance, but in normal times, Parliamentary sessions are short, their weekly hours limited. Up at Stormont on a fine summer day, it seems almost impossible that modern Belfast is only a few minutes away. When the British Government gave the Stormont building to Ulster in the twenties, they were creating a special setting for make-believe.

Londonderry, Ulster's other key city, is two hours drive across the province, into yet another existence. With a population of around 56,000, set on a hill by the river Foyle, its houses and businesses rise to the old walled town at the summit, and fall on the other side to the chaotic warren of slums and new housing blocks that is the Bogside, the Catholic heartland. Derry is a city steeped in Protestant tradition, yet most Catholic of all in its squalor and depression. On a fine day, it looks very pretty from a distance, but closer examination is disillusioning. /

To get out across the countryside, however, is a more cheering experience. Ulster, they say, is not as attractive as the South. But despite a landscape which finds most of its beauty in its barrenness, it can be enchanting. Gently rolling hills, green fields in the valleys, and streams and rivers in profusion create the air of serenity all the finest countryside needs. Hitchhikers stand by the roads in droves at weekends—for public transport is poor—hopping from one quiet town to the next. The towns themselves are often distinguished by groups of splendid eighteenth century houses along the wide main streets, although the civic buildings are usually grey Victorian piles, with the local Orange Hall prominent amongst them. But to think of discrimination, sectarianism and misery in these places, one must know them very well indeed.

In most areas of Ulster, although Catholics may represent the less affluent section of the community, there is nothing resembling social segregation. Perhaps the most bigoted members of the Orange Order or some local churches decline to mix with Catholics. But while Protestants in general may rail about Catholics in general, individually they will drink with them, go to parties with them and count them among their friends. It would be ridiculous to suppose that the kind of discrimination exists in daily life such as that in the Southern states of America. In the country especially, it's only relatively rarely that one hears of either Catholics or Protestants totally declining social contact with each other. In the cities, the gulf is more pronounced, largely because of the historical growth of traditional Catholic and Protestant areas. But even there, in normal times Catholics manage to live in Protestant streets and vice versa without great friction. Perhaps the most significant factor, however, is that anywhere in Ulster, among

34

friends, neighbours or enemies, everybody knows each other's religion, and nobody ever really forgets it. Ride with a Belfast taxi driver, and you will know within five minutes which church he belongs to. Be taken by friends to a neighbour's country dinner party, and on the way they will be more likely than not make some joke about the host being "a tame Orangeman" or a "rare old Fenian". This very knowledge ensures that when trouble comes, both sides think they know who they can trust. To many Protestants, however much they may like individual Catholics, each one could be—when the chips are down—a potential Republican.

And having stressed that on an individual basis relations are often cordial, at a communal level discrimination of a very pronounced kind has always existed. In business, some Protestant employers refuse to employ Catholics at all. Of those that do, many are careful never to let the proportion rise above 10 per cent or 20 per cent: more, and the Protestant work force can become restless, or worse. Lord Brookeborough once said that he knew people who employed Catholics, but would not do so himself. Other Unionist Ministers at different times stated openly that they believed priority in job vacancies should go to Protestants. And having been given a lead from the top of the province, the Protestant middle classes in Ulster usually followed. Where employers were uncertain, their Protestant extremist employees made up their minds for them. In recent years, there has been some improvement in the situation—but not nearly enough. It is only since World War II that a Catholic middle class began to prosper in Ulster, and there are still relatively few major Catholic-owned businesses

But if the Protestants—spurred on by the Orange Order, the Unionist hierarchy, and militant extremists—have practised discrimination, the Catholic leadership has traditionally given little help. The Church was, at least until 1968, the most powerful organised Catholic force in Ulster. It is headed by Cardinal Conway, who from his Cathedral in Armagh presides over the spiritual affairs of Irish Catholics in both South and North. For many years, the Church chose to "sit on the fence" when confronted with the major sectarian problems of Ulster. It is very rarely that it has given a clear and constructive lead to its flock in facing the realities of their situation. It has suffered some unfortunate differences of opinion and clashes of personality within its own hierarchy and has failed to produce any leader of the influence and forcefulness desperately needed in religious crisis. Most especially, in the context of Northern Ireland, it has outraged Protestant opinion by continuing to insist on exclusively Catholic schools for Catholic children. In many other parts of the world, of course, this is the case, and is accepted. But in the conditions prevailing in Ulster, Protestants claim to find it hard to stomach Catholic protest about discrimination and segregation when they themselves insist on Catholic education. To many Protestants, Catholic schools are a source of deep suspicion: it is there, they have an uneasy feeling, that little Catholics learn how to be Republicans and Nationalists.

But excluding education, it is only the Protestants who practise real discrimination. And among their ranks, there has never been any shortage of those ready to play on the population's worst sectarian fears. In every society there are always extremists and rabble rousers. In most places, their followings are small, their influence slight. But in Northern Ireland, they find a fertile breeding ground for every kind of bigotry, alarmism and terror. In 1968 and 1969, a number of notorious figures came to the fore in this role, of whom much more later. Enough now to say that extreme Protestant leaders and preachers have always had a hard core of support, urging on their followers a mistrust and bitter suspicion of Catholics which takes little to rouse it into violent action. Behind them, among the mass of Ulster Protestants, there has always been a legend that there are vast numbers of "moderates". In English terms, this is simply not so. There are indeed only a limited number of Protestants willing to fight and kill Catholics on the streets. But the Protestant majority are utterly unwilling to rouse themselves, to show sufficient enthusiasm to extend a genuine hand of welcome to Catholics, or to take active steps to isolate and curb their own militant brethren. The Unionist Government has always been equally lethargic. There may be few open Catholic-haters among Unionist M.P.s at Stormont, but there are also very few active peace-makers. A Government Commission* inquiring into the causes of the tragedies which began in 1968 reported in 1969:

> ". . . the train of events and incidents which began in Londonderry . . . has had as its background, on the one hand a widespread sense of political and social grievance for long unadmitted and therefore unredressed by successive Governments of

* Cameron Commission Report, paragraph 6.

Northern Ireland, and on the other, sentiments of fear and apprehension . . . of risks to the integrity and indeed continued existence of the state."

At the head of power in Ulster in the last days of peace was the curiously enigmatic Captain Terence O'Neill. O'Neill had been Prime Minister for five years, succeeding the vigorously right-wing figure of Lord Brookeborough in 1963. A modestly liberal man already mistrusted by many of his own party, he had had his fair share of political troubles since his succession. His main achievement had been to gain legal recognition for the Ulster Trades Union Movement, against heavy opposition from within his own party. His amazing talent for political survival against all the odds, which was to be displayed to advantage until April 1969, had already been called into play to defeat several conspiracies against his leadership from within the party.

He had, however, been involved in only one serious political clash that attracted notice outside Ulster. In 1965, he arranged in the deepest secrecy for the then Prime Minister of the Irish Republic, Mr. Sean Lemass, to visit him at Stormont for dis-cussions. There was no particular intent behind the move other than to get communication of some kind going once more between the North and South. But the talks themselves paled into insig-nificance when compared with the fury that followed them from extreme Protestant elements in the community. Although O'Neill paid a return visit in February 1965, he himself was never trusted again by right wing Protestants. It was not only that talks had taken place, but that O'Neill had organised them in such secrecy, knowing full well the storm that would surround any suggestion of such a meeting. In Ulster, liaison with the South amounts in certain quarters to treasonable correspondence with the enemy.

But even this affair had attracted amazingly little notice "across the water" in England. As the orchestra tuned up for the overture to the events that were to flash across the world in 1969, our picture of Ulster remained, as it had been for many years, very much blurred. We had read about it in our history books, ignored it, and laughed at it. We had seen photographs of grimy, smoky Belfast, and compared it unfavourably with the gaiety of Dublin. Perhaps we had fished or visited friends in Ulster, but we knew nothing. The English have occasional twinges of desire to get rid of Northern Ireland, but it clings to us like the Old Man of The

37

Sea. We had noticed it spasmodically during the forays of the Irish Republican Army, but these had died down to a trickle in recent years, and despite periodic wild statements from Dublin, the issue of Irish Partition seemed effectively forgotten. Those Englishmen who knew a little were aware that life was less than funny for a Catholic in that Protestant society, but a new generation of Britons had forgotten that their fathers had lived daily with the nightmare of Irish civil war and constant strife. When we heard murmurs of some parish-pump crisis over in Ulster, it hardly seemed the stuff of which melodrama is made:

> "Captain Terence O'Neill, Ulster's Prime Minister, was given a blunt warning by some of his backbenchers yesterday," ran a news report of November 1964, "that unless he moves quickly over the Royal Maternity Hospital rumpus, he could face defeat in Parliament on Tuesday. The warning was the frankest ever given to a Northern Ireland Prime Minister in 40 years of self-government. . . ."

Nor had it made much impact, earlier that year, when we read that the then British Prime Minister, Sir Alec Douglas-Home, had declined to meet Ulster Nationalist M.P.s to discuss religious and political discrimination. In October 1965, an *Observer* profile of O'Neill revealed that "with his small coterie of advisers, his administration sometimes resembles a medieval court, and the roots of his present power are perilously shallow. . . ." But an article in *The Times* less than two years later, highlighting reports of electoral discrimination against Catholics in Northern Ireland, was greeted in London with bland indifference. O'Neill himself wrote that "many of the criticisms now being directed at us are demonstrably ill-founded". Of final note, perhaps, was a television appearance in January 1968, by Labour Minister Mr. Richard Crossman: there was, he said, a strong case for regional parliaments for Scotland and Wales; the Northern Ireland system of a parliament for local affairs with M.P.s also attending Westminster had, after all, worked so well. . . .

No more than Mr. Crossman did we have a glimmering of what was to come. The Ulster Government's information officers, past masters in the art of whitewash, were still pumping out leaflet after leaflet on the astonishing "progress" of Ulster. Let them, perhaps, have the last word in a quote from the final paragraph of the Government's pamphlet on the history of Northern Ireland:

"Unfortunately, towards the end of 1968 communal disturbances arising out of the so-called 'Civil Rights' movement and reactions to it, developed into a threat to this progress. . . ."

The tale of Northern Ireland's reluctant struggle towards the twentieth century began, if one must choose a single date, with the doings of that "so-called Civil Rights movement" in Dungannon on August 24th 1968.

2

"A THREAT TO THIS PROGRESS . . ."

IN THE LATE summer of 1968, a group of Ulster citizens began serious agitation to demand from the Unionist Government certain changes in the pattern of Northern Irish society. The reforms which they sought—basic democratic rights for every Ulster citizen—were so patently reasonable that one might imagine that no civilized man of any religious belief could oppose them. What followed in the winter of 1968 and 1969 was only possible in a society where a tradition of suspicion and hatred has persisted for three hundred years.

In the late 1960's, Ulster as an entity was still, despite much measurable progress, in a parlous condition. Unemployment and the shortage of housing created a situation in which restlessness was inevitable. The growth of education and knowledge had created the same increased awareness and political consciousness in Northern Ireland as everywhere else in the Western world. In areas of England in the same economic state as Ulster, the poorer-paid sections of the community turned to the Labour Party in the hope of a better deal from government. One might have expected that in Northern Ireland too, working-class Catholics and working-class Protestants would have felt some unity of interest in reform and change. But working-class Protestants were still far more afraid of the Catholics than they were of poverty: they continued to vote for the reactionary, and by English standards far right-wing, Unionists. They were willing to do anything to avoid rocking their Constitutional boat, so they preferred to suffer in Unionist silence. Thus whatever the overall economic problems of Ulster, it was almost exclusively from the Catholics that political opposition to the forty-seven-year-old Government had to come.

But since the beginnings of the Northern Irish state, the Catholic Parliamentary Opposition had always submerged economic and domestic issues in the eternal wrangle about the very existence of Ulster. Long after any real prospect of a United Ireland had faded, the dream remained the political talisman of the Opposition. It was only a few years since they had discarded the policy of Abstention—elected M.P.s declining to take their places in the Ulster House of Commons to show their non-recognition of the Government. They tried to imagine that this somehow damaged the Unionists. In reality, of course, it merely gave them uncontrolled writ to run the province. But at least it spared the Opposition the indignity of sitting in the Stormont year after year, unable to accomplish any major change in policy, and treated like recalcitrant children by the massed ranks of Unionists. Today, their leather benches still look in almost pristine condition, while those of the Government, ingrained with years of Protestant trouser seats, seem to sag comfortably, well lived-in. The days of Abstention ended, but still the Unionists' only opposition stemmed from the ineffectual pinpricking of Nationalists and Republicans both inside and outside the Stormont. Whatever went on inside Ulster, the Government continued to have solid Protestant support and solid Catholic opposition.

But the growth of an increasingly educated Catholic middle class, and the passing of an older generation of single-mindedly Catholic Nationalist Ulstermen, turned some thinking Catholic minds in new directions. For years, all Opposition had been preoccupied with Partition. But in the 1960's, more and more people began to turn aside from this albatross, and consider the state of the province in which for better or worse they had to live. They did not like what they saw. First, there was the general economic condition of Northern Ireland. Beyond this, there was the statutory prejudice against the poorer classes, notably the Catholics, in elections. There was the statutory discrimination against Catholics in the organisation of local councils and ward boundaries; and the *de facto* discrimination against them in jobs and housing. What was remarkable was not that certain people began to stir, but that they had not done so before. But it has been well established all over the world that as soon as people have a little more, they want a lot more; as soon as they see the prize dangling near their grasp, they reach out to seize it. In any other society, the under-privileged of every religious denomination would have joined in any move to change the situation. In the conditions of rigidly sectarian political life in Ulster, it was inevitable that any reform movement should be almost exclusively Catholic based, however broad its declared intentions.

For many years, there had been a wide variety of small and unco-ordinated Catholic organisations scattered across the province. Some were largely social or devoted to tub-thumping for a United Ireland. Others had been established to try to promote better conditions for Catholics inside Ulster. There were Housing Action Committees in many places, and other groups of a more informal kind gathered around the handful of Nationalist and other Opposition M.P.s at Stormont. But there had never been any real unanimity between them—indeed they had frequently fought each other harder than the Unionists. Their impact on both Ulster and the outside world had been very slight.

But in February 1967, a group associated with the "Campaign for Social Justice in Northern Ireland", a small organisation created and based in Dungannon, a country town in County Tyrone, summoned a meeting in Belfast in an attempt to bring together some of the reform-minded elements in the community. Out of their discussions emerged the Northern Ireland Civil Rights Association, which was to form the skeleton of the whole movement of protest in Ulster in 1968 and 1969.

The essence of the founders' plans was that the new body should be completely non-sectarian. It brought together a loose alliance of Catholic Housing Action Committees from across the province. But it also urged a wide variety of Trades Unions, cultural groups, and political organisations of all kinds to join either as individuals or entities, if they accepted only the basic principles of civil rights. It was a very middle-class enterprise—cautious, decent, unsure of itself and very gentle in its outlook. At the outset, there was no really clearly defined programme, merely a pledge to attempt to bring to an end discrimination of all kinds in Ulster. A few liberal Protestants joined—and so, at an early stage, did certain members and supporters of the Irish Republican Army. The I.R.A., however, banned in both North and South, had changed in character a great deal even in the past ten years. Much of the steam had gone out of its emphasis on terrorism, and its numbers had declined. Many Nationalists both North and South of the Border who were determined to see an end to Partition called themselves I.R.A. men, but there were very few now who, as in the old days, regarded blowing up police stations as a really effective means of gaining their ends. There is no evidence that I.R.A. infiltration of the Civil Rights movement at its outset was intended to achieve anything more than gratify their liking for a

42

finger in every pie. The I.R.A. men affected the new movement's character far less than those open Nationalists and Republicans who also joined in the early days. And it was to be a young Nationalist Stormont M.P. who, in the summer of 1968, inspired a change in the character of the Civil Rights Association from which it was never to look back. Austin Currie, M.P. for East Tyrone, found the spark to move the C.R.A. into action.

From the beginning, the Association had concentrated its efforts on seeking remedies for individual and specific grievances, rather than agitating to impose changes of policy on the Ulster Government. But in the spring of 1968, a major discrimination incident developed in County Tyrone which was to catch the attention of all Northern Ireland. In Kinnard Park, in Caledon, a village not far from Dungannon, two Catholic families began illegally "squatting" in two new council houses just completed and intended for Protestant occupation.

Caledon was a Protestant and Unionist-dominated area, and local housing allocation was effectively in the hands of local councillors in each ward. In Kinnard Park, the two Catholic families from a neighbouring ward, sick like every other Catholic in the area of seeing themselves continually denied housing, moved into Nos. 9 and 11 with the encouragement of certain militant Catholic leaders. Wheels grind slowly in Ulster, but after two months, one of the families was ordered out. In their place, the house was given to a nineteen-year-old unmarried Protestant girl, Emily Beattie, the secretary to the local Unionist Councillor's solicitor. Like so many acts of Protestant injustice in Ulster, this one was a masterpiece of ineptitude. No one could ignore such blatant discrimination. When the other "squatting" family was evicted on June 18th, television cameras and the press were there in force. Austin Currie raised the issue in Stormont, but got nowhere. He and two others, therefore, decided on direct action. On June 20th, they publicly took over Miss Beattie's house. Their stay lasted a few hours before they were ejected by Miss Beattie's brother, a policeman, who later gained possession of the house himself.

But Currie, a shrewd and vigorous young man of militant leanings, had gained a priceless propaganda victory, and some badly needed publicity. Armed with these, he approached the Dungannon Campaign for Social Justice with a proposal for a protest march about the case in Dungannon. The Campaign for Social

Justice organisers put it to the Civil Rights Association. On July 27th, they met in Maghera, and after much heart-searching and misgiving about becoming involved in mass protest and demonstration, agreed to sponsor a march. After eighteen months of unspectacular leaflet campaigns and ill-attended church hall meetings, it was their first step towards action. A date was fixed for August 24th. It was decided that the protesters should march the three miles to Dungannon from the nearby village of Coalisland.

The Catholics of central Ulster greeted the news of the march with a mixture of bewilderment and excitement. Northern Ireland had seen many religious processions and get-togethers, but a serious political demonstration was a bizarre experience. It was customarily the Protestants who did the marching: the Orange Order—still a kind of masonic society whose key was vital to any Protestant in Ulster politics—the Derry Apprentice Boys, the Protestant extremist groups, all took to the streets at intervals in ritualistic homage to their belief. But for the Catholics, Dungannon promised unusual excitement. Plans went ahead in a carnival spirit, and nobody knew quite what to expect. In Dublin in the first week of August, the head of the I.R.A., Cathal Goulding, held a meeting of his executive to decide what part his force might play. He concluded that the C.R.A.'s activities could provide scope for exploitation, and twelve I.R.A. men, mostly locals from the County Tyrone organisation, were ordered to attend the march as observers. Some, on the day, acted as stewards, but without a hint of trouble or provocation.

Among the Protestant community, however, reaction to the news of the march was swift and predictable. One group of extremists warned the police that they were calling a meeting in Dungannon to coincide with the arrival of the protesters—this is a recognised tactic of sabotage in Ulster. More respectable Unionists expressed their feelings more discreetly, but both local Councillors and members of the Government warned that Dungannon's Protestants would give the marchers a hostile reception. Dungannon itself, a country town with a population of some 26,000, might almost have been created as a test case of Catholic grievance: while Protestant adults only outnumbered Catholics by a small fraction, Unionists held fourteen out of twenty-one seats on the Urban District Council. The most powerful Protestant residents made no bones about their sympathies: the Catholics proposed to march to the town's Market Square, but local Unionist leaders announced that this was considered Protestant territory, and would constitute provocation against the Protestant extremists. In the face of Protestant threats and demands, the police, late on the night of August 23rd, decided on the re-routing of the march: it was to be halted in Thomas Street, a quarter of a mile from the Market Square, and diverted around the town.

"Just stop any trouble", William Craig, the Home Affairs Minister, ordered his senior policemen before the march. In Ulster, there is no law against the carrying of offensive weapons, except firearms. On the 24th, when the Protestant counter-demonstrators gathered in the centre of Dungannon, many carried clubs and staves, but the police in the area did nothing but exchange greetings with them.

The Catholics, 2,500 strong, gathered at Coalisland, led by Austin Currie, Gerry Fitt—a Republican Labour M.P. at both Stormont and Westminster—and Miss Betty Sinclair, Chairman of the C.R.A. Miss Sinclair, who had been Chairman since the C.R.A.'s beginnings, reflected its character in August 1968. A prominent figure in the Ulster Trades Union Movement, a Communist for many years, fifty-seven years old and a grey-haired veteran of Irish politics, she was a lady of high principles but a quiet fighter. "I have been around too long to think you can take on governments with your bare hands," she would say cheerfully. Fine words, but already becoming out of fashion in the Ulster of 1968. Dungannon was the first occasion on which the C.R.A. leapt to life, and Miss Sinclair was obviously out of her depth facing it.

As the marchers gathered at Coalisland, a young Queen's University student, Miss Bernadette Devlin, was acquiring her first insight into the politics of demonstration. "There were masses of people milling around, selling civil rights rosettes and generally behaving as if they were at a carnival," she recounted. "The march was supposed to start at six o'clock on this fine August evening, but, of course, it started late, and it wasn't until about seven o'clock that we trudged off up the road led by a band of children playing accordions. We had been told that this was a non-sectarian, non-political march—for all that the demands we were making were political. Nevertheless, politically-minded young people had turned up with the banners of their associations —the Young Liberals, the Young Socialists, and so on—but they weren't allowed to carry them. . . ."*

* *The Price of My Soul*, op. cit.

45

So they loped up the road, their bands playing, singing Catholic songs, stopping off for drinks at the pubs, gaining strength as people came out of their houses to join them, chatting gaily and loving the newness of it all, till they came to Dungannon, and to the police cordon across the road to the Market Square.

The atmosphere deadened, the sight of more than a thousand Protestants hurling abuse from behind the police line brought first confusion then anger. Gerry Fitt harangued the police: "We are a lawful procession," he insisted. "You must let us through along our route."

The senior police officer was unimpressed: "You cannot proceed . . . there would be a likelihood of trouble."

The crowd of demonstrators hovered uncertain and simmering. Gerry Fitt and Austin Currie addressed them. Fitt talked very tough, flaying the police for their behaviour, rousing tempers, but himself uncertain what to do next. Finally, as chatter among the crowd of demonstrators breaking through the line grew more intense, he called: "Remember there are women and children among us!" Betty Sinclair, by now thoroughly alarmed, told her flock: "This is a non-political, peaceful demonstration. Anyone who wants to fight should get out and join the I.R.A." After another pause, she called for an end to the meeting after the singing of the civil rights anthem, "We Shall Overcome". As the singing ended, Miss Sinclair and her Executive gathered themselves up and left on their lorry. The marchers broke up, scattered and uncertain, leaving handfuls to sit and sing in the street for a few hours more. The police, new to the situation and like everyone else somewhat bemused, let them be. Their riot tenders and shields were unused; they had asserted their authority unchallenged. The Protestants were angry and aggrieved at the Catholic manner of venting their feelings, but they too drifted away into the town. The Dungannon March, which had roused such keen expectation and curiosity, fizzled out unremarkably. The marchers themselves, roused to a climax, found none. They went home somewhat confused: exhilarated in having done something together, in having presented a united front to pinprick the seemingly invincible Unionist armour; but frustrated in having been so easily turned aside from the goal they had set themselves. Market Square had been denied to them, they had been brought to a halt and dismissed. By the standards of America or the rest of Europe, this had been less a demonstration than an organised walk.

Yet Dungannon had awoken ideas, tactics, inspiration among many Catholics in Ulster. They began to think very hard indeed that night, and in the days that followed. Already the theory of non-sectarian opposition seemed a forlorn dream, with Nationalist M.P.s foremost in the ranks. No God-fearing Ulster Protestant would ever come forth to be seen in such company. Dungannon did nothing to widen the base of support for the Civil Rights movement, but it brought a thrill to Catholic bitterness such as had not been seen for very many years indeed. The publicity it gained faded quickly from the public consciousness, and left very little impact on the Ulster Government; only considerable annoyance. But it roused the keenest interest and brought about the most immediate consequences among certain Catholics in the second city of Ulster, Londonderry.

Londonderry, or Derry as everyone in Northern Ireland calls it, was not, like Dungannon, a place of spasmodic grievance and momentary unrest. The whole city, from the grimy stone walls of the old town to the slums of the Bogside below, was a sulky, pitiful, smarting depression. Its appalling unemployment, its wretched housing situation, its apparent cinderella role in the development of Ulster, made it a hotbed of latent bitterness. The Catholics felt it most, of course, because there were more of them and they made up most of the poorer sections of the community. But everyone in Derry, including the Protestants, felt that the Ulster Government had for years been passing them by. When a new town was planned for Northern Ireland, it was established in Craigavon. The new university went to Coleraine. New factories always seemed to be sited elsewhere, while in Derry old ones closed down. No one, it seemed, wanted to know about the place. And in the city itself, Protestant dominated, the Catholics felt that no one wanted to know about them. There was the gross inequity of the City Council's composition, and feeling about discrimination in jobs and housing. The Protestants had their share of problems, but the Catholics found theirs rather more burdensome. And on their sentiments, there were a number of men—most, not surprisingly, of left-wing leanings—who sought to inspire action. In the wake of the Dungannon march, which had set all Ulster talking, they decided to make a move.

The most active Catholic organisation in Londonderry was the Housing Action Committee, dominated by two young men named Eamonn McCann and Eamonn Melaugh. For some time,

47

the Committee had been attempting to organise sit-downs, demonstrations and protests against the City's housing policy, but with very little success and no response. But following Dungannon, this Committee invited the leaders of the Northern Ireland Civil Rights Association to attend a meeting with them to discuss the possibility of a further march in Derry itself. On August 31st, eight members of the C.R.A. executive arrived in the City to discuss the proposal. They felt that arrangements should be put in the hands of the most widely possible based interests in the community, and dispatched invitations to many organisations— excluding, however, the churches and the Unionist Party. But in the event, only five groups agreed to participate: the Londonderry Labour Party, the Londonderry Labour Party Young Socialists, the Derry Housing Action Committee, the Derry City Republican Club, and the James Connolly Society. Another meeting between the Derry activists and the C.R.A. executive was held at the City Hotel on September 7th. At this, a date was set for a march on October 5th, and an "October 5th Ad Hoc Committee" was established, with members from each of the five groups to organise it. On September 8th, in compliance with Ulster law, the secretary of the C.R.A. gave notice of the impending march to the Ministry of Home Affairs, and money for placards and posters was collected among Catholics in Derry. The march was planned to run from the Waterside Station on the east of the city to the very centre, the Diamond, in the Protestant heartland within the old city walls. Its theme, the C.R.A. intended, would be non-sectarian; liberal Protestants would be in the ranks, and Nationalist or Republican banners and flags were to be prohibited. In this way, they anticipated, their methods and their aims could be kept peaceful; they were utterly opposed to direct confrontation with the Government or with the Protestants on the streets. Somewhat naively, when they left the arrangements for the October 5th march in the hands of the Derry Ad Hoc Committee, they still did not appreciate the direction in which their movement was turning.

Young Eamonn McCann, who had been among the earliest to urge a major Civil Rights march in Derry, had not been nominated to the Ad Hoc Committee. But in the absence of anyone else either as capable, forceful or determined as himself, he became its driving figure. He was twenty-six years old, and almost the prototype Irish rebel: passionate, wild-haired, and handsome, with a gay indifference to logic on occasion. He had been a student at Queen's University, but had departed after a difference of opinion with the authorities. He had spent some time in England dabbling in labour agitation among the Irish on building sites. A socialist and a born orator, he was already an acute political operator. His early activities in Derry had provoked only tolerant amusement from older Catholics, but he had acquired a considerable following among his own generation. He believed, he was wont to say, in "revolution, not reform", but his theme song was too commonplace among the young to provoke much outside attention. Yet McCann, an enthusiastic amateur in politics, had been given the chance, by default of his elders, to tamper with the explosive tinder of Londonderry. Holding court in the City Hotel in Derry in the weeks before October 5th, he was a figure who would have frightened the life out of Betty Sinclair and her colleagues, had they cared to take an interest in what he was up to. Through the Housing Action Committee, he had an effective monopoly of the recognised channels of Catholic organisation in the city, and he used them. The October 5th march was, in the end, largely his handiwork.

For the events in Dungannon which had provoked so much new thought and action had brought out into the open the significant number of Catholics, mostly young, who were convinced that nothing less than a really shattering blow to the Unionist hierarchy would bring the reforms they sought. Feelings were already crystallising among the young activists at Queen's University, who were to play a prominent part a few weeks later. Across Northern Ireland, there were those who believed that to bring down Captain Terence O'Neill and his government would pave the way for what they wanted. They did not hate O'Neill so much—he was, by Ulster standards, a liberal—but his pace was too slow for them. They knew that he was hampered constantly by the hard-line Unionists: their answer was to bring those men out into the open and face them head on. They wanted to brush O'Neill aside in order to get to grips with the real enemy. In these first days, they were uncertain how to do this, as plans for October 5th went forward. But with staggering stupidity, it was the Unionists and the Protestant fanatics who themselves crashed forward to commence the battle, while the Catholics themselves were still in uncertain disarray.

At the Dungannon march on August 24th, Unionist M.P. John Taylor, a young engineer of determined Protestant outlook, had been prominent among those who had persuaded the police not to permit the marchers into the Market Square. Following the march, he made his feelings known to the Minister of Home Affairs, William Craig, who was already studying reports of known Republicans and I.R.A. men who had been present. A solid core of Unionist M.P.s, of whom Craig was one, took a bitter view of such Catholic activities, and were prepared to resort to any means to stamp on them. Craig himself, who was to become a central figure in the struggles of the next few months, had never lost touch with the hard-line grass roots elements among the Unionists during his own rise to power, and had never made any secret of his close links with them.

He was forty-five, a County Tyrone man who had been to Queen's University, served as an air gunner during the war, and built up a prosperous solicitor's practice in Lurgan since 1952. He became M.P. for Larne in 1960, and rose rapidly up the Unionist hierarchy until he was appointed Minister of Home Affairs in October 1966. He is a strongly-built, handsome figure, red-faced, talkative and in private, charming. But he has never enjoyed a reputation for "keeping his cool", and while an able administrator, his indiscretions and openly right wing associations had been a continual source of dismay to the few liberals in the Ulster cabinet. Anathema to the Catholics, close ally of the Protestant hard-liners, it was upon him that political responsibility for marches and parades fell in the autumn of 1968.

In the weeks before the march, two letters of protest were dispatched by local Unionist organisations in Derry, complaining that it would be offensive to most local inhabitants, objecting to the routing, and to the holding of any Catholic meeting near the War Memorial or any spot closely associated with the Siege of Derry in 1688, a memory still dear to so many Protestants. Then, on September 30th, came a third protest, from the General Committee of the Apprentice Boys of Derry, a powerful local Orange organisation which purportedly commemorates the activities of the original Apprentice Boys in 1688. This letter alleged that the march was merely a cover for a Republican and Nationalist parade, but said no more. Yet on October 1st, the same organisation suddenly gave notice that its "Annual Initiation Ceremony" would be held on the same day, at the same time, and along the same route as the Civil Rights march. The police, accepting the organisation's plan for its ceremony at face value, and mistrusting those organising the Civil Rights march, intimated to the Home Affairs Minister that there would be trouble. They also passed the word to him that in their view, if all processions were banned on October 5th, the Derry Apprentice Boys would be good enough to make their ceremony private. On October 3rd, Craig announced the banning of all marches either east of the river or within Derry's walls. A few liberal Unionist ministers were at once concerned at the inevitable effect on Catholic tempers, but could do little. A Protestant move that had been blatantly intended to force the Catholics off the field had been successful—at the eleventh hour, the marchers had been forced into a corner from which there was little escape.

Whatever the activities, or lack of them, on the part of Eamonn McCann and the organisers of the march, there had been so far nothing more sinister than a lack of forethought from most of those concerned. They could have reckoned on an attendance in hundreds' with notable abstentions from some Catholic leaders still very uncertain where the Civil Rights Association was leading. But with Craig's ban, in a flash the situation in Londonderry changed dramatically. Eamonn McCann and his colleagues were delighted: a priceless propaganda victory had been won before the start. The gloves were off and it was time for Catholics across Ulster to stand up and be counted. Craig's action had, on the one hand, united most Protestant thinking behind him. But on the other, it took the Civil Rights Association soaring to regions they had never dreamt of, and which frightened some of them very much. Whatever the C.R.A.'s original attractions, the moment their march was banned as the result of an apparent Protestant conspiracy, the whole weight of Ulster Catholic opposition rallied behind it. Those Stormont Opposition M.P.s who had been doubtful were won over. The people of the "Green Ghettos", the local Catholics of Bogside and Creggan Estate, were instantly awakened by the forbidden fruit. The old guard of the I.R.A. sent representatives incognito to act as stewards. Students from Queen's University moved into Derry. Three Westminster M.P.s came over to Ulster to act as observers. It was no longer a Civil Rights march, it was militant Catholic Ulster on the move. Only the executive of the Civil Rights Association, appalled by the confrontation now before them, considered drawing back.

On the evening of October 4th, a meeting was held in the City Hotel. Eamonn McCann and his colleagues, together with the

Derry Labour Party, were determined the march should proceed as planned. After a prolonged debate, a vote was taken. Other local people and some of the militants had managed to find their way into the meeting, and all of these joined in. It was agreed, despite the reservations of the C.R.A., that the march would proceed as planned. Police reinforcements had been brought in, scores of journalists and TV men had arrived in the city. The marchers had nothing to lose—their moral victory had been won by the ban: they stood only to face whatever kind of martyrdom they chose to risk. The Protestants believed this was a Nationalist Catholic conspiracy, an affront to their state, although the Apprentice Boys, who had provoked the ban, had already quietly arranged to go to their "Annual" initiation ceremony by car. Londonderry was in a ferment of excitement and expectation. Everyone in the city knew well that the Protestants had chosen to make this a showdown. The ban had ensured that on the morrow, there would be thousands of Catholics on the streets seeking to exercise the right to march to the centre of their city. Their other grievances suddenly became almost side issues.

On the afternoon of October 5th, some 2,000 people were gathered at the Waterside Station to the east of the Foyle River, across the Craigavon Bridge from the centre of Londonderry. Among them was Gerry Fitt, the Westminster and Stormont M.P. who was one of the oldest hands at Opposition politicking in Ulster; Eamonn McCann; Austin Currie; the three Westminster Labour M.P.s who had come over as observers—Russell Kerr, Mrs. Anne Kerr and John Ryan; Eddie McAteer, Nationalist leader of the Opposition at Stormont; John Hume, later to become a prominent Civil Rights leader in Derry; and Ivan Cooper, a Protestant member of the Derry Labour Party, and one of the most significant figures in the new Civil Rights drive because of it. No one had drawn up any real plan of action for the moment when, as everyone knew would happen, the march collided with the police blockade.

The police themselves drew up for action determined only on one purpose: that a ban on marches having been imposed, it would be upheld, and the demonstrators would not be allowed to enter the city of Derry. During the night, two water cannon mounted on armoured vehicles had been brought quietly into the town. About 130 officers were assembled for duty, armed with batons and revolvers, including two platoons of the Reserve Force, generally known as the "Riot Police". The County Inspector in charge of the R.U.C. Special Branch had been brought in to take command in place of the area County Inspector, who was on leave. At around 3.30 p.m., a senior police officer stepped through the police ranks to address the confused crowd of demonstrators milling in the forecourt of the Station, waiting for orders from their leaders. He called to them through a loudhailer: "Your march has been subjected to a ban by the Minister of Home Affairs because he fears there might be disorder." Then he added: "I must ask you to disperse. Women and children should not remain here." No leaders came forward from the crowd, who were still awaiting the arrival of Betty Sinclair, delayed on her journey from Belfast. There was a pause before Ivan Cooper suddenly took command. Cooper, the manager of a Derry shirt factory, was the employer of scores of Catholic workers. Twenty-five years old, a chubbily handsome young bachelor, he sympathised with the Catholic underprivileged despite an Ulster religious upbringing in the staunchly Protestant country on the edge of the city. Now, he faced the County Inspector and replied, "We have the democratic right to march through our own city peacably."

With that, the marchers suddenly formed up and took the assembled riot squads completely by surprise by abandoning their pre-arranged route and setting boldly off along Duke Street, the shortest cut to the Craigavon Bridge. Police riot tenders were hastily driven across the bridge to block the marchers as they sang their way towards the city. The police hurriedly spilled from their vehicles and formed a line in front of them, while others filled the side streets. They had barely deployed when the march, with Gerry Fitt, Cooper and Eddie McAteer at its head approached the bridge and marched up to the front of the police line.

Instantly, a series of scuffles broke out as several police without provocation—and without orders—drew their batons and clubbed the front line of marchers, including Fitt and McAteer. As the first police baton fell, others followed suit until half the front-line platoon were engaged. Mercifully, the marchers behind could not see what was happening at the front. Stewards forced the line back a few yards, the police were ordered to hold fast, and Fitt was dragged clear to be removed to hospital. Some twenty stewards—including several I.R.A. men—linked arms to hold back the main mass. At this moment, Betty Sinclair arrived, and getting a chair from the police, stood on it to address the crowd

"Don't be provoked into violence," she yelled through a loud-hailer. "We will stay here and hold a meeting. Don't get involved in a fight with the police; let's just wait here and discuss our problems."

The crowd, sullen and angry, didn't want to know. They called for Fitt, and were further outraged to learn that he had been injured. They called for "Eddie, Eddie", and McAteer rose, to another cry of rage when they saw the blood on his forehead. "Don't start a fight," he urged them. For half an hour, he and others addressed them at the junction of Duke Street and Craig-avon Bridge. Austin Currie spoke. Then Eamonn McCann, who told them they should either go home, hold a meeting where they stood, or make a non-violent, non-resistant attempt to breach the police lines.

Then, as they stood there, wavering and unsure, a bearded marcher standing a few yards from the police launched a banner, its slogan calling for fair housing allocation, at the ranks of the R.U.C. The County Inspector's patience was exhausted. He ordered his men to draw their batons. The riot squads tightened their chin straps and raised their shields. "Disperse this crowd," he demanded.

As the riot squads lunged forward, the water cannon roared into view, klaxons screaming. The marchers turned to flee; but fifty yards away, at the other end of Duke Street, were the second riot platoon. Unaware that their colleagues at the front of the march were smashing towards them, they followed their original brief: "Contain the crowd." They too moved in, hitting the demonstration from both sides. The water cannon came into action, police and demonstrators became hopelessly enmeshed, and the confrontation Betty Sinclair and the C.R.A. had dreaded so desperately was a hideous reality. It ceased to be a baton charge, it became a slaughter. The police broke ranks and hammered without mercy at anything within their range. Bloody demonstrators crawled aside into the alleys, a water cannon was trained at full velocity on a TV crew in a first floor window in Duke Street, onlookers as well as marchers scattered as the police bore in. The march became a shambles, with demonstrators fleeing desperately for refuge, and the crowd slowly thinned as they escaped through side streets and across a stretch of waste land. Small groups stopped to fight a rearguard action, hurling bricks and rubble at the oncoming police. The water cannon drove them off, then moved swiftly the length of the bridge to hose pedestrians off the pavements. Anyone trapped in the crossfire was hosed or batoned.

In half an hour, the march had ceased to exist. Demonstrators returned in small groups across the deserted bridge towards the City Hotel and the Bogside. Word travelled with them of what had taken place, and as they reached their own home areas, rage and bitterness went with them. The tough young men of the Bogside, most of whom had taken no part in the march, regarded the police action as a Protestant onslaught justifying instant revenge. As darkness fell, they armed themselves with bottles and stones and walked through the gates in the city walls in Butcher Street, where the Protestant commemorative buildings and monuments loom over Bogside, eternal reminders of the Papist defeat in the siege. They were bent on riot, and they knew how to provoke it. Tramping up the steep little hill from the Butcher Street gate to the Diamond, the central square which was the original destination of the afternoon's march, they gathered for battle. Inside the walls, in the warren of side-streets leading from the Diamond, live the Protestant working class of Derry, their houses as decrepit as those of the Bogside, their inhabitants too, in many cases, disenfranchised by the proprietorial voting qualifications. The party from the Bogside waved their Republican banners and chanted their Catholic slogans. Then they waited.

The Protestants poured from their terraced houses to return the hail of bottles and bricks from the Bogsiders. This was not civil rights or protest—just back to the old days for the hell of it: Catholic versus Protestant, three hundred years of history on their backs. The police hastily abandoned their positions half a mile away on Craigavon Bridge and screamed through the streets to separate them. They arrived to find a shambles of smashed shop fronts, streets littered with stones, and bleeding rioters seeking cover in the doorways, while a few looters moved in attempting to seize the spoils. The police had already suffered minor casualties in the fracas that afternoon. Although this time their opposition was only a few score youths, there was no question about their violent intentions. As a hail of missiles poured down on the police Landrovers, the riot squads massed their vehicles for a motorised charge, driving the rioters back down through the gates towards the Bogside. A few police stopped to hit out at the stragglers, while the Protestants laid down their weapons to watch from behind the police lines.

Then the riot squads moved on down to the Bogside itself. They sought to clear the pavements and force everyone indoors, but they were still baton-charging late into the night. As their vehicles roared through the narrow streets, volleys of missiles were hurled down from the windows of a new block of flats in Rossville Street. A small group of Catholics took advantage of a brief lull to break through a fence into a building site where contractors stored their supplies. They dragged out scaffolding tubes and debris and piled them across the roads—the first of Ulster's barricades—in an attempt to impede the police wagons coming into the Bogside. They fled to safety as an R.U.C. tender came into sight, stopped, and radioed police H.Q. three hundred yards away in Victoria Barracks. An armoured water cannon was diverted to the scene, and smashed its way through the flimsy structure. The roads were kept clear, but the battle continued.

Across the city, the Civil Rights leaders licked their wounds, horrified at what they had seen that afternoon and what was now developing around them. From the standpoint of the militants, this had been a triumph of propaganda, as news of the march flashed around the world. The Ulster police appeared totally discredited, revealed as the bully boys of the Unionist Government. Like the Administration of Chicago a month before, the Unionist Government had played into the hands of the demonstrators. The marchers had come, they had been banned, they had ventured forth, and they had been brutally suppressed on almost non-existent provocation. This, for all the world to see.

Yet all that night and early into the morning, guerilla warfare between Bogsiders and police rumbled on. As is Ulster's habit in war and peace, a brief truce broke out that Sunday morning while Protestants and Catholics repaired to their churches. But in the afternoon and that night, they fought on. In the early hours of Monday morning, as the skirmishers finally called a halt, they retired to their homes through streets littered with wreckage and debris. Eighteen policemen injured, seventy-seven civilians, police vehicles scarred and battered from the endless rain of missiles, shops and houses broken into and stricken; it seemed a heavy price. They were all tired, Protestants, Catholics, police—and very bitter. A frightening and yet familiar genie had been uncorked from the bottle and no one knew how or when it might be put back.

3

THE LOYALISTS OF ULSTER

On the morning of Monday, October 7th 1968, Ulster awoke to face a major crisis. As the shopkeepers of Derry ordered wooden shutters for their storefronts and the Civil Rights marchers trickled home with their anger, pictures and accounts of Northern Ireland's weekend were splashed across every newspaper in England and Ulster. The events in Londonderry had re-inspired all the old sentiments of hatred, fear and suspicion between Ulster Catholics and Protestants, but they had done more than that. Every household in England was reading the fantastic tale of what had been taking place across the Irish Sea, and they were staggered by what they saw. These things were unheard of in the relative tranquillity of modern Britain; many Englishmen had been unaware that the Northern Irish police carried guns, far less that they were equipped with water cannon. The papers were being read at Westminster, too, and a political storm was brewing among those many English M.P.s who wanted to know very quickly what had been going on under the aegis of British justice. The handful of Unionist M.P.s who represent Ulster at Westminster were already pressed to defend their province against the charges mounting against it. Calling the R.U.C. "the finest police force in the world", as one of them was to do, kept no one satisfied for very long. At the centre of the whirlwind, faced with the beginning of a new battle that in his heart he must have known he could not win, stood the Prime Minister of Northern Ireland, Captain Terence O'Neill.

At first sight, Terence O'Neill was the very caricature of an Ulster Unionist. Tall, narrow-faced, aloof, he had the manner of a rather arrogant public school housemaster, with his nasal voice and apparently contemptuous approach to public criticism. An Old Etonian and former Irish Guards officer (everyone who is anyone in Ulster clings desperately to military rank, however junior), he had the nexus of social and business connections across Britain that placed him firmly in the ranks of the Ulster Establishment. He was fifty-four, and had been a Unionist M.P. since 1946. A former Ulster Minister of Finance, he had succeeded Lord Brookeborough as Prime Minister in 1963.

But despite external appearances, O'Neill's political life since he became Prime Minister had been dominated by the conviction that change was needed in Ulster. He understood perfectly the impossibility of creating a modern society in Northern Ireland while discrimination and reaction prevailed, and he had constantly urged a more realistic approach to community relations. He was, without doubt, a very shrewd and able man. His problem was that in Ulster, he was Premier on the same political basis as Harold Wilson in England—as the elected leader of the majority party in the House of Commons. He held office only while he enjoyed the support of a majority of his own Parliamentary Party.

He was thus acutely aware that he could accomplish no major political change without the Unionists' support. Everything he did must be in the face of their boundlessly reactionary instincts. In public, his speeches were very cautious. He sought to nudge the Unionists gently and steadily forwards, step by step. He knew perfectly well that if he accelerated the pace dramatically, he would fall, to be replaced by some more acceptably quiescent figure. Even among his own Cabinet, he could not be sure of his ground. He had the gravest doubts about Craig, his Minister of Home Affairs, but needed very strong reason to be able to sack him. He knew that among his other Ministers, there was at least one highly ambitious man who was capable of resorting to almost any lengths to gain the Premiership himself. And he knew that his activities since he became Prime Minister, especially his meeting with the Premier of the Irish Republic, had already made him suspect in the eyes of many grass roots Unionists.

The Londonderry March placed him in a hopeless quandary. If he granted the Catholics a significant portion of their demands, he would face a major revolt from his own Party, which would help no one. If he did nothing, the Catholics would continue to press their case, escalating the situation to unknown perils. Whatever steps he took, he could count on the support of the British Labour Government at Westminster, but it was questionable how much this was worth at this stage. British Governments since the 1920's have always had a horror of becoming involved in the troubles of Ireland the political graveyard of so many of their predecessors, and while

Wilson and his colleagues might be sympathetic to O'Neill's problems, under no circumstances did they want to become directly enmeshed. The Constitution of Ulster gave the Ulster Government power over the province's domestic affairs, and Westminster were eager that they should continue to exercise it. They understood that the Catholics' demands were more than reasonable; as a Labour Government they loathed the Unionist Party; and as the overall Government of Britain, they were determined to do everything possible to urge reform on O'Neill and his Party and avoid any further bloodshed. But if it was humanly possible, they would do this at the furtherest distance from Belfast.

Nor did O'Neill himself have the slightest wish to hand over powers to Westminster or ask for their intervention. But he could at least use the threat of Westminster taking a hand as the ultimate weapon with which to browbeat his recalcitrant back-benchers: for the Unionist Party, any form of meddling from London was as repugnant as that of Federal intervention to the Southern states of America.* For the present, O'Neill sought to play for time, in the fervent hope that provincial tension would ease. He was desperately worried by his Minister of Home Affairs's handling of the situation, but could see no immediate answer save to wait and see. At this point also, he probably misjudged the full extent of the Catholic revolt which was developing. He accepted at least a proportion of his colleagues' insistence that this was a Republican and Nationalist-backed enterprise of a highly seditious nature. It was not until many weeks, or even months later that he seemed to grasp the far-reaching scope of the forces at play. This was partly, perhaps, because knowing his Protestant Ulstermen so well, he saw in the Catholic uprising the ruin of all his hopes for a gradual and peaceful reform of Northern Irish society.

So in the days following the Londonderry march, O'Neill embarked on a desperate two-pronged attempt to salvage the situation before everything crumbled around him. First, knowing so well the justice of many of the Catholic demands, he quietly began work on a limited crash reform programme which he could push through the Unionist Parliamentary Party, and which

* Much had changed since the days when the Protestants sought total political integration with Britain. As British ideas, ideals, and political thought had advanced, those of Ulster had been left behind. The gulf between English and Irish political feeling had created a new kind of reactionary isolationism and self-dependence among the Unionists at Stormont.

would answer at least some of the charges of injustice against the Government. He also summoned a Housing Conference which was attended by representatives of every local authority in Ulster. He emphasised to them the vital importance of maintaining the speed of the housing programme and of finding, and finding quickly, the means of establishing a fair Housing Allocation Programme. This met with some response, and the Corporation of Londonderry announced the switching of housing allocation from the personal discretion of the Mayor to a points system based on need. It was a trifle, but it was a beginning.

The second part of O'Neill's immediate post-Derry policy, however, left itself open to wide interpretation. In seeking to maintain a united front for his own Government, prevent Protestant unrest, and above all, if possible, dampen Catholic militance, O'Neill firmly defended the actions of the police on October 5th, and damned the organisers of the Civil Rights movement. In the weeks that followed, he preserved a semblance of unanimity among his own Government, but the public remarks of himself and his Cabinet widened still further the gulf between the Civil Rights alliance and the Ulster Establishment. While behind the scenes he struggled to find the means to hold the line, across the province over which he presided, ferment grew, and his own pronouncements did nothing to silence it.

"The police had no alternative," he said, following the Derry march. "If this march by Nationalists into a Unionist area had been allowed, we should not have been reading about scratches and bruises, but about fatal casualties. The police," he added, "are a very fine body."

Craig, the Minister of Home Affairs, was declining all demands for an inquiry into police conduct. Angrily defending his own actions, he threw charges with wild abandon. He even claimed that Cathal Goulding, head of the I.R.A., had been present in Derry, and was no whit abashed when Goulding proved he had been two hundred miles away, in the safety of the Republic across the Border. After a Cabinet meeting on October 8th, the Ulster Government issued a statement supporting all that had been done: "Ministers are satisfied that the action of the police was timely, and prevented an extremely dangerous situation from developing." A few days later, when the events in Derry were debated in the Ulster House of Commons, O'Neill said nothing to inspire the confidence of the Catholic protesters:

60

1a Early days: The Peoples' Democracy movement when they set out on their defiant New Year's march across Ulster on January 1st 1969.

1b Captain Terence O'Neill, Ulster's Prime Minister through the first months of Civil Rights militance.

2a Ian Paisley, self-styled Moderator of the Free Presbyterian Church of Ulster.

2b In Londonderry, the police brought out the water-cannon to smash the crowds as Catholic anger mounted.

"What have been presented as years of stagnation have, in fact, been years of immense economic and social progress—progress in whose benefits Protestant and Roman Catholic alike have shared. Our Government, caricatured as an inflexible and unreasonable autocracy, has not only accepted desirable change but urged it.

"But I must warn those who seek to impose changes upon us by violence or other forms of coercion that there is no course of action less likely to commend their cause to a majority of our people. In the last resort, change has to be *acceptable* change. Living happily together in a mixed community depends not upon legislation but upon a growth of trust and confidence. Neither internal violence nor attempts to engineer outside pressure is likely to promote such trust or encourage such confidence.

"For more than five years I have been trying to improve relations between the two sections of the community. What happened last weekend has certainly set us back a bit, but I will continue to hope, and to work, for better times ahead. But if we have further violence, further disorder, there will inevitably be, on both sides, a retreat into traditional attitudes, and the slender bridges men of goodwill have tried to build will tumble into a chasm. If these bridges should fall, many years may pass before they could be built again. Above all else, at this critical moment, we want a pause, a period of calm, an interval of restraint in word and action. This to my mind at the present time is more important than anything else. . . ."

Yet at that moment, O'Neill was promising the Catholics very little indeed.

In London, Prime Minister Harold Wilson had asked his Home Secretary, James Callaghan, for a report on the weekend in Derry. *The Times*, in a leading article on October 7th, said that "the refusal of Mr. William Craig, the Northern Ireland Minister of Home Affairs, to hold an inquiry into police methods in Londonderry cannot be the last word. His assurance that the police used no undue force echoes exactly that of Mayor Daley in Chicago last month." The next day, however, the paper followed up with a plea that Northern Ireland's affairs be left to the Northern Ireland Government, and that the British Government should not, at this stage, take a hand. But what had happened in Derry had made it certain that never again could the Ulster Government take action without coming under the closest scrutiny in London. The three Westminster M.P.s who had been on the march had sent a report

61

of what they had seen to the British Government. The Northern Ireland Labour Party sent a formal warning that more violence was likely if the situation was allowed to develop. From now on, Northern Ireland might be set aside from time to time, but it would not be forgotten.

In Belfast, a petrol bomb was thrown at a Presbyterian Church. Stormont Opposition Leader Eddie McAteer demanded Craig's dismissal, before leaving for Dublin for talks with the Republican Prime Minister, Jack Lynch—Lynch himself went to London shortly after for informal talks with Wilson about the Ulster situation. And in Derry, more minor incidents of violence took place. Yet while all Ireland and England were still talking about what had gone before, the protest movement, fired to far broader efforts by the effects of the October 5th march, were already launching into widespread new action.

Following the Derry march, the Civil Rights Association itself found much wider support, and a crystallisation of its aims. Branches of the Association began to spring up all over Ulster among the Catholic community, and a definite programme calling for specific reforms was drawn up. These were:

1 A universal franchise in local government elections in line with the franchise in the rest of the United Kingdom, abandoning Ulster's proprietorial voting qualification.

2 The re-drawing of electoral boundaries by an impartial Commission to ensure fair representation, e.g. to eliminate situations where Protestants could command disproportionate influence on councils.

3 Legislation against discrimination in employment at local government level and the creation of machinery to remedy local government grievances.

4 A compulsory Points System for housing to ensure fair allocation.

5 The repeal of the Special Powers Act.

6 The disbandment of the 'B' Special Police Reserve Force.

7 The withdrawal of the Public Order Bill.

These proposals were to form the basis of almost all Catholic demands throughout the civil rights struggle. With a formal organisation, a programme, a constitution and solid support within the community, the C.R.A. would have seemed well-established to press forward immediately with its campaign for change. But in the weeks following October 5th, its somewhat sedate and politically unsophisticated leadership appeared to become paralysed with shock at the forces they had conjured up. Betty Sinclair, the C.R.A.'s chairman, took a determinedly passive attitude to future policy: "The war is over," she said, "and now the discussions are about to begin." If she was content with truce, however, there were other bodies and new names who were willing and able to seize and follow through the initiatives the C.R.A. had opened up. First and prominent among these were certain of the students of Belfast's Queen's University.

As an institution, Queen's had for years been politically moribund, even by the standards of other British provincial universities. The students had shown little interest in the issues of war or peace, university conditions or the problems of Ulster. But a number of left wing Queen's students had attended the Dungannon and Derry marches, and found their way home outraged at what they had seen. On Sunday, October 6th, a small group of them organised a miniature demonstration in front of the suburban house of William Craig, the Home Affairs Minister. Craig, already furious about the row surrounding his handling of Derry, gave them short shrift. He appeared in his own doorway looking less than amused. "You don't know what it's all about. Push off you silly bloody fools!" he told the young protesters, to the delight of reporters on the spot, who ensured that the incident received widespread publicity. The next day, a group of students held a meeting at Queen's and decided on an immediate major protest against police brutality in Derry. On Tuesday, October 8th, the whole university reassembled to begin the new term, and another much larger gathering was held at which details of the march were decided to pursue the fight for six aims for Ulster: one man, one holding a march to Belfast City Hall at 2 p.m. the next day, the 9th, which would pass through Shaftesbury Square, near the deeply Protestant area of Sandy Row. Instantly, a Protestant extremist group issued notice that they would be holding a meeting in Shaftesbury Square on the afternoon of the 9th, to protest against the students' march. The students considered re-routing their own parade, but a majority decided to carry on as planned.

In the event, however, they accepted police changes of route to avoid Shaftesbury Square. About 1,000 of them set off on the afternoon of the 9th for City Hall, only to discover as they neared their goal that the Protestants were there before them. Around

63

1,000 had been at the meeting in Shaftesbury Square, but one group had assembled at City Hall, and the police blocked the road to keep the demonstrators away from them. The students, with complete restraint, sat down in Linenhall Street, and held their protest there for the next three hours. Some of their teachers, and even a few Unionists stayed with them. "We are not here to support Catholics but to draw attention to the social injustices that are common in this country," said one student. Eventually, the demonstration broke up, and they found their way back to Queen's University. But once home, furious at the behaviour of the Protestants and the frustrations of their protest, the marchers began an immediate meeting which went on far into the night. They formed a committee of ten to organise themselves. They decided to pursue the fight for six aims for Ulster: one man, one vote; fair drawing of electoral boundaries; freedom of speech and assembly; repeal of the Special Powers Act, and fair allocation of jobs and housing. The new movement was to be open to everyone, the committee would have executive power, but decisions would be taken by vote at meetings. The name People's Democracy some-how became attached, and it stuck. Its early leadership included Michael Farrell, a twenty-six-year-old lecturer at Belfast College of Technology; the ubiquitous Eamonn McCann; Cyril Toman; Kevin Boyle and Bernadette Devlin, herself just back from the Derry march. It aroused instant support within the University, and when its first march was held under the People's Democracy banner, on October 16th, 1,300 people took part. The marchers reached Belfast City Hall without incident, with only a handful of Protestant hecklers along the route, and even a significant number of Protestant moderates in its ranks. At this early phase, the group attracted a wide base of interest, and after its first peaceful activities, a reputation for moderation and reason. Queen's University continued as its headquarters, although much of its leadership was in non-student hands. There were allegations that it included too many strongly left wing and revolutionary elements, but it was difficult to find that these were responsible for any demonstrably malignant activities. From the outset, the People's Democracy channelled much untapped youthful enthusiasm, and some wild ideas and highly emotional pronouncements. But they could only be considered dangerous in a society in which some of those allegedly older and wiser allowed themselves to be roused to fury by them.

While the People's Democracy was being created in Belfast, however, those left behind in Derry to pick up the pieces after the October 5th march had been developing their own course. On October 9th, a representative meeting of Derry Civil Rights supporters was held, with Eamonn McCann in the chair. A new organisation was formed to co-ordinate activities in the city, known as the Derry Citizens' Action Committee, with a membership of sixteen. At this point, McCann himself departed for Belfast and the People's Democracy, proclaiming his view that the new group was "middle-aged, middle class and middle of the road", and thus not for him. Leadership of the Committee fell, somewhat by default, into the hands of a thirty-one-year-old local businessman, John Hume.

Hume knew all about poverty. He was the eldest of a family of seven, and his own father had been unemployed for twenty years. He had studied for the priesthood before opting out to become a teacher. He had been an early exponent of self-help to cure Derry's problems, and had helped to found a local Credit Union and the Derry Housing Association. He left teaching to start a new local smoked salmon industry, and its success gave him a degree of financial independence. He was widely respected among local Catholics for his work in the community, and well-known as a forceful and highly articulate speaker. A gentle looking figure, he had declined to join the leadership of the October 5th march, although on the day he participated in the ranks. He believed very strongly that the Civil Rights movement should seek the widest possible base of support, and above all that it should pursue its aims peacefully. He was a formidable figure, but also a very careful one. On the new Citizens' Action Committee, he became vice-chairman, with Ivan Cooper as chairman.

Hume's first move was a clear pointer to the way he intended to continue. Two weeks after the original October 5th march, he accomplished what the original protesters had intended. On October 19th, he and a large group of supporters occupied the Diamond in the centre of Derry for a sit-down demonstration. This Hume considered the most peaceful and least provocative form of protest—although it inspired the immediate resignation of the only Unionist on the Action Committee. His demonstration passed off entirely peacefully as a wary squad of Riot Police kept the bands of marauding Protestants at a distance. Encouraged by its success, he planned a far more ambitious gesture: his Committee and their supporters would march the whole length of the original October 5th march route from the Waterside Station. On November 2nd, they made the march to the Diamond, once more without major incident. A week later, Protestant extremists followed suit, but peace was maintained as Hume urged Catholics to stay away. He then, however, planned a further massive march to the city centre for November 16th.

On the 13th, despite the uneventful course of the last succession of marches, William Craig announced the banning of all marches within Derry city walls for a period of one month. O'Neill was furious, but could still do very little. The police had opposed the ban on the grounds that it was quite unenforceable. The Commission which later examined the events of the period found Craig's action "not only useless but mischievous". Every available riot squad man was drafted into Derry to face the expected massive confrontation with the Civil Rights marchers, but Ulster was terrified that this would be a hideous holocaust which no one could prevent. On the afternoon of the 16th, an incredible 15,000 strong crowd gathered at the Waterside Station to begin the march. Within a few minutes, they had moved across the Craig-avon Bridge with Hume at their head to face the hopelessly out-numbered riot squad in Carlisle Square, below the city walls, waiting to enforce the ban.

One of the police said later: "God, were we scared. We had never come up against a crowd like that. I didn't think I could, but I prayed for that Catholic, John Hume. All the men manning the barriers were thinking that if Hume couldn't keep control, and the mob got us, we would have been done for. . . ."

Hume's stewards were carefully mustered at the front of the march, arms linked to hold back the crowd. He himself walked to the police line and suggested that since he and his marchers had come out to break Craig's ban, the police might as well co-operate. A handful of marchers were allowed through the police ranks to make a token breach of the barriers. Hume, with the cheers ringing in his ears, explained to the crowd how he proposed to achieve the march's aims peacefully. With perfect obedience, they dispersed into small handfuls and made their way separately through the maze of streets to the Diamond—not, as the police could agree with relief, a formal procession. There they reassembled, and entirely peacefully they held their meeting. It was Hume's triumph. By organising ability and brilliant diplomacy, he had

66

vastly enlarged the scope of the Civil Rights movement in Derry, gained them massive publicity, and made major protest possible without bloodshed or a further outbreak of battle. A week later, on November 22nd, came news which appeared to justify all that he and his supporters had sought: The Ulster Government announced the first concessions to the Catholic demands.

On November 4th, Captain O'Neill and his Minister of Commerce, Brian Faulkner, and his Minister of Home Affairs, Craig, had attended talks in London with Prime Minister Harold Wilson. Wilson had made it abundantly clear that he was dissatisfied with the situation in Ulster, and that he expected to see some rapid progress. O'Neill, on his return to Belfast, had been able to ensure that the Unionist Party knew this. Alarmed at any prospect of Wilson stepping in, it was easier for them to accept action from O'Neill. On November 22nd, he announced a series of measures. First, the Corporation of Derry was to be suspended from its municipal functions, and replaced by a statutory Development Commission to accelerate progress in the city. Second, new steps were to be taken to remove housing allocation from the hands of local councillors and create a demonstrably fair system. The appointment of a government Ombudsman was announced, to deal with all complaints against government and local council bureaucracy. The Company Vote—an arrangement whereby businesses were entitled to special votes in local elections—was abolished. And a review of certain sections of the Special Powers Act was promised as soon as circumstance allowed.* The Unionist Parliamentary Party accepted the reforms. In Derry, the situation quietened. The more moderate Civil Rights advocates were prepared to give O'Neill a breathing space to see what he could do. For a brief moment, it appeared that something approaching normality could be restored.

But the very next day, trouble broke out in Dungannon. The People's Democracy had been making strenuous efforts to enlarge the scope of their movement across the province, and on November 23rd, a small group were holding a meeting in a restaurant in Dungannon's Market Square. Protestant extremists intervened to break it up by force, and there were incidents which caused even greater bitterness because the police appeared reluctant to take action against the Protestants. When another protest group, who had been planning a major march in Armagh for several weeks,

* At the time of writing, circumstance has still not "allowed".

announced that despite the Government Reforms, they would demonstrate as planned on November 30th, it became abundantly clear that very little had changed.

To the Catholics, there was no question that O'Neill's reform package was a very feeble answer indeed. Most especially, it did nothing to answer their loudest cry of "One man, one vote"— universal franchise in local elections. Derry might be temporarily satisfied with the promise of the Development Commission, but for Catholics across the rest of Ulster, O'Neill was offering very little that suggested rapid change. Partly also, perhaps, it was impossible then, as it continued to be in 1969, to feel great gratitude for reforms that were given so grudgingly. Throughout the Civil Rights struggle, at every step concessions were wrung forth in the face of open and insistent Unionist opposition. There was no admission that the Catholics were being given that which was long overdue to them. The atmosphere was one of unconcealed resentment: the Unionists made it clear that they were throwing a crust to the wolves only because the animals were becoming dangerous. There was no hint of conviction, of good feeling or of generosity behind the reforms. And in this situation, when so little was being given so reluctantly, it was unsurprising that the Armagh demonstrators decided to go ahead with their march.

Armagh, the ancient ecclesiastical capital of Ireland which still contains the residences of both the Roman Catholic and Protestant primates, had enjoyed a reasonably tranquil history in the years before 1968. The Unionists on the local council commanded a disproportionate number of seats, but local housing allocation had been arranged reasonably satisfactorily by a "live and let live" policy on the part of both religious sects. In the weeks following the October 5th Derry march, however, the town acquired its own local branch of the Northern Ireland Civil Rights Association, and this group was dominated from its outset by men of Republican and mostly militant Catholic leanings. It also included certain members of the Irish Republican Army.

On November 8th 1968, this new local branch held a public meeting at the Troddens Hotel, Armagh, which was also attended by representatives of the C.R.A. from Belfast, and a number of Nationalists, including Austin Currie. At this meeting, a decision was taken to hold a Civil Rights march in the city, and an Ad Hoc Committee of twenty-six members was appointed to organise it. On the same day, notice of its intended route was given to the police. In the succeeding weeks, detailed arrangements were made: three hundred stewards were nominated, the route was changed slightly after discussions with the police, and it was agreed that the only banners to be displayed would be those of the C.R.A.—once again, all provocative Republican emblems and flags were banned.

The local Protestants, however, objected to the proposed march in the strongest terms. Local members of the Orange Order and a number of Unionists demanded that it should be banned. Life in Armagh had for years pursued a reasonably tranquil course only because the Catholics kept quiet and made no trouble. Feeling had already been heightened by a Republican procession at Easter; it had been officially banned, but the police had not upheld the ban by force, and in the event it had taken place. Now the news of this new Catholic insult infuriated local Protestant feeling. On November 19th, one prominent local Protestant, Douglas Hutchinson, visited the police to reiterate insistence that the march should be banned, and to threaten the gravest consequences if it were allowed to proceed. It was made absolutely clear that if the march took place, the Protestant extremists would take their own countermeasures. The police offered Hutchinson no satisfaction, judging that the Catholic march presented no possible threat to the community. He retired discomfited, to make his own preparations. More significantly, so did another figure who had accompanied him to police headquarters: the Reverend Dr. Ian Kyle Paisley, the most prominent and the most formidable anti-Catholic in Northern Ireland.

In 1968 and 1969, many disorders ranging from scuffles to hideously bloody riots took place in Ulster. The circumstances varied, and the degree of the blame of the various participants. But beyond any shadow of doubt, no single man in Northern Ireland bears a greater share of blame for all the horror that took place than Ian Paisley, leader of the Protestant extremists. Legally, one may quibble about his exact responsibility in each holocaust that occurred. Overall, no man did more to arouse the feelings of fury, bigotry, ignorant fear and lust for blood. Paisley, a kind of nightmarish Ulster Elmer Gantry, was throughout the Northern Irish crisis a devastating threat to peace and sanity.

He was born in County Antrim, the son of a Baptist Minister who had broken away from his own denomination to found his own church. Educated at Ballymena Technical College, he studied at the Barrie School of Evangelism in South Wales, and took degrees at various somewhat questionable theological colleges in America, including the Bob Jones University at Greenville, South Carolina. He took a course of theological studies at the Belfast College of the Reformed Presbyterian Church, and then took up work with an "Evangelistic Mission Hall", at which he was ordained in 1946. He was always a loner, however; in 1951 he set up his own "Free Presbyterian Church of Ulster" which is not a recognised part of any British Presbyterian movement. In those early days, he had a church membership which numbered around 1,000. But between 1951 and 1968, he built up a following which must now number around 10,000 to 15,000 hard core supporters, in addition to many fringe adherents. Every one of his hard core loyalists will accept Paisley's word without question. He is still probably the only major figure in Ulster with a real personal following.

The man himself—forty-one in 1968—is an extraordinarily dramatic figure. Physically enormous in both height and girth, he has a deep, melodious voice which seems to roll with the hills; he has all the powers of a brilliant orator. His personal presence is entirely magnetic—there is nothing complex in suggesting that his female followers are fascinated by him for the most basic reasons. A teetotaller and non-smoker, married to an apparently uninspiring but devoted woman who lives only to further her husband's cause,* he can overwhelm even the most articulate face-to-face opponent by the sheer power and heat of his presence and voice. With a small, somewhat pointed head and large suspicious eyes mounted on that huge body, he would look grotesque were he not so formidable. To an outsider, he seems a buffoon. But in Ulster, he is accepted in deadly earnest. Over a period of years, a fundamentalist evangelist in the classic bible-thumping tradition, Paisley has become a symbol, the avenging fury of militant Protestantism in Ulster.

For the very essence of the creed he preaches, like that of Cooke and so many others before him, is that of Catholicism as the devil's own work, an unending threat to the life and security of every Protestant, and above all, a major danger to the existence of Ulster as a state. Paisley has flown to Rome to demonstrate outside St. Peter's against closer links between the Catholic Church and Protestantism. He has screamed vengeance on Cardinal Heenan when the latter preached in St. Paul's Cathedral in

* She is a Belfast City Councillor.

London. He has fought unceasingly against Civil Rights in Northern Ireland and he has sworn hellfire on any Protestant who seeks to give Catholics concessions within the province. He is the kind of Ulsterman who should by rights have died a thousand years ago. He and his supporters scream support for Britain while rejecting everything that Britain tries to stand for. They wave their Union Jacks as if they were magic symbols of Protestantism. Above all, they regard reform of Northern Ireland as the beginning of a hideous Catholic landslide that will drive Ulster into the Republic. In 1968, Paisley began a campaign for the deposition of Terence O'Neill, on the grounds that O'Neill was a threat to Ulster's survival because of his "surrender" to the Catholics.

For years, Paisley had been holding marches and demonstrations to bang the drum—very literally—for the Protestant religion. When the Civil Rights protesters began their agitation, it was Paisley's hand that guided almost every counter-move of the Protestant extremists, from the November 9th march in Derry to the attempted sabotage of the Queen's University demonstrations in Belfast. He has twelve churches around Ulster affiliated to his cause, and moves around them preaching his Sunday sermons amidst rumbled "Hallelujah's" from his congregations. His taste in church music includes "Our Fathers knew the Rome of old and evil is thy name". Callers telephoning his headquarters can frequently expect only a tape-recorded gospel message. In the autumn of 1968, the builders were already at work on an impressive new church half a mile down the road from his old headquarters in Ravenhill Road, Belfast, which he took over in 1969. It cost more than £150,000.

Immediately behind him stood a small group of totally dedicated followers who acted as his immediate staff. His wife was his secretary. His second-in-command was the bizarre figure of Major Ronald Bunting, a forty-five-year-old mathematics lecturer at the Belfast College of Technology. Bunting, some years before, had headed a local Ratepayers Association and been well-known for progressive socialist views—he had even campaigned for Gerry Fitt in his election battle for the Belfast Dock constituency. But having been converted to Paisley's camp, he played lieutenant for "the Doctor" with an unquestioning obedience and total devotion that silenced any doubts other Paisleyites might cast on his loyalties. He was the Commandant of an uncertainly defined body of Paisleyite supporters known as the Ulster Protestant Volunteers.

Both Paisley and Bunting always specialised in maintaining an air of mystery around certain of their activities, but it was well known that their two best-established organisations were the Ulster Constitution Defence Committee and the U.P.V. To the consternation of the more respectable sections of the Ulster authorities, the U.P.V. numbered in its ranks some members of the 'B' Special Reserve Police. The Ulster Constitution Defence Committee and the U.P.V. both had ramifications across all Ulster. The majority of their support stemmed from the Protestant working class and lower middle class, but Paisley had call on remarkable funds. No public accounts of his organisations were kept, but he was invariably in a position to find money for any enterprise he embarked on. At least some of it came from abroad, including the Bob Jones University; but he also collected handsomely each week at his church services in Ravenhill Road, Belfast, which were invariably well attended. Paisley had contacts, some of them extremely carefully-concealed, among almost every Protestant extremist group in Northern Ireland. His influence could not be overrated, nor the strength of his organisations. What they lacked in brainpower—and many of his aides were patently very stupid indeed—they made up in total devotion. If Paisley sent out the word that there was work to be done—of any kind—in defending Ulster's Constitution, the "loyalists of Ulster" would be right behind him. He had already served one prison sentence for leading a march through a Roman Catholic area of Belfast which deteriorated into a riot, and after which he declined to give an undertaking to keep the peace. He had never been seen with a weapon in his hand, but he had a remarkable facility for being in the vicinity of enterprises which concluded in violence. His feelings towards Catholics amounted to obsession, yet by no stretch of imagination was he mad. Far from it, an extremely shrewd and cunning mind moved behind the tub-thumping exterior. Paisley was, and perhaps still is, the cleverest political operator in Ulster. He understood precisely the motivation of his audiences, and of Ulster Protestants. He knew to needle point how to play on their deepest fears and apprehensions. And he never showed any sign of the handicap that often hampered his opponents—fear of the consequences of action.

In the days before the march in Armagh, red printed notices dropped through the letter boxes of many local shops and houses, unsigned and unidentified: "Ulster's Defenders", they read, "A friendly warning. Board up your windows. Remove all women and children from the CITY on SATURDAY 30th November. O'Neill must go." On November 28th, the police found posters on walls around the town: "For God and Ulster. S.O.S. To all Protestant religions. Don't let the Republicans, I.R.A., and C.R.A. make Armagh another Londonderry. Assemble in Armagh on Saturday, 30th November. Issued by U.C.D.C." The Ulster Constitution Defence Committee were at work. The police tore many of these posters down, amidst vehement protest from Paisley. The same day, Bunting informed the police of his intention to hold a "trooping of the colour" through a traditionally Catholic area of Armagh on the afternoon of the 30th. The police interpreted this as an attempt to get both marches banned—and thus achieve the aim of quashing the C.R.A.—or else to provoke confrontation with the Catholics. They told Bunting to have his meeting later in the afternoon, in a Protestant area of Armagh. The arguing stopped, and the town waited for the outcome of events. District Inspector Hedley Buchanan of Armagh police barracks resigned himself to a difficult weekend.

At 1 a.m. in the morning on November 30th, some thirty private cars drove into the centre of Armagh, and parked by the roadside. Paisley, Bunting, and more than one hundred of their supporters sat it out for the rest of the night by their vehicles in the silent darkness, informing the police that they intended to hold a religious meeting. At 8 a.m., the police opened roadblocks on the roads into the city, and during the next few hours removed two revolvers and more than two hundred other weapons, ranging from bill-hooks and scythes to sharpened metal pipes, from incoming "visitors". But as the crowd around Paisley gathered size, many of those present were still carrying staves and large lumps of timber; Paisley himself carried a blackthorn stick and Bunting a black walking stick. There were also, without doubt, firearms concealed among some of the party.

Soon after 11 a.m., Thomas Street, on the planned Civil Rights route, was blocked by a truck. Paisley was complaining to the police that he was prevented from holding his religious meeting. The District Inspector found many of the assembled Protestants already gathered for a hymn singing session, and called on them to disperse. He was ignored, and the police declined to move them by force. Soon after, more than a thousand Protestants converged *en masse* on Market Street, in the centre of the Civil Rights marchers' intended course, and again refused to move. In despair, the police,

350 strong, abandoned all hope of getting the Civil Rights marchers through, and erected blockades to keep Protestants and Catholics apart. When the Catholic marchers moved off from their starting point half a mile outside Armagh, 5,000 strong, they were told that the Protestants were waiting for them. Whatever the militant leanings of some of the march leaders, they were entirely unarmed, and accepted the police enjoinder to halt before they reached the police blockade.

They held their meeting where they stood, out of sight of the Protestant mob. The stewards held back the crowd and forestalled efforts by a few of the militants to break through. By 5 p.m., it seemed all over and the mass of marchers dispersed peacefully. Only a limited number of Catholics were in sight when they encountered an armed band of Protestant counter-demonstrators alongside the Catholic Cathedral in the centre of the city. The Catholics fell on them, enraged, and there was a minor battle before the police could separate them and restore order.

Yet evening came, fantastically, without a serious confrontation. Paisley and his men had come out prepared and determined to do battle if they had the chance. The Protestants had mobilised for war, and the Civil Rights movement knew it. The police, in one of their more creditable performances throughout the entire Civil Rights struggle, had narrowly averted disaster. But the cards had been called, and whatever O'Neill's reforms, whatever the protesters' moderation, it had been made utterly clear that the old lines were drawn. The question, from Armagh onwards, was not whether the old armies would clash, but when. As the People's Democracy pursued their little meetings in cafés and halls across the province to rally support for their cause, more and more often they would find Paisleyites battling them down. In Dungannon on December 4th, a local Civil Rights committee meeting became embattled with Protestants, one of whom fired a revolver at a cameraman. Paisley's statements became progressively more inflammatory. William Craig ordered some of the 'B' Specials to readiness for duty. Paisley and Bunting were charged with unlawful assembly for their part in the Armagh fiasco. And Terence O'Neill began a desperate bid to salvage something before it was too late. The story of December 1968 was that of the O'Neill Government's thrashings in the midst of an ever-speeding whirlpool.

On December 9th, the Prime Minister spoke to Ulster in a

television broadcast aimed at rallying "moderate" support across the province:

"Ulster," he said, "stands at the crossroads. I believe you know me well enough by now to appreciate that I am not a man given to extravagant language. But I must say to you this evening that our conduct over the coming days and weeks will decide our future. . . . In Londonderry and other places recently, a minority of agitators determined to subvert lawful authority played a part in setting light to highly inflammable material. But the tinder for that fire, in the form of grievances real or imaginary, had been piling up for years. And so I saw it as my duty to do two things. First, to be firm in the maintenance of law and order, and in resisting those elements which seek to profit from any disturbance. Second, to ally firmness with fairness, and to look for any underlying causes of dissension which were troubling decent and moderate people. . . ."

Ulster, he reminded his audience, owed everything—most of all a subsidy of £100 million a year—to the British and their Government. There could be no Unilateral Declaration of Independence, the Protestant extremists who thought in those terms were "lunatics". But disorder, both Catholic and Protestant, had to stop. The Catholics must stop demonstrating, and the Protestants must accept reforms:

"What kind of Ulster do you want?" he demanded. "A happy and respected province, in good standing with the rest of the United Kingdom? Or a place continually torn apart by riots and demonstrations, and regarded by the rest of Britain as a political outcast? As always in a democracy, the choice is yours. . . ."

It was a moving speech and a forceful one, and it very nearly succeeded. Letters of support for O'Neill poured into the local newspapers, 135,000 people signed petitions endorsing his policies, much emotion and endless public good feeling was lavished on his intentions. He had played for public backing, and it seemed that he had won it. Thus armed, he moved two days later to fire Craig.

William Craig had for weeks been one of O'Neill's major problems. With Craig as Home Affairs Minister, the chances of maintaining peace in Ulster were drastically reduced. His initial ban on the October 5th march had caused one kind of havoc, his subsequent ridiculous ban on all Londonderry marches had provoked further chaos and weakening of central authority. Then, he made a final blunder. He made public remarks which appeared to imply that he favoured a kind of Unilateral Declaration of Independence from Britain, turning Ulster into a separate state. It was all O'Neill needed. On December 11th, he dismissed him.

On this action, O'Neill managed to get the backing of his Parliamentary Party. He had weathered a very dangerous stretch indeed, had negotiated at least a series of modest reforms, and had by implication quashed the Protestant extremists by his successful appeal to the province. With Westminster, he knew he was on safe ground. As early as November, he had seriously considered resigning in the midst of the growing chaos around him. But the British Government, specifically both Mr. Wilson and Mr. Callaghan, had made it clear that they were most anxious that he should stay in the saddle. Any alternative Premier could only be worse—both in ability and political leanings. If O'Neill could be kept in power, they wanted him there.

In England, it appeared to many people that Northern Ireland had escaped from the brink of tragedy. In a Leader on December 7th, *The Times* had urged the Civil Rights marchers to ease up their efforts as "useful concessions have already been won from the Stormont Government". On December 12th, following the sacking of Craig and the news that the Unionist backbenchers had supported O'Neill with only four abstainers, the paper's reporter decided: "The Northern Ireland Constitutional crisis ended here this evening with a victory for Captain O'Neill, the Prime Minister, which exceeded his best expectations. . . . A resounding victory was recorded here which has been a special triumph for the thousands of people of moderate views in Northern Ireland. . . . Commonsense views had tended in the past to become obscured by the more spectacular activities of the minorities. . . ." In such a haze of apparent goodwill, it was easy to ignore the wild warnings of Gerry Fitt, who was already suggesting that Ulster could be on the brink of civil war.

The weeks following the O'Neill broadcast marked an uneasy lull. An attempt was made to begin again: the Northern Irish Attorney-General announced that all summonses relating to the disorders of October and November would be adjourned until May 1969. Most of the Civil Rights groups imposed a moratorium on their own activities while they waited to see what real fruits O'Neill's efforts would bring. Hints were given that "One man, one vote" legislation might be forthcoming—although not effective until 1971. A solitary Unionist, William Fitzsimmons, the Minister of Development, attempted a unique gesture of goodwill towards suspicious Catholicism: he resigned from the Orange Order, whose influence on Unionist policy many Catholics mistrusted so much. There was wild noise-making from Paisley on December 14th, when amidst much hubbub, a sacred cow of Ulster returned home: the aged gun-running ship *Clyde Valley*, which had supplied the Protestants in the desperate days of the battle to prevent Home Rule, was brought back to Northern Ireland to find a final resting place. Paisley attempted to turn this event into a major historic drama, but his efforts won him little more than the curious interest of some local Protestants in Larne, the port at which the ship arrived, and some flag-waving pictures in the local papers. On December 18th, the Apprentice Boys of Derry held one of their annual ritualistic ceremonies in Londonderry, but it passed off without incident. As Ulster approached Christmas, for the first time since October there was some spirit of gaiety in the air. Week after week, it had seemed that violence was being avoided only by a hairsbreadth. Yet as the days dragged on with only sporadic incidents, people began to hope again. They had already cursed the newspapers and television for the prominent publicity that had been given to Ulster's agonies since October 5th, and they derived comfort from the fact that thus far, the great majority of the province had remained untouched by the crises of Derry, Dungannon and Armagh. Up at Stormont, peaceful and still amidst those acres of green lawns and leafless trees, it was easy to feel that perhaps, after all, it was all going to be alright. The Civil Rights movement had sprung so suddenly out of the clouds, thrusting the province into the spotlight of embarrassing attention and violent unrest. Now, some of their demands had been granted, and they seemed to have shut up. In Ireland, tempers can rise and fall so quickly. Ulster had had its storms before, and they had blown over. Santa Claus, perhaps, could produce at least a Happy New Year.

Then, on December 20th 1968, the People's Democracy announced a new Civil Rights march across the length of Ulster. It was to begin on New Year's Day.

4

BURNTOLLET AND AFTER

IF, IN THE weeks following Terence O'Neill's bid for peace, many Ulster Catholics seemed willing to call a truce, elements of the People's Democracy movement were not. At a large People's Democracy meeting attended by many Queen's University students a few weeks earlier, a massive Civil Rights march planned for December 14th had been called off. But when the university dispersed for the Christmas vacation, effective control of the P.D. was left in the hands of the small group of activists still enthusiastic enough to keep the movement alive during the holiday. Their number, not surprisingly, included the most militant and the most left wing of an already radical movement. Michael Farrell, Loudon Seth and Kevin Boyle were the most prominent among them, and the most determined that protest in Ulster should not "lie down and die" merely because O'Neill appealed for calm. They felt that this was only another ploy on the part of reactionary elements attempting to maintain the status quo. Many of them were already of avowedly socialist principles—not that there should be anything unreasonable about that in a Western democracy—and they had time and energy to burn.

A Queen's-based group known as the Young Socialist Alliance had already decided to hold a march at the beginning of the New Year, regardless of who did or did not join them. In this knowledge, a small People's Democracy meeting controlled by the activists took place on December 20th. The decision was taken to march once again—more ambitiously than ever, across the length of the province from Belfast to Londonderry, a distance of some seventy-five miles, setting out on January 1st and arriving on the 4th.

The news of this new protest caused consternation among both Catholics and Protestants throughout Northern Ireland. Captain William Long, the Home Affairs Minister who had replaced Craig, summoned the leaders to see him and attempted to dissuade them from marching. They were not to be deterred, but Long declined to ban the march altogether, and so preparations went ahead. Of the two other major Civil Rights organisations, the Derry Citizens' Action Committee was already observing an informal moratorium on mass protest, but they reluctantly agreed to look after the marchers' reception when they reached their destination. The Civil Rights Association itself, increasingly passive and divided within its ranks, gave the People's Democracy £25 towards their costs as a hesitant gesture of goodwill. A number of leading Catholics, however, expressed open misgivings about the wisdom of the march at such a delicate moment—notably Eddie McAteer, increasingly obsolescent in the new climate in Northern Ireland, but nonetheless a respected old-time opposition man.

But the People's Democracy leaders, long past listening to such as McAteer, continued with their planning. Cars and a minibus were arranged to back up the march, accommodation and food were organised for the stops along the route, and word was sent out to the faithful. On the morning of January 1st 1969, some sixty marchers assembled outside the City Hall in Belfast.

The questions at issue in determining whether People's Democracy were justified in their decision to come out on the streets once more were hardly those governing demonstrations in any other society. For all Ulster knew perfectly well, as the province entered the New Year, that the Protestant militants were spoiling for battle. Armagh had been an overture which left no doubts as to the likely nature of the performance. When the People's Democracy planned their march, they were doing so in the almost certain knowledge that it would be forcibly opposed. An admittedly left wing body, they were taking the road in a society in which socialism is considered a form of the plague, and student protest something approaching treason. They knew that even if only a minority of the Protestants were prepared to oppose them openly, the great majority were passively against them. In many other parts of the world, perhaps, there would not have been the overriding fear of really serious violence which dominated Northern Irish thinking at this time. In other countries, there can be a riot one day and then a return to complete tranquillity. But in Ireland, one did not have to be a very old man to remember full-scale civil war, nor have to be very perceptive to see how little the conditions that created it had altered. Beyond this even, there is the uneasy suspicion that the Irish are particularly prone to belligerence. Ireland has always had more than its share of those who like a good fight for its own sake—some of them showed themselves in 1969—and are very much more easily provoked for it. Many societies simply would not tolerate the attitude of men like Paisley and those who followed him when they came out for battle in Armagh. Yet for all the condemnation poured on the militant Protestants by O'Neill and his more responsible colleagues, Ulster as a whole seemed quite unwilling to treat them as the social pariahs they deserved to be. The events of the autumn of 1968 might seem, in abstract judgement, less frightening than they appeared to some of those on the spot: the damage had not been insufferably great, no deaths had occurred, nor even much permanent injury. But in the peculiar climate of Northern Ireland, in the conditions then prevailing, it was abundantly clear on January 1st that a really serious holocaust could be sparked off. It was those who feared this above all else—including many liberals —who disapproved strongly of the People's Democracy march on the grounds that it was impossibly dangerous tinder at such a time.

But the marchers too had a very deeply-felt sense of purpose. If the aim of the Civil Rights movement when it sprang to life in October 1968 had been to create a more equitable society in Ulster, on New Year's Day they were still very far from that goal. O'Neill and those like him urged patience on the Catholics on the grounds that all would come in good time, as change acceptable to the Protestants was gently pushed through. But if the Civil Rights movement looked for some sign of a radical change of heart by the Unionists or the whole Protestant population, they sought in vain. The young leaders of the People's Democracy were marching because they were determined to maintain the impetus of all that had gone before, when it seemed to them to be slipping. More than that, they were going out to exercise the right of protest procession in a peaceful manner. The main burden of the charge against them is that they did so knowing they would be opposed, and this was no time to seek martyrdom. But to them, the march was the means of exposing the sickening nature of the society in which they lived. Lest there should be any doubt as to their thoughts, Bernadette Devlin has clarified them*: "Our function in marching from Belfast to Derry," she admits, "was to break the truce, to re-launch the civil rights movement as a mass movement, and to show people that O'Neill was, in fact, offering them

* *The Price of My Soul*, op. cit.

nothing. We knew we wouldn't finish without getting molested, and we were accused of going out looking for trouble. What we really wanted to do was pull the carpet off the floor to show the dirt that was under it, so that we could sweep it up; and to show the uselessness of the tactics of both the Unionist Party, who were stretching the carpet to prevent the dirt coming out, and of the civil rights campaigners, who were tidying round the edges of the carpet and forgetting the real problems underneath."

People's Democracy sought to extend the nature of the Civil Rights struggle from a merely Catholic fight for legal justice to a broad cry for social reform: they demanded not only a bigger slice of the Ulster cake for Catholics, but a bigger cake; not only a share of the Protestants' economic and social problems, but general change on classic socialist lines. Inevitably, of course, in the climate of Ulster, their support—apart from students—came almost exclusively from Catholics, and the Protestants merely classified them as the most radical and thus most dangerous of all the Civil Rights organisations. People's Democracy also lost the support of the more conservative Catholics, which meant most of the older ones, and they remained a very young group indeed, with most of the youthful vices. Especially, People's Democracy, over-come with idealism of one kind and another, had very little sense of political reality. The new Civil Rights leaders who were develop-ing elsewhere across the province were learning fast how to com-bine a degree of militance with a sense of the possible. But People's Democracy, in their anxiety to rock the Protestant boat (a very understandable objective) chose to ignore the bitter conse-quences of getting their opponents thoroughly roused: that the moderates in favour of gentle reform would be swept aside by the right wingers. Beyond any doubt, the People's Democracy's actions contributed more than those of any other body to the subsequent downfall of Terence O'Neill. Many of their number had openly desired it. And whatever attitude an observer chooses to take to-wards their decision to march on January 1st, it is difficult to follow the reasoning of their policy towards the Prime Minister. The political thinking which inspired the January 1st march was very naïve, whatever the justice of the cause they sought to promote.

The small band of marchers who left Belfast soon after 9 a.m. on the morning of New Year's Day were in uncertain humour. And already, Ronald Bunting and a group of his flag-waving and jeering cohorts were there to see them off. Bunting and his men walked in front of the marchers to the outskirts of the city, still reasonably good-tempered in their abuse. But the Paisleyites— which is Ulster's usual name for the Protestant extremists—left the march after a mile or two, and the People's Democracy group, now swollen to around a hundred, arrived in Templepatrick for lunch without serious incident.

But that afternoon, as they approached Antrim, the goal of their first day, they found Bunting waiting for them on Antrim Bridge. Around him were gathered his supporters—men he called "farmers, shopkeepers, and some of the landed gentry of the area". They were clustered about the Lambeg Drum—a large, ugly instrument, much beloved of the Protestants with its dull, heavy thud—banging away steadily. There were not very many of them nor did they look very imposing, but they had their effect.

A cordon of police had been extended across the road to separate them from the marchers. The marchers asked the police to clear the way as they were doing for the traffic, which was still moving through steadily. The County Inspector parleyed with Bunting, but came back and told them that this was not possible. Eventually, after much argument, police tenders were made available to ferry the marchers to the hall on the other side of Antrim where they were to stay the night.

All the next day, January 2nd, was spent in spasmodic progress across County Antrim, partly on foot, partly by car, often re-routed by the police, and continually interrupted by negotiation and confrontation. With every hour, Bunting's force was growing, and the first signs of weapons appeared amongst them. Every stage of the day, the Paisleyites were there first. There would be altercations, abuse and the firm refusal of the police to move the counter-marchers. James Chichester-Clark, the Minister of Agriculture, whose home lay near the route, appeared with his brother Robin, an Ulster Westminster M.P. The two of them appeared to feel that any police diversion of the march was preferable to police action to remove the Paisleyites. As the *Belfast Telegraph*—the most influential Ulster paper, of moderate but far from committed Catholic views—noted in a Leader: "For how long would the police permit a Roman Catholic crowd to stand in the way of a parade of Protestants, militant or otherwise?" Massive press and television coverage was already accompanying the march, and feeling grew as it became clear that the police were totally unwilling to ease its path. Local Catholics along the route were joining in increasing numbers. By that night, when they stopped at Brackaghreilly Hall near Maghera, guerilla parties of roaming Protestants armed with sticks, bottles and rocks were already becoming a serious threat, and a number of incidents broke out. During the hours of darkness, around 1,000 Protestants swept through Maghera smashing the windows of shops and houses and hurling in bottles and stones. A Protestant deputation called on James Chichester-Clark at his home late in the evening and demanded that he ask for the march to be forbidden to pass through the town. That ever-obliging gentleman telephoned the Home Affairs Minister and put the request. Long deferred an answer. But the next morning, when the marchers set out to go back through Maghera before continuing their journey, the police prevented them, and they had to set out directly over the Glenshane Pass towards Dungiven, their next target. By now some five hundred strong, they arrived in Dungiven to find a warm reception from local Catholics who turned out in large numbers to cheer them in, feed them and prepare them for the next stage. Michael Farrell addressed the crowd, reiterating the demands of the protest for an end to discrimination, and adding that many of the reforms they sought were non-sectarian, and would benefit both Protestants and Catholics. They then set out for Feeney, a little village next along their route.

But they had scarcely gone a mile when the police halted them again, and insisted that several of their intended stops were in Protestant country, and would provoke trouble. This time, the marchers decided they had had enough. Massing in front of the police line, they forced their way through the row of officers standing with linked arms. Aside from their exasperation with re-routing, they had begun to have very serious doubts about the policy guiding police action. They had genuine fears that the police re-routing could divert them straight into the hands of a Protestant crowd. This had already happened once. So when one of their scouts reported that contrary to police remarks, the road ahead appeared entirely clear, they broke through. They reached the village of Claudy, their destination for the night, without incident.

During that evening, Captain Long, the Home Affairs Minister, appeared on television to say that he had met during the day with Dr. Paisley and Major Bunting, and that their meeting had been "very congenial". He added that the followers of Dr. Paisley had been entirely non-violent during the march. Following the afternoon meeting, the incredible Bunting had held a press conference

83

at the Stormont Building, during which he was asked whether he had ordered his men to harass the Civil Rights march. He replied: "I have given a request to the Loyal Citizens of Ulster, and thank God they have responded. And I think they have hindered it, and I think to a certain extent they have harried it. . . ." It was then suggested that the Paisleyites should have ignored the march. Bunting replied: "You can't ignore the devil, brother."

The next day, January 4th, was intended to be the last of the march. But while the marchers slept in Claudy, guarded by groups of local Catholics as restless Protestants roamed the town, preparations began for the final act of the drama. In Londonderry Guildhall, Paisley and Bunting held a "religious" meeting attended by around a thousand Protestants. Paisley asked the meeting if the marchers were to be allowed to enter Protestant Derry freely; he reminded them of Derry's history of Protestant resistance to Catholic onslaught, and he inquired if this spirit had died. The meeting was roused to enthusiastic yells of defiance. Bunting then rose. If anyone felt like taking positive action, they should meet him the next day at a pre-arranged spot along the road, ready for a long job.

Catholic Derry, however, had by now got word of Paisley's assembly. A huge crowd of furious Catholics gathered outside the Guildhall, enraged by the activities of the Paisleyites in the past three days. John Hume and Ivan Cooper—even Eamonn McCann —addressed them in a desperate effort to keep the peace, urging them to save their feelings for the next day, when they could welcome the marchers into the city. But tempers were too high. Bunting's car was discovered around the corner and set on fire. Stones and bottles began to fly in the direction of the Guildhall. Then, as the situation hung in the balance, the besieged Paisleyites broke out: armed with broken furniture and banister rails, they sallied from the hall driving the Catholics fleeing before them. There was a major fracas in the streets at the centre of the city as police struggled desperately to separate the rioters. Eventually, the crowds were broken up. But the atmosphere in Derry was dangerously tense in the aftermath.

Outside the city on the road to Claudy, other strange activities were taking place that night. In Killaloo Orange Hall outside Claudy, a group of Protestants met under mysterious circumstances. Certain planning was done relating to the Catholics' march the next day. Also during the hours of darkness, truckloads of newly quarried stones and empty bottles were taken out into the countryside and dumped by the road along which the march would pass. The Catholics, both in Derry and Claudy, had the strongest suspicions that something was afoot, but no one knew precisely what was being organised.

On the morning of January 4th, the marchers held a prolonged discussion on whether to call off their plans for the day as a result of the night's events in Derry, and the air of acute tension and Protestant "troop movements". But after an hour-long debate, in which Eammon McCann took a prominently militant role, they determined to see it through to the end. The circumstances were not auspicious.

Throughout the past three days, minor scuffles had been taking place continually between Protestants, marchers, and local Catholics. A Catholic monument along the march route had been damaged by explosives—it was fifty yards from a police station, but no arrests had been made. Protestants had been infuriated still further because at times, some marchers had carried the hated Republican banner. The police had already given grounds for suspicion that they would not extend themselves to defend the march, and in fairness to them, the relatively small Ulster police force was being stretched to the limit to maintain some semblance of order. Major Ronald Bunting, on the other hand, had given every sign that he was gathering all the forces he could muster for the final phase of the march. While his public pronouncements might make him seem ridiculous, the Major was no mean organiser. With his receding hairline, sad face and prominently protruding ears, he always appeared in public to be Paisley's somewhat zombie-like shadow. But while this might be true in terms of policy, in tactical planning he was no fool. Many of Bunting's enterprises may never enjoy the benefit of public scrutiny. But those that have come to light show all the qualities of shrewd judgement. Bunting could never be a leader in his own right, but he was the ideal lieutenant. On the night of January 3rd, he appears to have been very busy indeed. As the marchers finally left Claudy on the morning of the 4th at 10.15 a.m., with the students in front and local people behind, some Protestants standing by the roadside yelled to them that they weren't home yet. But most of the little town turned out to see them off in good spirits.

At Cumber Church, only a little way up the road, the police halted the march. The leaders were warned by the senior officer that an opposition group perhaps fifty strong was assembled on high ground a few hundred yards ahead. The officer was most insistent that the opposition was thus limited, but admitted that he could not guarantee to get the marchers through in safety. Nevertheless, they determined to press on. For the first time in the march, some forty steel-helmeted police were placed in the forefront. Then, five hundred strong, they advanced up the road towards Derry. Minute after minute went by without event. Only a few handfuls of obviously ill-intentioned youths were following them on a parallel course in the fields above the road. They were in a narrow lane bordered on both sides by hedges and trees as they approached the Burntollet Bridge across the river Faughan. It was as they reached the bridge that the Protestants attacked.

About three hundred of them, commencing a hail of rocks at the marchers on the road, smashed forward with nail-studded clubs, sticks and bottles. Some were on the high ground above the road, others behind the hedges along it, yet others swarming about the road ahead. As marchers fled into the fields for cover, they were seized and kicked into unconsciousness. Bloodstained men, women and young girls were cowering for refuge where there was none. The attackers wore white armbands to distinguish them from their victims, and were pouring down ammunition in plenty.

"A curtain of bricks and boulders and bottles brought the march to a halt," says Bernadette Devlin. "From the lanes burst hordes of screaming people wielding planks of wood, bottles, laths, iron bars, crowbars, cudgels studded with nails, and they waded into the march beating hell out of everybody."

Some were hurling marchers into the river, others attacking them as they fled into the riverbed for cover. Screaming people were dashing bleeding back down the road to Claudy, while the forefront of the march desperately attempted to press on up the Derry road clutching their injured. But the march had become a shambles of weeping women and bloodstained men, as a storm of Protestant abuse followed them. Many were still lying unconscious where they had been thrown. A considerable proportion of the wounded were girls. The ambush had been complete, the results devastating. No one who was at Burntollet could ever forget it.

Most incredible of all, the police appeared utterly indifferent to everything that passed. Many of the police had chatted amiably with the Protestants as they had watched the marchers come up. Others had stood by and watched while marchers were clubbed and kicked. No attempt was made to arrest the attackers or even to impede them. Bunting and his men had stormed down without interference, and it seemed impossible that the police could have been unaware that such a highly organised force was waiting. Beyond even this, numbers of men who were clearly identified as 'B' Special reserve police were among the attackers. The regular police seemed reluctant to assist the wounded. Only the first ranks of helmeted police at the front of the march had swept through in cohesion, bearing behind them the front lines of marchers. These, rallying somewhat as stragglers caught up, staggered on towards Derry, shattered by what they had experienced. Behind them lay the last of the wounded and a few gangs of Protestants striding off towards their cars, parked across the fields. Behind them also lay the ruins of Terence O'Neill's "slender bridges of goodwill".

The marchers came into Derry through Irish Street. Here, they found more Protestants waiting for them. There was a further serious battle as slates and rocks hurtled down and more marchers were injured. As they arrived at last at City Hall, where the Citizens' Action Committee had prepared to meet them, much of Derry relapsed into sectarian struggle. For the remaining hours of the afternoon and evening, Protestants made periodic assaults on the Catholics around City Hall, Catholics from the Bogside came out to do battle. And some of the police disgraced themselves. Parties of police, at last given their chance to "get" the Papists, assaulted Catholics at random—a number of them elderly—smashed into Catholic homes, and even fought their way into a department store where they batoned several customers. When at last quiet of a kind returned, Derry was in a shell-shocked stupor.

The truce was broken, Ulster was once again splashed across every newspaper and television newsreel in Ireland and England. For a few days, Derry broke down: the Bogside slammed itself shut in the face of the police, a "pirate" radio station calling itself Radio Free Derry began propagandising on the air waves, and it was a matter of desperate negotiation before the Bogsiders finally agreed to let the police return to patrols in their area; 163 people had been treated in hospital following the weekend. The results of Burntollet and the chaos that followed it altered the entire face of the Northern Irish crisis.

First, the polarisation between Catholics and Protestants increased immeasurably. Many Catholics who had hitherto wavered were now totally committed to Civil Rights solidarity. The

Protestants, who considered that it was Catholic militance which had brought about the tragedy, became even more enraged with the activities of the protesters.

Second, the relationship such as had existed between the Catholics and the police broke down irrevocably. On January 11th, in the predominantly Catholic town of Newry, near the border with the Republic, a Civil Rights Association–People's Democracy march took place which ended in open battle with the police when they attempted to divert the parade from its route. Police tenders were set on fire, anarchy prevailed for several hours, and militant Catholics joined determined assaults on the police lines. The police on the ground handled the situation with remarkable tactical skill and restraint, minimising the extent of the riot. But the attempts of Michael Farrell, Kevin Boyle and John Hume to keep the peace failed hopelessly. Several efforts were made to occupy public buildings, and the Post Office was damaged. It was a new type of affray, in that despite threats prior to the march, the Protestant extremists played no part. This was simply an attempt at revenge for the events of Burntollet and Derry. It achieved nothing save further heightening of feeling, and set the stamp on relations between Catholics and police.

But Newry, while it contributed significantly in heating the climate of feeling across the province, was almost a diversion in the current of events following Burntollet. From January 5th until early in April, it was not riots but politics that thrust Ulster into the headlines. The People's Democracy's New Year march threw the switch on a long chain of political crises that upturned the face of Ulster's Government. If the People's Democracy's aim had been to shake the very roots of the O'Neill Administration, they succeeded completely.

Terence O'Neill returned from a holiday in England that Sunday, January 5th, furiously angry and deeply depressed. He saw in what had happened, in the "meddling" of a few hundred wild young students, the ruin of all his endeavours. Immediately following his return, he put out a hasty statement which reflected his exasperation:

"I want the people of Ulster to understand in plain terms the events which have taken place since January 1st. The march to Londonderry, planned by the so-called People's Democracy was, from the outset, a foolhardy and irresponsible undertaking

88

—two things have happened. Some of the marchers and those who supported them in Londonderry itself have shown themselves to be mere hooligans, ready to attack the police and others. And at various places people have attempted to take the law into their own hands in efforts to impede the march. These efforts include disgraceful violence. . . .

"It deserves to be remembered that it was the refusal of decent people, both Roman Catholic and Protestant, to be provoked which made the last I.R.A. campaign such a failure. Peaceful contempt will bring marches to an end where violence only tends to recruit further marchers. . . ."

O'Neill praised the police for all their efforts and said they had done the best job possible under the circumstances. Then he added:

"But clearly Ulster has now had enough. We are all sick of marchers and counter-marchers. Unless these warring minorities rapidly return to their senses we will have to consider a further reinforcement of the regular police by greater use of the Special Constabulary for normal police work.

"It is also high time that certain students returned to the studies for which they have the support of the taxpayer, and learned a little more about the nature of our society before displaying again such arrogance towards those who have built up the facilities they enjoy. . . .

"Enough is enough. We have heard sufficient for now about civil rights; let us hear a little about civic responsibility."

In the near-hysterical atmosphere following the events in Derry, it was an ill-considered speech; whatever truth there might be in what he said, it served only to infuriate further the Catholics, without appeasing the Protestants. O'Neill seemed to be trying to brush them all aside like so many buzzing flies, to be talking to them like an irritated schoolmaster with some trying pupils. The Catholic community wanted regret and real sympathy for what had happened—also some very solid promises that nothing like it could ever occur again. This they were denied. An inquiry was set up to examine the conduct of the police,* but the Ministry of

* The inquiry found cause for police disciplinary action against 16 policemen, but the charges were dropped at the beginning of 1970 when efforts were being made to permit the R.U.C. to start yet again with a clean slate. Formal indictments against the men had already been dropped in the general amnesty that was announced in May.

Home Affairs stonewalled every question about their actions, and fought hard to prevent the role of the off-duty 'B' Specials at Burntollet being seriously examined. Above all, at this moment, it was the ultimate outrage to the Catholics that O'Neill should mention calling up more of the infamous Specials as a remedy for what had gone before. Eamonn McCann said: "At least it meant an end to the fiction that O'Neill was a fair-minded liberal, dedicated to solving social problems. No one in Derry could place any further trust in promises and assurances made by him and people like him. . . ."

O'Neill's position among the Unionists and Protestants upon whom he depended for power was now rocking dangerously. First, there was their fury about the increasing demands from the Catholics for intervention by Harold Wilson and the Westminster government. Wilson had been making it very clear publicly in England that his sympathies lay with the Catholics. He and his government had also been in close consultation with O'Neill. The Unionists began to feel more and more that O'Neill was party to some private conspiracy with Westminster that threatened the independent jurisdiction of Stormont. In a sense, in trying to strengthen O'Neill's hand, Wilson weakened it by threatening O'Neill's essential power base among his Party. Beyond this, as Unionist M.P.s' doubts about O'Neill had grown, there had seemed only one overwhelming reason for maintaining him in power—if he could be relied on to guard Protestant interests while keeping the Catholics under something resembling control. After January 5th, it was abundantly clear that O'Neill's influence with the Catholic community was waning very fast—or at least his ability to keep them quiet. When this failure was allied to fears of his dealings with Westminster, the Unionists' restlessness swelled to the point of open revolt.

On Monday, January 6th, O'Neill was faced with the impossible problem of securing law and order within the province—a task at which many Unionists already considered him weak and inept—while somehow continuing to keep his reform programme in being. First, and to the Catholics most devastating, after a three-hour Cabinet meeting on that day, he announced that the Home Affairs Minister was being given powers for a large scale call up of 'B' Specials to protect the interest of the country "from the irresponsibility of the few". In consultation with his senior police chiefs, he determined that more men had to be found from somewhere. The R.U.C. with its total strength of 3,200 could only concentrate five hundred men in any one place at any one time, and this was alarmingly few in the growing climate of violence. The 'B' Specials' call-up was intended to make it possible to relieve some R.U.C. men of normal police duties to be available for riot control. To the Catholics, it seemed tantamount to unleashing the wolves upon them. But O'Neill insisted that since his first reform programme had been announced "the Government has given the clearest possible evidence of their determination to implement these proposals, and there is no justification whatever for the continuing agitation which is bound to make the task more difficult, and to damage the best interests of the province".

On January 9th, he paid a sudden surprise visit to London for more talks with the British Government, vigorously denying the growing rumours that troops would have to be called in to ensure the peace. In Belfast and across Ulster, however, it seemed to many people that he was rapidly losing control. The even louder threats of the Catholic militants, the carnival atmosphere of the Newry riot, the walk-out of Paisley and Bunting from the Armagh court where they were being tried for their part in the November disturbance, and talk of more major Civil Rights marches being planned all contributed to the unease.

Then, on January 15th, he announced the setting-up of a Commission to examine the causes and nature of the crisis since October. Initially, the news was welcomed by both Catholic and Protestant extremists. But on January 23rd, Brian Faulkner, Deputy Prime Minister and Minister of Commerce, resigned from the O'Neill government. The mounting anger among the Unionist Party burst.

Brian Faulkner was the ablest man in the Administration. The forty-seven-year-old son of a prominent local businessman, he had become the youngest-ever M.P. in the Ulster House of Commons and then the most successful Minister of Commerce the province had ever known. A tough, white-haired, decisive figure, he was one of the most articulate men in Ulster politics, also one of the most ambitious. He walked out on O'Neill after a violently acrimonious exchange of letters. He said he believed O'Neill was allowing the province to tear itself apart by his in-activity; that if he believed (as Faulkner claimed to) in universal adult suffrage and major reform, he should take these measures straight to his party and push them through, while taking a firm line to restore law and order. "I am forced to the conclusion," he said in his resignation letter, "that not only is the party tearing itself to pieces, but conditions in the country are such that the work of my department is imperilled." Most specifically, he condemned the setting up of the Commission of Inquiry as "an abdication of authority". O'Neill should not, Faulkner demanded, sit back and let some outside Commission tell him what he and Ulster should be doing.

And O'Neill, in his letter of acceptance, threw away the political tradition of polite gestures of thanks and acknowledgements. He offered his own ideas on the shortcomings of his Minister of Commerce. Faulkner, he said, had neither objected to the setting-up of the Commission when it had been discussed, nor had he shown any sign of his convictions before. Following the events of October 5th, claimed O'Neill, it had been Faulkner who demanded that there should be no surrender to the Catholics under duress.

The reality was that O'Neill believed, with some very good reason, that it was not wholly altruistic idealism that persuaded Faulkner to quit. Faulkner had had a long-time reputation in Ulster as a right winger. These were the first signs he had shown of liberal pretensions. It was difficult not to suspect that Faulkner sensed the ship sinking beneath him, and sought to make his own play at the critical moment. Above all else, the Minister of Commerce appeared to be a highly ambitious political realist, and at a time when the future of the O'Neill government hung narrowly in the balance, he saw a chance to be in at the kill. William Craig, the sacked Home Affairs Minister, already had one group of disenchanted Unionist M.P.s gathered around him. Faulkner's departure drastically eroded the support O'Neill had left.

Then, two days later, came a further blow. The Minister of Health and Social Services, William Morgan, also resigned. Morgan was a much less significant figure in the Government than Faulkner, but his action, following so closely that of the Commerce Minister, showed the way the wind was blowing. On the 28th, still seeking to convince the province that he was determined to take a tough line with disorder, O'Neill introduced to Parliament changes in the Public Order Act, making it illegal to hold sit-down demonstrations that obstructed highways and outlawing the occupation of public buildings.* But the Nationalists were talking of a cam-

* After much delay and violent Catholic opposition, these measures became law early in 1970.

92

3a The Royal Ulster Constabulary included armoured cars and personnel carriers in their standard armoury.

3b In April 1969, 21-year-old Bernadette Devlin swept to celebrity when she was elected Westminster MP for Mid-Ulster.

4a In the Shankill Road, Belfast, heart of Protestant Ulster, cars were overturned and set on fire as rioters seethed with indignation at the Catholics' demands for Civil Rights.

4b In Londonderry, the police became desperate as warfare with the Catholics of the Bogside grew in intensity.

paign of civil disobedience, and Paisley and Bunting—having declined the province-wide adjournment of disorder cases until May—were each sentenced to three months' imprisonment for their behaviour at Armagh, thus achieving the role they sought as Protestant martyrs. When O'Neill appeared to address an evening meeting at Newtownards Town Hall, he was greeted by a jeering mob outside. By January 30th, thirteen Unionist backbench M.P.s were known to be seeking a change in the Government's leadership, and another Junior Minister, Joseph Burns, resigned— possibly after some pressure from his local constituency association. All the remainder of O'Neill's government claimed to be solidly behind him, but even with both Faulkner and Morgan still keeping quiet, a majority of his backbenchers were openly opposed to him.

Now, there was open discussion of O'Neill's chances of survival. It appeared that he had three choices: either to resign immediately and leave the Parliamentary party to elect a new leader and Prime Minister; or to call an election to seek public support for his policies; or to try to sit it out where he was. The latter alternative seemed the least practicable, and O'Neill had battled on for too long now to abandon everything and resign without a fight. He was left to weigh the odds of an election, knowing as he did so that it would further isolate every warring element in the province. Paisley had already announced that if Ulster went to the polls, the Protestant extremists would fight as many seats as they could. The Civil Rights supporters, sensing that the political battle was immediately more important than anything they might do on the streets, were preparing to enter the lists. And the Unionists, now clearly divided between those who wanted O'Neill out and those who would fight for him to stay in office, were split down the middle. The only factors favouring O'Neill were that he still enjoyed an obviously large measure of moderate public support; and that Faulkner and Craig, his most obvious rivals for the premiership, had both made enough enemies in their political careers to create a pro-O'Neill group if only because the alternatives seemed worse. When it came to the point, O'Neill could reckon that many Unionist waverers would back him in the hope of staving off a total split within the Party. Nevertheless, although the cards clearly lay somewhat in his favour, he also knew that the forces opposed to him represented a strong and very solid minority. If he called an election, thus openly declaring war on

4—U1969 * *

them, he had to defeat them impressively to maintain his own credibility. A mere narrow victory leaving the opposition unscathed would prove nothing. Yet more than ever, he could not see how to continue governing his unruly province without smashing his Parliamentary opponents. At the beginning of February, the Unionist M.P.s opposed to him held a meeting at Portadown to discuss their course of action. It was widely reported in the press, earning those taking part the name of The Portadown Junta, and finally formalising the rift in the Unionist Party. O'Neill saw that his public position was becoming untenable with Civil Rights supporters on one side of him, Paisleyites on another, and now a formidable detachment of his own Party declaring open war. On February 3rd, he held a seven-hour Cabinet meeting at Stormont. The next day, Parliament was dissolved and a General Election, not legally due until 1970, was called for February 24th.

5

THE FALL OF O'NEILL

THE GENERAL ELECTION summoned by Terence O'Neill in February 1969 offered Northern Irish voters their first cliff-hanging political choice since the creation of Ulster. It opened up divisions and issues such as had never been seen in the history of the province. And yet it also showed conclusively how deep was the gulf between the multitude of contending factions. O'Neill entered the fray needing strong Catholic support for his candidates in order to oust his own right-wing opponents. He had only a third of his Parliamentary Party openly against him, but his own forces were in such disarray that the minority had been able to force all the initiatives. Yet from the outset of the campaign, the actions of every splinter group showed that there was no mood for alliance even against common enemies. Thirteen parties and factions put up candidates in various of the fifty-two constituencies. The 942,000 registered electors of Ulster were in principle delighted to be offered a "real" choice at last. But it quickly became apparent that whatever the long-term benefits of this expansion of the political area, in immediate terms the fragmentation was disastrous.

The basic election struggle, as confusing for the participants as for the onlookers, was between the rivals within the Unionist Party. Each "official" Unionist candidate was chosen by his own local constituency association. Clearly, O'Neill had hopes that in at least some areas, the local associations would deny re-nomination to M.P.s who opposed him. This did not occur. The "official" Unionist candidates in almost every constituency were those who had been M.P.s, whether pro-O'Neill or anti-O'Neill. In the campaign, both sides issued the same leaflets and were entitled to use of the same Party machine. They differed only, in effect, about the premiership of O'Neill and policy towards Civil Rights. The electorate knew very well the issues at stake, but both sides attempted to blur their attitudes to the greatest possible extent in an effort to keep their options open.

The Unionist battle was complicated still further by the fact that neither side was willing to leave "official" Unionists to be elected in seats safe against Catholic opposition. New factions sprung up in many constituencies: where anti-O'Neill men had been nominated as "official" Unionist candidates, pro-O'Neill Unionists stood as "unofficial" Unionists. Likewise, in some places where pro-O'Neillites were the "official" candidates, anti-O'Neill candidates emerged. These splits extended the political battle that had hitherto been openly waged only at Stormont to every local Party group in the province. Old alliances and traditional friendships were cast aside and new ones forged, and the campaign began with all the bitterness of internecine strife.

In five constituencies, too, Ian Paisley mounted his own "Protestant Unionist" candidates. His deputy, Ronald Bunting, opposed O'Neill's Minister of Commerce, Roy Bradford, in the Victoria division of Belfast. And Paisley himself took on the Prime Minister in Bannside, County Antrim.

The Opposition at Stormont had traditionally been based on the Nationalists, the Republican Labour Party and the Northern Ireland Labour Party (affiliated to that in England). But in 1969, two significant new forces took to the hustings. First, the People's Democracy introduced candidates in eight constituencies. Michael Farrell came in against O'Neill in Bannside, Eamonn McCann against Eddie McAteer in the Foyle Division of Derry, and Bernadette Devlin—the first time her name had been heard across the province—against James Chichester-Clark in South Derry. It was clear that their chances of success were very slim indeed, but they decided that if everyone else was to try conventional politicking for a change, so would they. They sought the widest publicity for their political platform, and this was the obvious way to get it. And more significant even than the stand of the People's Democracy was that of Ivan Cooper and John Hume. Both stood for election against sitting Nationalist M.P.s, in mid-Derry and Foyle respectively, as Independents. The other traditional Opposition parties mounted candidates, too, but it was on the Unionists, the Paisleyites, People's Democracy and the Independents that every eye was turned.

As the election campaign began, it was clear that the overriding issue was the survival of O'Neill and his modestly progressive policies. By the Left, he stood accused of cowardice—of rating the unity of the Unionist Party above the importance of reform, and of being a repressive force in the struggle for Civil Rights. People's Democracy, who issued a manifesto broadly restating their original aims and continuing to emphasise their demands for general social change, were firmly anti-O'Neill. Meanwhile, the Right charged O'Neill with indecision, failure to maintain law and order, collusion with the Westminster Labour government. Ian Paisley insisted that he was threatening the very existence of the Protestant state. By now, ominous talk of a possible take-over of Stormont's powers by Westminster had become general. O'Neill sought to capitalise on this by suggesting that Ulster could only keep its self-government by progressive policies. The right-wingers blamed O'Neill for any danger of a sell-out to Westminster that might exist.

From the beginning of the campaign, mutual personal abuse was general and bitter. Yet to many people's vast relief and astonishment, the election continued on its course without violence or street clashes. For three weeks, across the length and breadth of Ulster, the population reverted to a battle of words. It was soon evident that the People's Democracy, while they were getting their share of publicity, were making little decisive impact on the electorate, and represented a force only capable of vote-splitting. Equally, in most constituencies, the "unofficial" pro-O'Neill candidates were losing the battle against the "official" anti-O'Neillites. Despite all the activity and rhetoric, no faction was gaining or losing significant ground. But one constituency attracted intense interest: that of Terence O'Neill himself.

O'Neill is a Parliamentary debater of great ability and skill. But he had never in his entire political career been forced to fight a really tough electoral battle among the people. When, notably late in the campaign, he at last turned aside from provincial problems to considering the safety of his own seat, he found himself in poor case. Yet as a matter of policy, he declined to hold or address any public meetings in the Bannside, and restricted himself to touring the area in person, walking the streets and visiting the small factories talking to the people. But he has never had the common touch. It was embarrassing to watch him as he stopped to chat to his voters: he could ask about the weather and make some remark about the job a factory hand was doing, but after that he was lost. He seemed reluctant to discuss politics with the people, to come out of the shell he had created around himself and play the extrovert part real electoral politics demands. In the last ten days before the election, his amblings around the Bannside in the snow left spectators bemused and sceptical.

For in addition to Michael Farrell's efforts against him, drawing away his support from the Left such as it was, O'Neill was being challenged by Ian Paisley in a campaign that rattled the very bones of Ulster Protestantism. Almost every night, Paisley was there with his fife and drum band, the Shankill Road Young Conquerors. Muffled in an overcoat and fur hat, sash across his massive chest, Paisley careered from housing estate to meeting hall, from village square round the little streets, proclaiming the downfall of O'Neill and the rallying-cry of salvation of Protestantism with that fantastic voice and superb showmanship. Even in icy weather, the crowds came out to hear him. He called on them to sing "Ulster's Battle Hymn"—O God Our Help in Ages Past; he told them how "Popery takes you down into the darkness"; he led them in his parades behind the band—and they loved it. Paisley appealed to the romantic, tub-thumping, excited taste in the country community: all the fun, and religion too. He told them that what he did, he did for the name of the Lord; and that made it all seem all right. As O'Neill made his lonely trudges by day, Paisley brought the fair to town every night. It was obvious that the Prime Minister was in deep trouble.

As election day drew near across the province, however, it was also depressingly clear how little real debate was taking place in most Unionist constituencies about the issues of Civil Rights or reform. Perhaps it was inevitable that in any political system which wields much responsibility with little power, this should be so. But undoubtedly, the highlights were being provided exclusively by the outbursts of personal hostility and back-stabbing. In County Fermanagh, John Brooke, son of old Lord Brookeborough—still a much-revered figure among old-style Protestants—was standing as an anti-O'Neillite. His father came out in open opposition to O'Neill, further deepening the Party split, and provoking reciprocal public hostility from the O'Neill camp. Up in County Derry, the clash between Hume and Cooper and the Nationalists —New Opposition against Old—saddened and depressed many Catholics. Nevertheless, there was no shadow of doubt who most intelligent moderates wished to win: Hume and Cooper were both men of exceptional ability and articulateness, with a strong sense of political reality. Nationalism as a political platform had long since become a kind of harmless sacred cow, whatever the virtues of some of its M.P.s as individuals.

At O'Neill's last press conference before polling, he appealed to the electorate to support "those candidates who have the whole country's interests at heart. While party unity is important, it is not as important as the unity of Northern Ireland". But even as he said this, he must have known full well that the omens were not promising. When the results were announced during the night of February 24th, most of his worst fears had been realised. Technically, he had won, but his opponents were almost unshaken. The cross-voting he had hoped for so desperately had failed to take place. The electorate had voted on the old sectarian lines, the old men were almost all back in the Stormont, and his personal prestige had suffered a crippling blow. The gamble had failed, the lines were as before. The electorate voted two-to-one in his favour for pro-O'Neill Unionists against all other opposition, but eleven firmly anti-O'Neill Unionists were back in Stormont. Of his major opponents, only William Morgan and William Hinds lost their seats. Three Independent O'Neill Unionists had been elected, and the Party had gained one seat overall. But this was not the kind of victory O'Neill sought. Only among the Opposition had there been notable developments: both John Hume and Ivan Cooper were elected, and Eddie McAteer, after twenty-two years in Stormont, was out. Bernadette Devlin had lost in South Derry, but she had collected nearly 6,000 votes against the Minister of Agriculture, Major James Chichester-Clark. The Paisleyites had scored significant numbers of votes in several constituencies, although Major Bunting had fared poorly against Roy Bradford. The upheaval had shown Ulster politics a new face, but it proved only that Ulstermen do not easily change their minds.

And for O'Neill, facing this provincial situation, there was a further shock that was in many ways the most damaging of all: in his own constituency, the Prime Minister of Northern Ireland had been elected by an overall minority of voters: Michael Farrell had won over 2,000 votes for People's Democracy; and, devastatingly, Ian Paisley scored 6,331 against O'Neill's own 7,745. "The Prime Minister," boomed Paisley in his triumph, "is despised, discredited, and disgraced!" Not yet that, perhaps, but badly wounded. O'Neill made no effort to conceal his own dismay. He appeared haggard and grim on the morning following the election to admit, in a masterpiece of understatement: "I had hoped that this would be the dawn of a new Ulster. It has not broken as fully as I would have hoped. . . ."

O'Neill's continued survival now hung in the balance. Those Unionist M.P.s who had stood by him assured him of their support, but it was plain that it would take little to make them waver. At a party meeting on February 28th, ten M.P.s walked out on a vote of confidence, although the remainder backed him 23–1 with one abstention. In the weeks following the election, while another brief lull in the battling in the streets and in Stormont prevailed, he had few choices left. All he could try to do was push forward his reform programme with all speed, pray for a truce from disturbances and rioting, and fight determinedly to hold his remaining support among his party. On March 12th, he reshuffled his Cabinet in an effort to strengthen his hand; but on March 31st, at a meeting of the full Unionist Council, the grass roots body of the party, he won a vote of confidence by only 338 votes to 263. In the climate of Ulster that spring, such a majority was not enough.

It was now, too, that for reasons far removed from those of conventional politics, his position began to collapse irrevocably. On March 31st, a major explosion smashed electricity installations at Castlereagh, on the outskirts of Belfast. The Irish Republican Army were instantly blamed, and new accusations of infirmity of control were hurled at O'Neill. On April 4th, as People's Democracy supporters were on an Easter March from Belfast to Dublin, violence flared in Lurgan with police and Paisleyites. A series of unorganised sit-downs and spasmodic attempts at civil disobedience broke out. On April 20th, another major explosion affecting water supplies occurred, and for the first time British troops from the permanent 2,500 strong garrison were ordered on duty to guard key installations; in some places, 'B' Specials were already mobilised on the same tasks.

On Saturday, April 19th, spasmodic Civil Rights demonstrations took place at various points in the province, including one spontaneous sit-in in Londonderry. John Hume tried to disperse it without success, and a crowd of Paisleyites gathered. The two factions became engaged in fighting, and the police turned out to deal with them. They drove the rioters back into the Bogside, where heavy fighting developed as Bogsiders, assuming they were under new police attack, came out in force to do battle. A major confrontation developed. At one point police fired shots when one of their vehicles was under assault, and savage guerilla warfare continued into the night with both police and Bogsiders suffering heavy casualties. The next day, it was only by desperate efforts on the part of Civil Rights leaders and senior churchmen that more serious rioting was averted. After extended negotiation, the new Home Affairs Minister, Robert Porter, was persuaded to order the police out of the Bogside. They withdrew, and John Hume and others narrowly succeeded in restoring the peace.

Ian Paisley was in jail: he had been out on bail during the election, but was now serving his sentence for his part in the Armagh troubles, along with Ronald Bunting. But towards the end of the month, sectarian clashes began to occur in Belfast, and the riot police were engaged on several occasions in breaking up small disturbances. Also, ominously, the first evictions were taking place: Catholic families living in Protestant streets in the most sensitive areas were beginning to receive the threats that were to mount in volume and intensity to alarming proportions later in the summer —"get out or be burnt out".

In the face of all this, O'Neill's grip was slipping very fast indeed. The Unionists were furious about the new outbreaks of violence, and whatever the realities of necessity, the introduction of British troops to guard installations seemed to usher in an unhappy new phase: these men were not under the control of Stormont, but obeyed orders direct from Westminster: it appeared to be further evidence of the British Government's deepening involvement in Ulster's affairs. The explosions, too, heightened anti-Catholic feeling among Protestants. There was the general conviction— including, most pronouncedly, among the police—that these were the work of the I.R.A., and they inspired fear of a new campaign of I.R.A. terrorism. The main aim of many Protestants at such a moment was inevitably that of keeping the Catholics—and hence the Civil Rights advocates—quiet. On every side, the Government appeared to be failing. And while Protestant concern about the Catholics increased, the British public and their politicians were suddenly inspired to a new wave of noisy support for the Civil Rights movement: on to the scene, with a shattering impact, swept Miss Bernadette Devlin.

On December 10th 1968, the death of George Forrest, Unionist M.P. representing Mid-Ulster in the Westminster House of Commons, had created a vacancy in a marginally-held seat. When a by-election was called for April 17th 1969, the Unionists nominated the late M.P.'s widow, Mrs Anna Forrest, to succeed him.

Mid-Ulster had always been a wayward constituency in which in the past the Catholics had voted consistently for Republicans—including one while he was serving a prison sentence for I.R.A. work. But the Unionists, as always, felt secure. Mrs Forrest was an uninspiring figure, but she was well-known among local Protestants, had the support of the Unionist machine, and went dutifully on her rounds of the little villages and towns assuring the faithful that she would do the right thing by them when she was elected.

And at the beginning of April, elected she appeared likely to be. The opposition factions had learnt nothing, it seemed, from the Stormont election. Republicans, Nationalists, People's Democracy and the rest were still arguing bitterly among themselves. They had managed to agree that in principle, it made sense to put up one candidate supported by them all. But they were still struggling furiously to decide who it should be. A series of meetings around the constituency had settled nothing. The names of Austin Currie, a Republican named Kevin Agnew, and even that of John Hume had been mentioned. But only in the final, frantic moments, did anyone give real thought to the possibility of Miss Bernadette Devlin. She was known in the area, she had impressed certain people with her gift for words and with her showing in the Stormont election, but she was still, after all, a twenty-one-year-old final year psychology student at Queen's University. Then, at the final selection meeting on April 2nd, in a bid to save the unity of the opposition's campaign, Kevin Agnew and Austin Currie withdrew. Bernadette Devlin was chosen from the possibles who were left, a compromise choice to fight as the "unity" candidate. A young friend who had worked for her during the Stormont campaign, Loudon Seth, became her agent, and Eamonn McCann her press agent. In a frenzy of last-minute activity, her deposit money was found, her nomination papers were sent in, and the Catholic population gathered behind her to mount a campaign. In two weeks, initially almost unnoticed, latterly inundated with press and TV men, she stormed her way to election victory on a platform of general social reform, carried along by her particular force of personality and the weakness of the opposition. On April 17th, by a majority of 4,211 votes, on an astonishingly high 91·5 per cent poll, she became the youngest ever woman M.P. in the House of Commons, a popular sensation, and an entirely new factor in the Ulster crisis.

On April 22nd, she made her first appearance at Westminster, at the beginning of the emergency debate on the Northern Ireland situation. In a maiden speech that was received as a triumph by both politicians and the press, she became a celebrity overnight. Her remarks to the Commons were everything an Englishman might expect from the fighting Irish, and vastly more dramatic coming from a girl of 22: first, she slammed into the previous speaker, Ulster Unionist M.P. Robin Chichester-Clark, for his lack of understanding of her people. Then she said:

"Ever since October 5th, it has been the deliberate and unashamed policy of the Unionist Government to force the image on the Civil Rights movement that it is nothing more than a Catholic uprising. The people of the Civil Rights movement have struggled desperately to overcome this image, but it is impossible when the ruling minority is the Government and controls political matters and the so-called impartial forces of law and order. . . .

"The people of Ulster can no longer be fooled. There are always those of us who can see no difference between the Paisleyite faction and the O'Neill faction—except that the unfortunate Paisleyite faction do not have hyphenated surnames. . . ."

She described police attacks on the Bogside, and how she had played a part in attempting to resist them. Then:

"I can no longer say to people who put their trust in me: 'Do not worry about it—Westminster is looking after you'. Westminster is itself at fault because it has condoned the existence of . . . and has, sitting on its benches, members of that party who by deliberate policy keep down the ordinary people . . . I would have said that any Socialist government worth its guts would have got rid of them long ago."

Bernadette Devlin is a formidable speaker, both in the text and tone of what she says. With her biting Irish accent and forceful style, she can command an audience superbly. In the atmosphere of the House of Commons, which is so seldom granted real drama in these days, she was a stunning theatrical success. Reports of her doings which came back to Ulster further infuriated the Protestants, for in those early days of her fame, she contributed significantly to forcing Ulster's crisis back into the forefront of English affairs. There gathered around her the left wing elements of the People's Democracy and its adjuncts who saw in her the most useful weapon for pressing their cause both in England and Ulster. After her maiden speech, it was very rarely in the next few months that she appeared in the House of Commons. But she had become a new force in her own right, and considerable consequence was to turn around her doings.

She came from a lower middle-class background in Cookstown, North Tyrone; convent educated and then a student at Queen's, both her parents were dead: during the election campaign, she'd crack about her opponent: "She may be a genuine widow, but I'm a genuine orphan!" At Queen's, she had become initially mildly involved in politics, and then, with the formation of the People's Democracy, completely committed. Yet until she stood against Chichester-Clark in February, no one had really heard of her.

Very small, with her long dark hair, chaotic teeth and stubby features, in the early days she looked frankly awful. Westminster and fame won her some new clothes and an improved turnout, but appearance would never be her strong point; she still seemed to favour jeans and a sweater for everyday wear, and she never pretended to care what she looked like. Yet with her head sunk on her body, those deep set eyes glaring at the world, she appeared fiercely determined and very defensive. Nervous and often ill at ease (much more than she ever admitted), she hated the harassment of the press and the impossibility of escape from the flashlights. She was also, despite all her facility for words, politically very naïve, as many of her pronouncements revealed. In the Ulster situation of 1969, her ferocious incitements to the Catholics alarmed moderate opinion very much indeed. She admitted that if all else failed, she believed in resort to violence. She had no capacity for seeing events or personalities other than in black and white. She was also surrounded by a number of very shrewd and determined advisers, notable among them Eamonn McCann. Her agent, Loudon Seth, became her closest companion, and a number of other People's Democracy leaders gathered in her counsels. It frequently appeared that if she herself was somewhat bewildered by a situation, there were others around her who were not. Her militance and political isolation increased with the passing months, and as it did so, her popularity waned both with the press and in London. Her influence among the Ulster Catholic community at large was never nearly as great as many reports pretended. She had been elected because peculiar circumstances brought her to the fore, and she possessed a certain crude political skill. But across Ulster, while she remained for a time a symbol of Catholic success, her views were not widely shared, and her influence was slender. She continued to be important for only two reasons: because publicity had made her name and face familiar to everyone in England and Ulster; and because the press continued to give her every word and deed relentless coverage, creating a freewheeling publicity situation that none of those concerned seemed either willing or able to control.

But she cannot be ignored, if only because she has become the most famous individual in the Ulster crisis. For that alone, her role must be recognised. She was the classic case of a personality created by the accident of events, and maintained there by the attention of the press. Her tragedy now is that she is too harshly condemned. *She* has changed very little; the world's attitude to her has. Suddenly, flaws have been pinpointed and exposed which should have been apparent from the outset. She has been treated like a toy of which people have grown tired, and it is not surprising if she is bitter about it. Her vices and weaknesses are those of any other twenty-two-year-old anywhere in the world: impulsiveness, unsophistication, lack of emotional self-control and judgement. Perhaps now not enough credit is given for her basic wit, intelligence and courage, all three of which she possesses in large measure. In 1969, she was, like Ian Paisley, a luxury Ulster could ill afford. But it is very difficult to throw the blame for this at her door. Many times, she was as bewildered and uncertain as everyone else. Perhaps it was her greatest misfortune to be trapped from the outset with a group of youthful advisers whose aims were not always synonymous with her interests, even though she might persuade herself that they were. She gained vast rewards and enormous celebrity for her efforts to do what she thought right for "her people" in Ulster in 1969. But she also paid a bitter price. She has said and done many silly things, but never, most observers would probably agree, from unjustified malice. In the light of subsequent events, the new M.P. for Mid-Ulster merited much sympathy and not a little patience in April 1969.

To Terence O'Neill, however, she could be judged only as another thorn in the side. On April 22nd, the day she went to Westminster for the big debate, he and the Unionist Party were beginning discussions on a critical question: that of the granting of "one man, one vote"—universal franchise in local elections—the most strident of all Catholic cries for justice. The atmosphere was not auspicious. In addition to the Derry violence the previous weekend, ten post offices in Belfast had been bombed. An electricity pylon was blown up. The water installation blasts * had already caused a shortage in certain parts of Belfast; army helicopters and armoured cars were engaged on the much-publicised guard duties, and the air was charged with constant accusation and threat. Ivan Cooper, the new Civil Rights M.P., was warning:

"We are now closer to bloodshed in this province than at any time since the 1920's. This province is being ripped asunder, and in particular, the city of Londonderry is being torn to shreds, while the Government stand idly by and allow this to happen."

Brian Faulkner, the ousted Commerce Minister, said he thought it was time everyone recognised that the whole Civil Rights effort had got out of control. In a sense, he was right.

In February, at its Annual General Meeting, the Northern Ireland Civil Rights Association had been heavily infiltrated by the People's Democracy, and Betty Sinclair had been deposed as Chairman amidst some rancour, to be replaced by a compromise moderate, Frank Gogarty; Michael Farrell and Kevin Boyle of the People's Democracy became members of the Executive. The move had been intended by the People's Democracy forces to concentrate the Civil Rights Association and People's Democracy efforts on a broad front, but in the event, the C.R.A. was still doing little, while even the People's Democracy had made few moves in the streets save for their somewhat half-hearted Easter march. The Derry Citizens' Action Committee had been keeping their supporters off the streets as far as possible for many weeks, and there had been very little officially organised Civil Rights activity for some time. Yet spontaneous demonstrations and sit-ins kept breaking out, sometimes sparking incidents, and there was a feeling that protest was dissolving into anarchy and sectarian feuding. John Hume, Ivan Cooper and the others might deplore it, but in April, Catholics were increasingly militant and yet less and

* The sabotage outbreaks in the spring of 1969 and subsequently early in 1970 highlighted the all-too widespread availability of explosives in Ulster, where the Explosives Act had in the past been very loosely enforced. In 1969, there were 107 premises in the province licensed for the storing of explosives, as against only 491 in the whole of England and Wales, with their enormously greater population and area. There is, however, some sign that the law is now to be more rigorously enforced in Ulster.

less organised. Even responsible members of the Government had come to feel that even if there was a chance of negotiating some kind of "peace terms", it was getting harder and harder to find anyone to negotiate with. Thus far, the only hopeful signs in the entire situation were that no one had been killed and the reform programme was making some kind of progress. The rhetoric was becoming more violent and tempers were getting shorter. But O'Neill still hoped for his small miracle from "One man, one vote": it was his only card left.

The Unionist Parliamentary Party met at Stormont for two and a half hours on the morning of Tuesday, April 22nd, to discuss the crisis, with particular reference to the "One man, one vote" proposals. Terence O'Neill and his quietly liberal Home Affairs Minister, Robert Porter, made short speechs at the outset before the debate became general. O'Neill's Cabinet appeared reasonably solid behind him. But even among those not openly opposed to him, there were a number of waverers with acute doubts as to whether the time was right to introduce such a measure. When the meeting broke up, the issue had still not been decided. Tempers had been roused, and the M.P.s emerged in an angry silence. During the course of the meeting, O'Neill had told them that if they failed to approve the universal franchise measures he would feel forced to resign. At that stage, there was still no sign of any major crack in the forces he felt he could rely on for support. But when discussion transferred from a Stormont Committee Room to the Commons Chamber for a full Parliamentary debate that afternoon, O'Neill declined to speak. He preferred to keep out of sight until he had some genuine "peace proposals" to offer. At Westminster, too, the Government was distressed that there was no firm news of developments to be brandished in the British House of Commons.

The next day, the Unionists reassembled to conclude their secret debate. The news, when it came, seemed all that O'Neill had hoped for: the Party had agreed to support the "One man, one vote" proposals by twenty-eight votes to twenty-two—Unionist Senators had also participated in the decision. But it was followed almost immediately by the announcement that Major James Chichester-Clark, the Minister of Agriculture, had resigned from the Government because he disagreed with the timing of the decision. Chichester-Clark, to those outside Ulster, seemed a barely articulate and almost insignificant figure in the Administration.

Yet it was abundantly clear that his resignation was a serious blow to O'Neill. He had informed O'Neill before the meeting began, in a sudden aside that greatly surprised the Prime Minister, that overnight he had suffered a change of heart. It is certain that some of Chichester-Clark's constituents had already expressed their strong opposition to the franchise proposals, and there is some evidence to suggest that the Major found himself under pressure concerning the vital meeting. What is clearer, however, is that Chichester-Clark has always been a man who believes in doing the "right" thing at the "right" time. He is a firm believer in acting by the book, in "following form". In all his heart-searching about O'Neill's actions, there must have been an ingrained resistance to O'Neill's erratic and sometimes sledge-hammering attitude towards his own Party. Chichester-Clark may have been uncertain what positive action could be taken towards solving Ulster's crisis, but at least he was convinced that certain measures should not be taken. Introducing "One man, one vote" in such a way when Protestant feeling was so high was, he thought, a highly dangerous step.

In his formal letter of resignation to O'Neill, he said:

". . . You are aware that for the last two days I have been concerned about the proposals to move to universal franchise at the next local government election. I have been worried, not because I am against the principle of the franchise—indeed I think it will come and is right to come—but I question firstly whether this concession will stop the activity in the street. Secondly, I feel that our supporters will lose all faith in the determination of the present Government. . . ."

O'Neill had won, but at further cost to his credibility as Prime Minister. Eddie McAteer said: "The grudging and inglorious concession of an obvious right will not cleanse the Government. Why, oh why, are we to pay so dearly for a basic freedom?" William Craig embarked on a new series of violent attacks on the Prime Minister, saying that "by all normal standards, Captain O'Neill should have resigned a long time ago. He has no support to justify his remaining in office more than a matter of days. To do so would be an insult to all normal democratic standards." The Prime Minister himself also knew that the vote in the Parliamentary Party was vital, but not yet conclusive. The proposals still had to go before a meeting of the Unionist Standing Committee, and then of the full Unionist Council. If the M.P.s had been reluctant, the grass roots could be expected to be rebellious. O'Neill's chances of surviving a vote in either body looked poor.

Then in the last days of April, the overall situation across the province deteriorated even further. On the night of April 23rd, another water pipeline at Clady, twelve miles from Belfast, was blown up by anonymous saboteurs. It was followed by yet another explosion on a critical pipeline at Annalong in County Down. Belfast's water situation was becoming critical. In some areas, water was turned off for most of the day. Taps were set up in the street at which residents queued to draw supplies in buckets. Hotel bathrooms began to wear signs asking guests to report to reception after using the lavatories so that they could be refilled by hand. Tempers were fraying fast, and rage against the I.R.A., still the alleged culprits, mounted still further. Now, everyone in Belfast was learning the price of crisis—the hard way. Police road blocks were checking vehicles all around the explosion areas— the first time police had been seen in significant numbers armed with sub-machine guns and rifles. Mrs Eileen Paisley led 6,000 Protestants on a march through the streets of Belfast calling for the release of her husband; and in some Roman Catholic areas of the city, police were engaged in sporadic action with petrol bomb throwers. It was announced that more British troops were coming to Ulster to strengthen the guard on installations; and in a Leading article, *The Times* suggested that the moment might be approaching for Westminster to consider direct intervention in the government of Ulster. For Terence O'Neill, assessing the situation in the last week of April, there seemed no way of putting the brake on a skid into total confusion.

At this moment, many of the paper reforms originally sought by the Catholics in October 1968 were being implemented. Whatever the outcome of the Unionist Standing Committee and Council meetings, the "One man, one vote" proposals were now too far advanced to be shelved altogether. A full scale reorganisation of Ulster's local authorities to reduce both their number (ridiculously large for such a tiny province) and their powers (which had been so grossly abused) was already under way. Housing allocation was being put on a "points system" basis which should ensure obvious fairness, and a permanent Commissioner for Complaints—an Ombudsman—was to be appointed to replace the interim appointee who was already in office.

Yet as these reforms progressed slowly towards becoming reality, other unfortunate truths were becoming clear. First, there was little the Catholics could see for themselves as having been achieved—all the measures were still only promises. Second, both the hated Special Powers Act and the 'B' Specials were still in existence. New grievances had been created since the outset of the disturbances, notably as a result of police action in suppressing them. It was also becoming slowly clear to Catholics, as it had to Negro Civil Rights advocates in America, that legislative reform can only go a very limited way towards securing full Civil Rights. Much can only be achieved by good will on both sides. There had been talk of a Race Relations Bill outlawing discrimination of any kind, such as exists in England. But not only had this not been implemented but it seemed unlikely to have a real effect even if it was. No, what was needed was a change of heart, partly from the Catholics, but much more from the Protestants. And this had still not occurred. Indeed the reverse was true, feelings and tensions were at their highest for many years. The Unionists had to bear a heavy part of the blame: reforms which meant so little on paper could mean a great deal if they were given willingly and with obvious good intention. But as Eddie McAteer remarked, the Unionists had throughout given their concessions desperately grudgingly, quite plainly only because of the external pressures upon them to do so. As such, they were worth very little.

Furthermore, the Catholics had experienced a major change of heart in their attitude to their own demands. Whereas once they had expected that their gains would have to be wrested from Stormont, now, more and more, they began to have much higher hopes of Westminster. Talk of Westminster intervention, of a complete elimination of Stormont and direct rule by the London Labour Government, had reached the proportions of serious debate. The Catholics attached very high expectation to this occurring. Although only a very limited number were prepared to accept violence as a means of speeding Westminster's coming, many more cherished a secret feeling that disturbances could only benefit their prospects. Over the recent weeks, they had seen Westminster politicians become progressively more voluble in their support of Civil Rights demands. Now, British troops were involved, albeit only on the fringes, and if O'Neill fell, there were some who were convinced that Westminster would step in to suspend Stormont and prevent a right wing takeover. "One man, one vote", which had seemed so important the previous October—and was still a vital symbol—had in practical terms now waned as a concession towards peace. It was too late for all that kind of thing. Six months ago, it might have gone far to silence the Catholics. Now, the militants, the activists, the People's Democracy, were demanding far broader reforms and changes, and would not return to tending their gardens merely for some technical change of the political structure. The true Civil Rights advocates, the Humes and the Coopers, had long since abandoned marching for reforms, and were saving their energies for preventing sectarian riot and demanding action on the excesses of the police. These were fast becoming full time jobs. The Civil Rights structure was fragmented, and parts of it had become in effect revolutionary.

The situation on the streets was disintegrating partly because the credibility of the police had fallen so low, partly because there were so many fringe elements on both sides seeking to cash in, and partly because even if only a few were directly engaged in fighting, the majority were emotionally too involved to support the kind of actions needed to stop them. A state of spiritual and emotional anarchy existed, an infirmity of collective will which prevented any firm action by the society as a whole. What happened in Ulster in 1969 was a fascinating kind of warning: society depends so heavily on the credibility of the police and of the government behind them, and in Ulster it was utterly shattered in a few short months. Morality became confused—among the Catholics, it was no longer wrong to assault policemen, it was almost virtuous, because the police had behaved as the armed forces of the enemy. Among the Protestants, the Paisleyites were gaining ground faster than ever, and there seemed no power, least of all the police, willing to keep them in check. There was, throughout 1969, a very strong hooligan element on both sides who sought violence for no other reason than the joy of the fight. By April 1969, these forces were heavily engaged, and once again, it seemed impossible to check them, because they claimed to act as the "irregular troops" of the two factions, and were so treated. Hooligans caused trouble in Derry, and if they were Catholic hooligans, the police automatically drove them into the Bogside "where they belong". This, of course, merely served to make the confrontation general, through no wish of the Bogsiders. But they were by now sufficiently alarmed to "stand to arms" whenever the police appeared brandishing riot shields and batons.

The new element in the disorders provided by the sabotage efforts achieved precisely what it obviously intended: a further heightening of tension and raising of tempers and fears, together with an added undermining of Terence O'Neill's position. It was blamed on the Catholics, because the I.R.A. had indulged in this type of activity so often before. There was known to be a Protestant extremist group named the Ulster Volunteer Force (also illegal) which similarly preached violence, but it suited many interests better to regard the explosions as the work of the I.R.A. It was not until very many months later that it was revealed to be indeed the work of Protestants, and by then the damage had been done. The police, it always appeared to their discredit, had been most unwilling to pursue detailed investigation into the possibility that the demolitions were Protestant work until they were heavily pressured to do so; again, this was long afterwards.

By April, it was also clear how limited was the overall entanglement of the Irish Republic in Northern Irish affairs. Forty years ago, in a similar situation, the Republic would probably have been sending guerillas into Ulster the moment Catholics became engaged with the police. But since October 1968, while the Dublin Government had made many wild statements, held "crisis" cabinet meetings and damned the Unionist Government, there had been virtually no real action from the South in the face of the Ulster crisis. There too, while a united Ireland remained a dreamy goal for the future, the harsher realities of economic and social problems within their own state had turned the thoughts of the Dublin Government to their own worries. There had been a scattering of demonstrations in Dublin in support of the Ulster Catholics, wild promises and threats from the I.R.A., and much noise: but in broad terms, the South had stayed out. In truth, of course, there was little they could do, short of sending their army across the Border; and they had grown too realistic over the years to think much about that. Civil Rights leaders commuted to and from Dublin, the Republic's newspapers carried heavy coverage of events in the North, but there was no international incident. Stray I.R.A. men became momentarily involved in incidents and events, and some of the group's militants screamed for action. But in practical terms, they did nothing. Unfortunately, at the end of April it was not what they did that counted, but what they were thought to be doing. At that moment, this was supposed to include commencing a new terrorist campaign.

On April 27th, new trouble broke out in the Roman Catholic area of Armagh, when for a brief phase barricades were thrown up and windows were shattered in an early morning disturbance. A time bomb was found outside a Roman Catholic church near Belfast. And Terence O'Neill knew that on Friday, May 2nd, he faced the Unionist Standing Committee on his universal franchise proposals. He knew that among his Parliamentary supporters, several were wavering at the prospect of the Standing Committee meeting. His opponents were continuing to hammer him mercilessly in public and to undermine him vigorously in private. His own Party members, of whatever political conviction, were holding him responsible for splitting the Unionists more disastrously and seemingly irrevocably every day. He knew that Harold Wilson and his Government still desperately wanted him to hang on, to avert the danger of their having to intervene themselves. Contingency plans had already been drawn up for a possible use of British troops for riot control if the situation worsened, but Wilson was deeply anxious to avoid such action if it was humanly possible. Technically, O'Neill could still press on with his reforms if he was defeated by the Unionist Council, but it would in practice be exceedingly difficult to do so, since he would lose even more support among his remaining Parliamentary supporters. And William Craig, ever popular among Unionist grass roots right wingers, was saying: "What we see on the streets of our province will look like a Sunday school picnic if Westminster tries to take our Parliament away."

Over the weekend of April 26th and 27th, O'Neill, in consultation with his closest supporters and friends, debated his position once more, now that his ability to govern Ulster seemed at last finally shattered. For weeks, he had hung on in the face of all the odds, in an attempt to keep his policies moving forward. He had the satisfaction of knowing that what he had done could not be reversed, whoever was Prime Minister. Now, he was influenced by two considerations. At this stage he still had a government in being with some degree of consensus on basic policy. If he stayed in office, this remaining support would be whittled away by the right wingers until when he fell, the extremists would automatically be in a position to seize the reins. Yet if he quit now, there was the strongest probability of maintaining his forces in being, and thus his policies. In addition, if this could be done, at least some degree of Stormont's independence of Westminster could be preserved.

If the right wingers took over, without doubt Westminster would feel compelled to step in and suspend the Ulster Government. Yet if O'Neill's policies continued, while Westminster would hold the firmest of watching briefs, it was unlikely that they would intervene drastically. O'Neill faced the facts: he himself, and all that he stood for, had become the most dramatic point of conflict in the Unionist Party. He felt that if he resigned, some of the divisions might also still heal.

Weighing all these thoughts, and the certainty that he still held sufficient influence to be able to exert considerable pressure on the election of his successor, O'Neill determined on resignation. On April 28th, after informing his Parliamentary Party at an informal meeting at Stormont Castle, he issued a statement announcing his departure as leader of the Unionist Party, and thus as Prime Minister, the latter to take effect as soon as the Party had chosen a successor. "A new leader committed on his record to progressive principles, but unhampered by personal animosities, may have a better chance of carrying on the works which I have begun," he said. The following evening, in an emotional television broadcast to the province, he looked back on his achievements and expressed his hopes:

". . . To those of you who have so loyally supported me . . . I want to say this: Do not be dismayed. What you and I were trying to do together was right. Morally right, politically right, right for our country and all who seek to live at peace within it. . . .

"For too long we have been torn and divided. Ours is called a Christian country. We could have enriched our politics with our Christianity; but far too often we have debased our Christianity with our politics. We seem to have forgotten that love of neighbour stands beside love of God as a fundamental principle of our religion.

". . . Democratic government must rest upon the consent not just of those who elect the governing party, but of the people as a whole.

". . . We *must* go forward; for British public and parliamentary opinion would not tolerate our going back . . . look about you at the present state of our country and try to answer the question 'Is this *really* the kind of Ulster that you want?' I asked you that question once before; and now, as then, it is only you who can answer."

O'Neill's departure as Prime Minister marked the clear ending of the first phase of the Ulster crisis of 1969. He went partly as the sacrificial lamb, in order that some of what he believed in could continue. He is remembered more kindly since his passing than while he was Prime Minister, although to Ulster Protestant extremists, his name will always evoke hatred. His basic aims were just, reasonable and progressive. He was far abler and more articulate than any of his colleagues. Yet his power rested on no firm base. His early, disastrous miscalculations about the real strength of the Catholic revolt, which he regarded as a fatal interference with his own pace of reform, cost him the support of the Catholics. His dallying with reform and with Westminster, not to mention the intellectual isolation in which he seemed to exist, broke his support with the Protestants. Only a remarkable talent for political survival kept him going as long as he did. From the beginning, he was in an impossible position—knowing that without his Party he could do nothing, but that to keep in step with his Party he must continually hold back. He made mistakes and rash judgements at key moments, for certain; but in an intolerable situation, he could have done little more. At that moment Ulster needed a great and charismatic leader to pull her safely together. There was none. Having to make do with what she had, she could have done no better than Terence O'Neill. He salvaged all that could be saved from a blazing ship, and doused the fires as best he could. His resignation may have preserved the body of Ulster Government, but after his fall, it was in effect decapitated. No individual again had the influence on events that O'Neill managed to wield from October 1968 to April 1969.

6

TO THE BRINK

THE PROTESTANTS IN the Shankill Road area of Belfast lit bonfires in the streets to celebrate the resignation of Terence O'Neill. To Paisley and his brethren, O'Neill had been the ally of Catholicism, the betrayer of Protestantism. One of Paisley's lieutenants, Ivan Foster, said: "We see this as the hand of God. We have seen this man consistently as a traitor and a very dangerous man to the Protestant province." The British Government, officially silent, none the less waited with much anxiety to see what the future would bring. Many Catholics, faced with the reality of political upheaval were concerned that the Unionist right wing might at last have gained its triumph.

Within hours of the announcement of O'Neill's departure, it was public knowledge that there were three major candidates to succeed him: Brian Faulkner, ex-Minister of Commerce; James Chichester-Clark, late Minister of Agriculture; and John Andrews, Leader of the Senate. Andrews, however, was never a real contender. Days before O'Neill's announcement, private discussions had been going on in an effort to find an acceptable successor. Andrews had been approached as a first choice, an uninspiring but reasonable man who could rally the Party. He declined in the firmest terms—in no small measure, perhaps, because his father had been Ulster's second Prime Minister, and had been stabbed in the back by his own Party in a manner that left his son with some unfortunate memories.

The issue turned, then, on Faulkner and Chichester-Clark. To become Prime Minister, one or other must be elected by a majority of the Unionist Parliamentary Party, and thus be able to command a majority in the Ulster House of Commons. Faulkner, the abler and the better known, could count on the support of the Unionist right wingers, a hard core of around a dozen, including William Craig. Yet beyond these, he had to find a number of uncommitted votes, and it was the search for them and the uncertainty of his degree of success, that kept Ulster in suspense in the days before May 1st, the date of the decision. Faulkner wanted power, and he wanted it badly. He was highly articulate, shrewd and careful. The political bookmakers gave him a shade of the odds against the apparently faceless figure of his rival. Major James Chichester-Clark, like O'Neill a product of Eton and the Irish Guards, was forty-six years old, and an M.P. since 1960. Married with two daughters and a comfortable country home, he seemed most at ease in the shooting field or casting a trout fly. Big, bluff, craggy and yet apparently wholly inarticulate, he hardly seemed the stuff of which political leaders are made. He was very obviously a decent man—which is an undervalued quality in Ulster politics—but he seemed to lack any air of drive or purpose. Stories of his blunderings were already manifold: asked by an American TV interviewer if he was worried that the riots would affect Ulster's tourist industry, he smiled pleasantly and replied: "Well, I must admit that I can't imagine what any American would want to come here for at the best of times. . . ." His accent was every foreigner's caricature of a British upper class drawl, easy-going and un-hurried. Immensely courteous, an obvious believer in doing the right thing at the right time, he was still regarded in political circles as a man who had never had an original idea in his life. For months on end, interviewers and pundits struggled to plumb the inner reaches of Chichester-Clark's mind. But as an American wit once said of Hollywood: "You've got to strip the gloss off the surface to get to the tinsel underneath." Much probing produced few new insights.

Yet Terence O'Neill and his former colleagues in Government saw in Chichester-Clark the man they needed to maintain the Stormont in being. The very qualities of outward simplicity and adhesion to tradition and "form" were those that made him popular and trusted among the rank and file of the Unionist Party. If Chichester-Clark said something must be done ("sorry about that, but that's the way it is") then something had to be done. Honourable and straightforward, once convinced of a course, he would stick to it. Conservative by upbringing and inclination, he was nevertheless pliable enough to accept at least some of the pressure from Westminster that would undoubtedly be exerted. He was, in effect, the identikit moderate, by nature more a follower than a leader, but motivated by a strong sense of duty.

There were suggestions, later, that there had been collusion between O'Neill and Chichester-Clark about the latter's resignation a few days before the fall of O'Neill. But it seems almost impossible, on the evidence, that this was the case. No, for his own strange reasons Chichester-Clark had felt obliged to express his protest about all this racing headlong towards change. But now, in a new situation, he accepted the role in which he was being cast as the compromise choice, and with it the energetic backing of the O'Neill group. The pundits tended to predict Faulkner as the winner, because Faulkner was the more impressive personality; but in the event, O'Neill's last major act before retiring almost completely from the Ulster political scene was to provide the support that made Major James Chichester-Clark Prime Minister of Ulster.

The Unionist Parliamentary Party met at Stormont on the morning of May 1st, and Chichester-Clark was elected to power by the paper-thin majority of seventeen votes to sixteen—that of O'Neill himself being decisive. The battle over, the vanquished moved to make the decision unanimous, and Brian Faulkner agreed that he would serve in the new Government if asked. Chichester-Clark, emerging to face a press conference, said he was prepared to press on with the "One man, one vote" proposals now that they had been agreed on by the Party. He proceeded at once to try to heal the breaches in the Unionist ranks by naming Faulkner Minister of Development, and three other right-wingers as junior ministers. It quickly became clear that the grass roots Unionists would endorse his Premiership, and when the Party's Standing Committee met a few days later, in the general surge of goodwill towards the new Leader they also voted massive support for the "One man, one vote" proposals. Chichester-Clark launched out on his task in many ways ill-equipped in character, but for a time at least, with his rear protected from Unionist dissidence.

The Catholics greeted the coming of Chichester-Clark with mingled apathy, suspicion, and scepticism. John Hume said: "The difficulty is to see how this solves anything. There are clearly two irreconcilable forces in the Unionist Party with two different views on what sort of society there should be in Northern Ireland. The problems of the last six months are largely due to the Government's inability to govern and to deal with problems because they have been held to ransom by the right wing in the Unionist Party. The question is: will Chichester-Clark be able to ignore these pressures?" To the Catholics, the admission of the right-wingers to the Cabinet was an alarming sign. Most especially, the new Parliamentary Secretary to the Minister of Home Affairs was John Taylor, a prominent hard-liner, now in a job where he would be directly concerned with peace-keeping. Still, to most Catholics a victory for Faulkner could only have been worse, although one Civil Rights leader remarked with a shrug: "Tweedledee has beaten Tweedledum by a short head. . . ." The Catholics were long past caring much, or expecting much from the Unionists, of whatever political shade. Their own leaders were deeply divided among themselves, between all the factions of left and right within their own ranks, and had already lost much of their control over the policy of protest. There were too many splinter groups, too many hooligans, too many personal feuds: such men as Hume and Cooper still commanded great respect, but their ability also to gain obedience was waning fast. Many figures, most of them young, who had never been on a Civil Rights march were now roused for battle. And in bordering Catholic and Protestant areas in towns and villages across the length of Ulster, it was mutual fear and hatred that was causing outbursts of violence from both sides— not idealism or political aims. In the Protestant streets, they hung up the Union Jack, the flag of Britain, as the banner of their sect. At the high moments of crisis, a flag would dangle from almost every house and window. Some of the Catholic militants, more for lack of any other emblem than for real belief in its significance, would wave the Republican Tricolour. Only Northern Ireland could need legislation like the Flags and Emblems Act, which enabled a police officer to demand the lowering of a flag if he thought its presence was likely to provoke disorder—as it often did.

And while responsible Catholics were doing everything possible to persuade their people to "keep their cool", there was now too much anger across the land. The Paisleyites taunted and provoked them at every turn, while young Catholics would never miss the chance to toss a stone at a policeman or kick the cars in a Protestant street. It was partly the disappearance of any clearly definable goal that had created this situation. Back in October, when the sensation of rebellion was fresh and the mood was explorative and hopeful, it had been possible for the dissident leaders to reach a measure of agreement. But now, the Government had been shaken to its roots, many of the simple aims of October had been achieved, and yet still there was no feeling of victory.

Perhaps this was the tragedy, above all: in some indefinable way, both Protestants and Catholics felt there was some tangible victory to be won, although they did not know what. The Catholics were a little drunk on the heady sensations of revolt: they had made Ulster a focal point of English affairs, they had made their cause ring through every home in Britain. They had had their M.P.s elected and their voices taken seriously—yet even now, they felt that they had not won. The Protestants, likewise, knew only that the Catholics had disturbed the tranquillity of their province, and therefore must be defeated. What defeat meant, they did not know. But it was clear to them that it had not yet been achieved. They hated the press—above all the English press—for its support of Catholic demands and harsh coverage of Paisley and the extremists. They could spit on and occasionally manhandle reporters, they could damn interfering English politicians, and they could single out "traitors" for their hatred. But this was not enough. Somehow, somewhere, there lay something more to be found. At the beginning of May 1969, both sides felt this, and were in a state of continual restlessness as a result. But their frustrations and unchannelled gropings were still unsatisfied. They knew what they hated, and even had ideas as to why. But how to conquer it they did not know.

On May 6th, Chichester-Clark took his first decisive action as Prime Minister, and one which was to provoke controversy from that day forward: he announced an amnesty for all "political" offences since the disturbances began, and the dropping of all charges pending. Ian Paisley and Ronald Bunting were immediately released from gaol amidst general extremist Protestant rejoicing, and the indictments against others who included Bernadette Devlin, Ivan Cooper, Gerry Fitt, Eddie McAteer and Austin Currie were all set aside. Amidst general acclamation, the Prime Minister was trying to begin again. Paisley, freed, told his followers he would support Chichester-Clark, who, he said, had told him he would stand "four square for the defence of Ulster". The Catholics accepted their reprieves with grudging acknowledgement, as little more than their due in view of the circumstances in which they had been charged. But it appeared that the Premier's decision had given a marginal boost to the chances of peace.

But a dangerous precedent had been set. Any chance of justice being done in respect of the Burntollet attackers or the April rioters had vanished. A wearying and yet furious debate began that dragged on for many months, as to why certain people should be imprisoned for offences for which others had got off scot free. It became more difficult in the future to take decisions on the arrest and conviction of those engaged in disturbances, and created new cause for grievance, among those who felt that their persecutors were going unscathed. Law and order has broken down not when people commit offences, but when they do so with impunity.

The trouble was, of course, that since October the police had been so wildly selective in their enforcement of the law and so erratic in their behaviour that their decisions had become almost meaningless. In the climate of May, perhaps it was best to stop attempting to apportion blame for what had happened and try again. But in so doing, the Government tacitly admitted that many of those who had been charged with law-breaking had had grounds for doing so. Once the Prime Minister had accepted this, it became infinitely more difficult to insist in the future that these grounds no longer existed.

And having tried to set aside the past, Major Chichester-Clark now had to look to the future. He had already announced his intention to continue the reform policy, and could not see his way to promising much more. Faced with the dangerous situation around the province, his most serious problem was to find the forces to deal with the threat. He announced the call up of retired members of the R.U.C. under the age of sixty for service with the new supplementary police reserve, while warning that anyone who construed the amnesty as a sign of weakness would be making a great mistake. But even discounting the misbehaviour of elements of the R.U.C. in recent disturbances, he knew that in sheer numbers, they were in a very weak position. Confronted with major violence, however skilfully and justly they were handled, the force was far too small for serious riot action with its 3,000 men spread so thinly across the province. On many occasions, the police behaved with exemplary courage and restraint, and under sound leadership—which unfortunately they lacked in many places—they had done and were to do some fine work. But Chichester-Clark knew that there were not enough of them, and that when they became tired and—in extreme situations—very frightened, there was a grave danger of a catastrophe. Yet he could not and would not ask for British troops to be made available for riot duty. The decision would be so utterly foreign to Britain, so repugnant to the British Government, so enraging to the Protestants. The men of the R.U.C. had to prepare to face the future as best they could, relieved of as much routine police work as possible. Meanwhile, Chichester-Clark could only seek to hold the ring.

Throughout the months of May and June, it seemed that the gods were smiling on him. The new Government was able to find its feet in office interrupted by only limited alarms and restlessness. The Londonderry Development Commission, which had superseded the City Council, announced a major programme for jobs and housing. Lord Cameron's Commission, appointed by the Government to investigate the causes and consequences of the disturbances since October, began to hear evidence in Derry. Chichester-Clark himself paid a visit to Harold Wilson in London late in May with Robert Porter, his Home Affairs Minister, and Brian Faulkner. The Government pumped out frantic streams of propaganda on the figures for new housing and industrial development, and on July 2nd issued a White Paper on the future of local government. Effective from 1971, most of the cumberous mass of local authorities that had dogged the province's progress would be swept away, to be replaced by seventeen new area councils. Local Electoral boundaries would be re-drawn, the Government promised, by an independent body. Only William Craig and his allies seemed to find fault with the White Paper, but then Craig was becoming increasingly wild in his pronouncements, and isolated from the centres of power. To the Civil Rights leaders, another vital goal was in sight.

The only Unionist right wingers who were provoking open trouble were the members of the Fermanagh local Party Association: they expelled the Duke of Westminster and four other Unionists from their number for supporting "unofficial" pro-O'Neill candidates at the February election. But by the end of June, the overall prospect of the province seemed sufficiently hopeful for Chichester-Clark to tour the Bogside in person without incident.

On the streets, the situation remained uneasy but manageable. It was reckoned that a million pounds worth of damage had already been done in the rioting,* but through the early months of summer, while there were incidents of petrol-bombing, no major wrecking took place. There were a few scattered Civil

* In January, the Government had agreed to pay half the cost of all injury claims and the full cost of all property damage claims arising out of the disturbances.

Rights marches and a half-hearted picket of public buildings across the province, but none of these had the weight of Civil Rights organisation behind them. Bernadette Devlin addressed meetings and counselled with the People's Democracy leaders, but attracted little stir or excitement. Many marches by various bodies were planned and then cancelled for fear of provoking trouble. The Stormont Opposition harangued Chichester-Clark for his tardiness in announcing the dates when the promised reforms would go through, but devoted more energy to quarrelling among themselves.

The Paisleyites held a number of rallies, their freed leader hastening from town to town continuing to spread the word among the faithful. In all his time as Prime Minister, O'Neill had always declined to meet Paisley on any pretext, on the grounds that to do so lent him credibility, but on July 10th, Chichester-Clark saw him to discuss demonstrations, following a series of minor Civil Rights assemblies in Armagh, Lurgan, Dungannon and Downpatrick on July 7th.

Yet still the peace held. Chichester-Clark had survived his critical first two months without a major division in his own Party, without overt intervention from Westminster, and without a serious clash on the streets. The reform programme, flourished as a magic wand at both English politicians and Catholic leaders, seemed to be effective in keeping violence at bay. Responsible elements in the Catholic community were avoiding demonstrations for fear of chaos, if not because of satisfaction with what had been achieved. The new Prime Minister had settled in without distinction, yet without disaster, and seemed in the process to have acquired at least a limited measure of self-confidence.

Then, on Saturday, July 12th, came Orange Day. Every year, the anniversary of the Battle of the Boyne, in which William defeated the Catholics is marked by major Protestant celebrations and marches. On this July 12th, despite all the perils facing the province, the Orangemen were allowed to march as usual. The result was disastrous. In Londonderry, Dungiven and Lurgan, rioting broke out. Dungiven Orange Hall was burnt by raging Catholics, and a group of police trapped inside escaped only after a desperate baton charge. In Derry, throughout Saturday night and Sunday morning, the police were engaged in a major battle when Catholics turned out to fight the Protestants in the streets, and for the first time there was serious looting, while Civil

Rights leaders tried in vain to keep the peace. Chichester-Clark returned hastily from holiday in England, and Eamonn McCann said: "This has nothing to do with Civil Rights. The old primaeval instincts have come to the surface. It is a religious war." In Derry, two people were wounded by shots from police who found themselves cornered, and the first attempts at sniping took place, mercifully with little effect. The Catholics threw up barricades in efforts to keep the police out of Bogside, largely ineffectually—these were still the days when fighting was scattered and chaotic—but they added to the confusion. Derry Citizens' Action Committee condemned the looting and hooliganism, but to no avail. That July weekend, it was plain that there were considerable numbers of Derrymen who found that smashing their own city was a more effective outlet for frustration than marching and demonstrating.

Throughout the next fortnight, the situation worsened. All Civil Rights marches were banned. There were intermittent sectarian clashes in Belfast, more petrol bombing in Londonderry, and on July 21st, 20,000 Catholics attended the funeral of a man who had died of a coronary following an incident during the riots in the city. 'B' Specials had been put on standby in Derry to the fury of many Catholics and protests from Labour M.P.s at Westminster. On July 18th, a petrol bomb damaged William Craig's house on the outskirts of Belfast—although Craig himself was not at home at the time. The Civil Rights Association made attempts to reassert itself without notable success, and on July 30th, there was an incident when police—watched by Ian Paisley—removed Civil Rights squatters from Dungannon Council Offices.

On August 2nd weekend, serious rioting broke out in Belfast. Protestants and Catholics became involved in a long series of bitter struggles with the police. Much of the Protestant Shankill Road was severely damaged, a Catholic block of flats nearby was besieged, and both sides fought it out from behind hastily erected barricades. The police, behaving throughout the weekend with the utmost restraint, were pushed to their limits to contain the situation. Frequently under fire from stones and petrol bombs from both sides, they somehow held on, and prevented the worst excesses of the rioters. Hopelessly outnumbered and without hope of major reinforcement, squads of police roared through the dark streets in armoured personnel carriers, attempting to break up mobs wherever they found them. The streets were littered with debris, broken glass, and rocks; many shops were blackened where

5a In the Bogside in August, police drove rioters harassing a Protestant procession into the Bogside. The Bogsiders mobilised to fight off the police "invasion".

5b If the Catholics hated the Royal Ulster Constabulary, their fear of the police reserve force, the Protestant 'B' Specials, was great enough to send them to the barricades when the Specials were mobilised.

6a Late on the first night of the Bogside siege, the police began to hurl tear gas against the Catholic lines in an attempt to drive back the defenders.

6b Fires broke out in the Bogside as Catholic petrol bombs fired at the police set buildings ablaze, and Protestant guerillas began to attack Catholic property wherever they could find it.

petrol bombs had licked the brickwork; and overturned cars burned where they lay. It was almost impossible to make arrests, completely impractical to contain every spot at once. Eighty civilians and seventeen police were injured; when quiet finally returned on Tuesday morning, it was more because of weariness on all sides than any change of heart.

That week, Chichester-Clark was under pressure on every front. He went to London for discussions with the Home Secretary, Mr Callaghan, still resolutely declining to discuss in public the possibility that troops might be called in. Nevertheless, 150 men of the British army's permanent garrison had already been moved into quarters in the naval base in Derry, following the July 12th riots. On all sides Chichester-Clark heard condemnation of the rioting, yet no one offered any answer as to how it was to be stopped. Above all, however, he heard warnings about the march of the Derry Apprentice Boys.

On August 12th, every year, the second great annual Protestant celebration takes place; the Derry Apprentice Boys, a kind of militant Protestant masonic society, stage a march through the streets of Londonderry to commemorate the seventeenth century siege. It is an occasion which, at the best of times, arouses distaste among the Catholics. In 1969, following the events of July 12th, every reasonable individual both in Ulster and in England foresaw the gravest consequences if the march took place. In the extraordinary climate of Ulster, it constituted a mad provocation to the Catholic extremists. True, the Governor of the Apprentice Boys was holding talks with Catholic leaders in an effort to ensure that it would pass off peacefully. But there was already plentiful evidence that negotiations with the leaders was no guarantee against action by other elements. Yet Chichester-Clark, like every other member of his Cabinet except two,* was himself a member of the Orange Order, a close friend and traditional ally of many of the Apprentice Boys, and fully alive to the Protestant anger that would follow any effort to have the march cancelled. Of all the actions for which he was responsible in 1969, his decision to permit the Apprentice Boys' March to take place resulted in the most devastating consequences. Yet as a Protestant and a conservative well aware of the dangers of a revolt from his own right wing, he could not bring himself to ban it. Police reinforcements were organised, every step to ensure peaceful procession was taken. But with the

* Phelim O'Neill, Minister of Agriculture, and William Fitzsimmons.

5—U1969 * *

concurrence of Derry Development Commission it was agreed that the march should go ahead as planned.

That sunny August, there was still a strange feeling of make-believe about Ulster. Riots had taken place indeed, but they had withered away again after one day, or two or three. The destruction, by the standards of American race riots, for example, had been limited. The casualties had been unpleasant, but not yet fatal. Many people talked very seriously about the awful dangers of the situation, of the risk of a really calamitous outbreak, yet in a way, nobody really believed it. Too many people were too young to remember what happens when passions are really roused, and all semblance of control is lost. Every weekday, the shops still did a busy trade and people went about their business fascinated and talkative, yet not deeply perturbed. The middle classes, most of all, had very little conception of what was happening around them; they could hardly imagine the effect of a petrol bomb if it catches a man's clothing, or of a broken paving stone catching a human head. Much of Ulster had been wholly untouched by the events since October—only a very small percentage of the population had even seen a rock hurled. It had all been heavily reported in the press, certainly, but the only effect of this was to induce many Ulstermen to blame the press for grossly exaggerating the perils of the situation. In Belfast, it was only the hidden depths of the Catholic and Protestant ghettos that had seen the face of crisis. In Londonderry, a much smaller city, the violence had been more obtrusive, but still no one had seen men dying or dead. All Britain, including Ulster, had known many years of peace—even the last I.R.A. campaign had had more effect in the telling than in the reality. Englishmen, especially, were very accustomed to reading in their newspapers about crisis, only to find that a few days later, it would be a different "crisis", and the old one had faded away with the clouds. Very few Englishmen and not many Ulstermen were genuinely frightened by what had been taking place around them. Angry, bewildered, sometimes interested perhaps—but they could not really imagine that all the talk about "the guns coming out soon" could be more than the anxiety of pessimists. It seems important to establish this tacit optimism, because in the light of what followed, it is easy to analyse the ingredients and say that it was entirely forseeable. Perhaps it should have been. But in the early August days it was fear of repetition of what had taken place, not real anticipation of worse in the future, that inspired journalists, politicians, and most of the people of Ulster and England. Only with the benefit of hindsight may one see more clearly the conditions that created the battles that were to follow.

By August 12th 1969, the Ulster crisis had created a momentum of its own. The leaders of almost every faction, having done so much to create the situation which existed, were by now strategically impotent. They had it in their power to make tactical movements of varying importance, but command of the direction in which the province was moving had been utterly lost.

Major Chichester-Clark and his government at Stormont were not doing anything disastrously wrong, but nor did they seem able to find any grip which could break the stalemate. The Cabinet was composed of men of varying personal ability, but no real powers of leadership. Brian Faulkner was the best possible man to be handling the Ministry of Development, but his efforts would pay long-term rewards rather than offer any short-term solutions. Robert Porter, the Minister of Home Affairs, was both intelligent and reasonable but very nervous by temperament and quite lacking in personal presence. Physically small, with receding hairline and worried eyes, he could never disguise the effects of the strain under which he was working. Roy Bradford, the Minister of Commerce, a younger and more publicly effective figure, still appeared unable to offer any original guidance or communicate usefully in public with either Protestants or Catholics. These three, along with the Prime Minister, stood at the centre of power, yet none seemed able to do more than make statements and speeches denouncing violence and promising reforms soon. Their supporting team of civil servants appeared to feel that their first duty was to protect the Government from public criticism. The arts of concealment, evasion and whitewash became almost a fetish. At this stage, more important than anything else was the public image of the Government, the impression it created on those it governed. There was a lamentable failure in this direction throughout the key phases of crisis. Stormont Castle engendered the air—whether true or not did not matter—of being concerned with the Government's survival, above all of doing only what was needed to secure its own position. This at least was the feeling created among the Catholics, with critical effect on events.

It was partly brought about by the difference of background and way of life between governed and governing. The Protestants might put up with the Unionist hierachy and system of promotion apparently contentedly, but the Catholics found rule by the squire-archy of Ulster almost a specific grievance. Chichester-Clark was a man hopelessly far removed from them, not only because he was at the seat of power in 1969, but because he had been there all his life. The English class system—what is left of it—pales besides that of Ulster, where the aristocracy still have a clinging grip on power at every level, and middle-class politicians on the way to the top merely struggle to live and behave like their public school-educated colleagues. The Unionist Party is an alliance between the English public school-educated landed gentry and the Protestant middle-class business sector, with the former the dominant element. At a key moment in Ulster's history, when much depended on the level of liaison between those in government and those on the streets, no real contact existed, or could exist. Both sides lived in mutual incomprehension and mistrust. Much had been done to bring in legislative reform, yet through this critical failure of communication, little was really understood.

Although other towns around the province might become embroiled, and embroiled seriously, in the sectarian struggle, it was on Belfast and Londonderry that everything hinged, and where by mid-August tensions were highest. The situation among the Catholics was deadlocked. The main Civil Rights organisations were talking much but doing little, because of the risks in the situation. They also saw that the Unionist Government were un-willing and largely unable to grant much further reform in the immediate situation. The People's Democracy, still the most militant faction, were attempting to influence Catholics around Ulster to renewed Civil Rights action, but with only limited success. Personal relations between moderates and extremists in many places were very frayed, and there was endless argument about future policy. Among the Protestants, Ian Paisley and his deputies had been working all-out for many months, creating a climate of anti-Catholic feeling and anger that was never still. Paisley's theme was that Protestants were being denied their civil rights by the Catholic struggle for theirs. He never explained logically what he meant by this, but he persuaded Protestants in significant numbers that Catholic efforts towards reform were directly threatening Protestant interests. A vigorously energetic figure, throughout the year he had been travelling constantly across the province, gaining much publicity for his views and unquestionably swelling the ranks of his supporters. He was a specialist in embarrassing the authorities and the press by continued pin-pricking and argument over trivial details of law, and the Protestants loved him for it. His influence in undermining the efforts towards peace cannot be underestimated. He used his considerable talents solely towards "keeping the pot boiling". In this he was immensely successful, aided and spurred by the activities of Catholic hooligan elements.

In both Londonderry and Belfast, where clearly defined Catholic and Protestant areas border one another closely, it took very little to create an incident. For while in normal times street brawls and mutual abuse burnt out on communal apathy, when the general temper was so high it took only two men fighting or shouting at each other to have a hundred ranged behind them within minutes, indifferent to what started it, only knowing that the enemy was gathering. The gradual escalation of the struggle had warmed everyone to acceptable violence. Rumours spread and roused feeling almost instantly. Both sides would accept everything said about the enemy as true. Word that the Protestants were stoning a Catholic house in, say, Hooker Street, Belfast, would rouse the entire area to grab stones and petrol bombs without any thought of seeking the facts. Above all, the Catholics now hated the police passionately, and needed little provocation to join battle with them. The tales of police action in Derry in January and April had spread the length of the province. The Catholics had never liked the R.U.C. Now, they considered its officers had forfeited any right they might ever have had to obedience or even tolerance. The very sight of a policeman was enough to send the Catholics looking to their weapons.

The police themselves were weary to death of continual riot duty, outnumbered and unable to take really effective action. In general—certain notable encounters in Belfast set aside—they could count on the Protestants to be at their side both in heart and body whenever they were engaged, while the Catholics seemed invariably to be the enemy. Any feelings of impartiality they might have had were long since shattered. They had had enough. The number who were prepared to do malicious damage to Catholic life and property still seemed limited, but very many more officers were simply unwilling to risk their necks defending the Catholics. The senior officers of the police were very rarely prompted in any of their actions by malice. But in harsh fact, many of them appeared quite incompetent to command in the situation which had developed. The whole force, even after so long in action, was lamentably ill-trained in riot tactics, and discipline invariably collapsed under pressure. The Inspector-General, Anthony Peacocke, an officer nearing retirement, was a pleasant and courteous man of an old breed who plainly lacked the force-fulness and foresight his difficult job demanded. The reluctance at all levels to discipline officers for even blatant derelection of duty left an unhappy impression on many outside observers.

Finally, and by now vitally significant, there was the British Government at Westminster. Still, at this eleventh hour, they shrank from intervention. For many months, they had been pressuring Stormont relentlessly to speed up the pace of reform. They had watched with growing anxiety while the situation on the street deteriorated. But they felt unable to do more unless the situation altered considerably. When O'Neill was still Premier, there had been discussions about the possibility of using British troops for riot control duties, and Westminster had emphasised to the Ulster Government that any use of the army could mean a serious re-evaluation of Northern Ireland's constitutional relation-ship with Britain. It was impossible, London argued, merely to bring in a few soldiers to aid the police, and then withdraw them a few days later. Once the army came in, the complexities of the situation became acute.

But in the last days before August 12th, as it became increasingly clear how close Ulster was coming to total breakdown of law and order, those concerned began to debate the situation once more in a harsher and more realistic light. Chichester-Clark argued that if his lawfully elected Government at Stormont came closer to facing illegal rebellion, it was the duty of the British Government to give him the force to uphold the Government's authority, without strings attached. But Westminster were at all costs anxious to avoid any use of troops that might suggest that they were being employed by the Protestants to crush the Catholics. Above all, there must be no question of troops being placed under Stormont's authority—they would have to remain under London's control. In the end, a vague compromise was reached which papered over the misgivings of both sides: if troops had to be called in to keep the peace on a short-term basis, there would be no necessity to upturn the Constitutional authority of Stormont; only if the troops had to remain for some length of time under London's orders would the dreaded "re-evaluation" have to take place. Westminster, increasingly alarmed that some use of troops might become necessary, were still making decisions in the fervent hope that any involvement would be strictly limited to short-term tactical assistance. Behind the thinking of both sides lay no clearly-defined plan, only the certainty of certain things that could not be permitted. Chichester-Clark hoped that he could have his soldiers in dire extremity without a Westminster take over. Callaghan reluctantly accepted that if the situation deteriorated, it would be impossible to refuse military aid altogether.

At Chichester-Clark's latest meeting with Callaghan on August 8th, the Derry Apprentice Boys' March had been discussed, but no pressure had been brought to bear on him to ban it. For he made it clear that if a ban was imposed and then ignored, the risks of serious violence in enforcing it would be even greater than those of allowing it to take place. But London had organised every kind of contingency plan. The commander of the British Army garrison, Lt.-General Sir Ian Freeland, had been warned that he could be called on at any moment. Many of his 2,700 men had been briefed, issued with riot equipment, and put on stand-by. It may be argued that still, the Home Office in London did not appreciate the extent to which Stormont and the R.U.C.'s credibility had collapsed among the Catholic community; but it would also be impossible to underrate the risks of intervention by London against the wishes of Stormont. London now had to wait until Chichester-Clark officially asked for the aid of British troops. On August 12th, the Westminster Government was anxious and unhappy, but still firmly opposed to drastic action if it could be avoided, and optimistic enough for several of its senior ministers to be on holiday in the country.

Then, on to this messy and uncertain battlefield, came the parade of the Apprentice Boys of Derry.

7

THE BOGSIDE AND BELFAST

THE SOLEMN PROCESSION of the Derry Apprentice Boys began in perfect tranquillity on the morning of August 12th. There were thousands of them, in their sober suits and bowler hats with their pipe bands and flute bands and drum bands, their wives watching from the city walls all dressed up in Sunday best. The Catholics, in the Bogside below the city, complained that they felt like animals in a zoo as spectators and Apprentice Boys gazed down over the parapets to peer into the Catholic cauldron below. In the Bogside, they could hear the sound of the bands, and the Protestant tunes—the endless renderings of "The Wearing of the Sash" and "Derry Walls". By general consent and after much hard work by the moderate Catholic leaders, most Catholics stayed at home during the march, sick of Protestants and police cordons and riot tenders and drumbeating. But they were irritated, ill-humoured and not a little apprehensive.

There had been Protestant threats and constant rumours that this had been chosen as the day when the Bogside was going to be "hammered". After the events of January, April and July, the Catholics were edgy and easily susceptible to the wildest reports. In their square half mile of dull streets and wasteland, dominated by the new ten-storey tower block in Rossville Street, news travelled very fast indeed. Most of the Civil Rights leaders were in town, Bernadette Devlin was there, and Eamonn McCann. Eddie McAteer, gloomiest of the prophets, had already forecast that this day could "raise the curtain on the last terrible act of the age-old Irish drama". His remarks were considered histrionic. Yet among the Bogsiders, especially the younger ones, there were those who were ready for trouble of any kind. A month before, the Derry Citizens' Defence Committee had been formed in the Bogside, with twenty members led by two middle-aged local Catholics, Paddy Doherty and Sean Keenan, and including Eamonn McCann. Their declared aim was to defend the area from any further incursions by Protestants or police. Barricades of paving stones, scaffolding and debris were already in place in many streets on the afternoon of the 12th. In some places, petrol bombs had been made. There were even those who had learnt on which radio wavelengths the police communicated, and could monitor them. There was a hard core of men who were determined that if there was any repetition of the events of January, there would be resistance. Beyond these, there were many more people who needed very little to rouse them to join the action. The Bogside was a very close community in which everyone knew everyone else, little was kept secret, and fears and trials were a shared experience. The atmosphere was emotional and highly charged; the Bogsiders had come to expect the worst, and when it happened, to take the most desperate view of the situation. Many of them, also, were not only no longer willing to accept the police, but for many months had been longing for a confrontation with them on their own terms. While on August 12th they might not be prepared to cross town to court trouble, they were ready for it if it came to them. Late that afternoon, it did.

As part of the Apprentice Boys' parade passed through Waterloo Place, close to the Foyle River below the city walls, a group of Catholic youths began to throw stones at the parade. Young Protestants in the crowd retaliated, and a skirmish developed. The police, ready in full riot kit, moved in to break it up, and the situation worsened. Police and Catholics became engaged at close quarters. Then, somewhat reinforced and now more organised, the R.U.C. began to drive the hooligans down the street—towards the Bogside. Once more, they were making the disastrous error of automatically forcing rioters back into the Catholic area. As the police line battled forward, by now being constantly reinforced, the R.U.C. faced a heavy rearguard action.

Then the Bogside Catholics mobilised. Seeing the conflict approaching, and caring only that a heavy contingent of police were moving into the Bogside, they poured from their houses and flats to engage them. Around William Street and Rossville Street, a major action began. By 5 p.m., it had become a battle around the barricades. The Catholics were frantically strengthening their defences at every nearby approach to the Bogside, breaking up paving stones to hurl at the police, and commencing a heavy fire with petrol bombs. The tension heightened when it was reported that a police radio conversation had been intercepted, in which

H.Q. had ordered the men not to enter the Bogside, but that the senior officer on the spot had reported back that he was going in regardless. Not that it mattered, by now. The police had been checked by the murderous barrage pouring down on them. Their numbers were increasing rapidly as all available strength was brought into the area, equipped with riot shields, batons and visored helmets. But it was impossible to penetrate in the face of the storm of missiles that greeted every charge. The siege of Bogside, begun so suddenly, settled into a prolonged and bitter struggle.

As darkness fell, it only intensified. Late that night, tear gas began to come over from the police lines in quantity. As the volunteers at the barricades—men, women and small children—tired, others came forward to replace them. The entire community was in it now, and their operations were becoming organised. A raid on a Post Office depot brought in large supplies of petrol; every spare hand turned to filling bottles, jamming rags in the necks, and passing them in milk bottle crates to the front line. Major fires were springing up, lighting the sky. The police sheltered behind corners organising for their attacks, then charged forward launching tear gas as they came. All through the night and the next day, and the next night, the engagement continued. The police had become utterly determined that the Catholics must be crushed, and the Catholics were equally sure, now, that they must win or perish. They were certain that after what had passed, there could be no going back. Protestants appeared behind the police lines; some hurled petrol bombs from vantage points overlooking the Bogside; others fired Catholic shops outside the barricades; others still borrowed helmets and riot shields from exhausted policemen and joined the fighting cordon. On the roof of the Rossville Street flats, the Republican tricolour was broken out. The roof was manned by teenagers who maintained the fire of petrol bombs almost continuously, letting out wild war whoops whenever flames burst on a human target. The police, enraged by seeing colleagues set on fire or smashed down by flying rocks, responded with massive quantities of C.S. tear gas—both cartridges from projectors and grenades hurled by hand.

This provoked only more maddened fury from the Bogsiders. They tied handkerchiefs soaked in lemon juice around their faces or smeared themselves with vaseline to subdue the worst effects, or tried to smother the gas containers with wet blankets as they landed. Bernadette Devlin raced around the area in jeans and a sweater, urging the Bogsiders to ever greater efforts through a loudhailer, organising the filling of petrol bombs, screaming at the defenders to man the barricades. "She really seemed to feel the revolution had come," said one observer. "She was completely carried away by it all. She was sure there was nothing left for the British Government to do but suspend the Constitution and chuck out the police." The excitement, the very real thrill, overwhelmed the Bogsiders. Having convinced themselves that the police and the Protestants were bent on murder and that surrender meant disaster, they threw themselves into the fray with inexhaustible energy. They had first aid stations, a fire fighting squad and a highly effective intelligence system to warn them of police deployments and impending action. Over it all hung the gas. The police were no longer pretending to use it for specific purposes—they merely maintained a continuous choking, retching blanket of the stuff over the Bogside. In their gas masks and helmets and visors, they looked far more sinister than they proved: for all their efforts were in vain. Painfully moving forward inch by inch, they would gain a few yards, only to be driven back by Catholic counter-attack. Paving stones were being smashed in dozens for ammunition, and the police, by now exhausted and despairing, were hurling some of them back. Elsewhere across the city, as Wednesday dragged into Thursday, some semblance of normality continued in daylight, with only street diversion signs to indicate that anything was amiss. But at night, marauding Protestants were wreaking havoc where they could find targets. In addition to Catholic property, they attacked the City Hotel in Shipquay Place, headquarters of the press; the police appeared reluctant in the extreme to intervene—it was forty-five minutes before aid arrived to succour some dozen of very shaken journalists.

As the battle entered its third day, the situation seemed deadlocked. The police were adamant—with very good reason—that they could not simply withdraw. With Catholics and Protestants in arms, any madness was possible. There was every prospect that the Catholics would sally out into the city, and if they did not, the Protestants would sally in, outraged after seeing what the Catholics had been doing to "their" police. Yet the Bogsiders were hanging on, and there appeared no means to deal with them, even with up to 600 police deployed at some climactic moments.

Meanwhile elsewhere, events in Derry were driving others to

action. Almost since the siege began, the Bogside leaders had been appealing frantically for help in telephone calls to British Ministers, the Ulster Government, and other Catholic communities across Ulster. They had also been begging the Irish Republic's government for aid and medical supplies and gas masks. Their requests brought little response, but the Bogside struggle roused Dublin in a manner that had not been seen since the Civil Rights campaign began.

While most Irishmen in the South had been expressing loud support for their Catholic brethren since October (and for forty years before that), until now they had done singularly little about it. There had been much coming and going of Civil Rights leaders from the North to Dublin, and the Southern Irish papers had given every disturbance heavy coverage. Yet until the Bogside, it had been more a talking point than a provocation to action. But as the siege stretched on, feelings in the South rose. There were demonstrations and minor disturbances in Dublin, calls on the Irish Government to intervene, and young men seeking passage north to join the struggle. The I.R.A. issued noisy calls to arms, which caused much concern although producing little result. Above all, there was a feeling that no matter what, the Irish Government should do something.

Jack Lynch, the Premier, found himself in an acute dilemma. In theory, the Irish Government's political commitment to the concept of one Ireland was as great as ever, no matter how the issue had been allowed to fade in recent years. Lynch himself had been chosen as a compromise Leader. Now, factions on all sides of him were demanding contrary decisions. In this situation, he was under considerable pressure from his militants, both within and without the Cabinet, to take some effective action to show the South's attitude at a moment when Catholics were fighting for their lives. In terms of political reality, however, he knew very well that short of sending the Irish army to invade Ulster, there was little he could do. He sought, therefore, in the next few days, to take the least possible practical action while making the maximum amount of noise.

On Wednesday, he made a wildly emotional televised speech in support of the Bogside Catholics, and announced that he was ordering the setting up of Irish Army field hospitals near the Border to take casualties from Derry. He also sent his Foreign Minister to the United Nations to demand a U.N. peace-keeping force in Ulster, saying that British troops would not be acceptable (although he did later propose a mixed British-Irish army force). As he spoke, he knew perfectly that there would be no U.N. force, and that all his drumbeating in reality amounted to nothing, for he was powerless. But on the Ulster Catholics and Protestants who heard his remarks, the effect was galvanising. The Protestants were already in a state of acute alarm about events in Derry, and now feared that the Republic was building up to some even greater threat. The Catholics, taking Lynch's fighting speech at its face value, and acting on the pleas from the Bogside to take the heat off Derry, turned out on the streets. The combination of excitement, alcohol (heavy drinking always played a part in Ulster's serious disturbances), and Lynch's remarks had them ready for anything. That night violence broke out in Belfast, Armagh, Dungiven, Dungannon, Enniskillen and Coalisland, when police stations were attacked by Catholic mobs. In Dungiven and Dungannon, shooting took place.

On Thursday morning, Chichester-Clark at Stormont faced a critical situation. The police in Derry were at breaking point, while the Bogsiders showed no sign of weakening, and the destruction was growing worse hourly. It was clear that violence was spreading, and the growing hysteria in Dublin was creating a new element in the chaos. Television viewers were watching the nightly film of the rioting and becoming worked up to a pitch of anger and excitement. There were reports—however tendentious—that the I.R.A. was frantically gathering men to come north and join the Catholics with arms. The Derry police had already felt compelled to open fire themselves on several occasions, and a number of people had been wounded. More than two hundred casualties had been reported in the city, and terrified Catholic refugees were trickling across the Border into the Republic as the Bogsiders cleared out some of their women and children, and some other Catholics fled from Protestant areas. Chichester-Clark described Lynch's speech as "a clumsy and intolerable intrusion into our internal affairs", and had appeared on television himself on Wednesday night to warn that he would not hesitate to seek "other than police aid" if the situation demanded it. But in the Bogside, Bernadette Devlin, asked if her behaviour befitted a British M.P., was yelling back: "Tell them I didn't go to Westminster to join their bloody club!"

In England, Home Secretary James Callaghan flew to see Harold

Wilson in the Scilly Isles, where he was on holiday, to discuss the crisis. As he was airborne on his return journey, a radio message was brought to him from the Home Office: the Ulster Government had asked for British troops in Londonderry.

A few hours earlier, the dreaded 'B' Specials had been fully mobilised. Westminster had been led to suppose, when Stormont originally informed them, that the Specials would only be used for routine police duties, to free R.U.C. men for riot control. Above all, it had been clearly understood that the Specials would not be brought into "sensitive" areas. Yet now the Specials were already moving into Derry in their old-fashioned uniforms with high collars and peaked caps, armed with rifles, revolvers and sub-machine guns. County police chiefs had in fact been authorised to use the Specials wherever they were needed. In Derry, they were beginning to join the cordon around the Bogside, while many stood idly watching Protestants attacking Catholics outside the barricade perimeter. Chichester-Clark claimed privately that the situation was such that had the Specials not been officially mobilised, they would have mobilised themselves with even more disastrous results. And Ian Paisley had been threatening to call out the Ulster Protestant Volunteers, his terrifying personal army. It was a sign of the chaos that no one could suggest any effective countermeasure even if Paisley fulfilled his threat—so laughable in a reasonable society, so real in Ulster. Civil Rights, protest, demonstration—none of this meant anything any longer. The Bogside represented a serious challenge to Stormont's authority, and both sides interpreted it as such, and were rallying their forces to join in the battle. Chichester-Clark felt that Ulster stood within a hairsbreadth of real civil war, and for the first and only time throughout 1968 and 1969, this was almost true.

In his plane, Callaghan did not hesitate. General Freeland, the Commander-in-Chief Northern Ireland, already had warning from his own intelligence officers quietly observing on the spot that the police in Derry could not be expected to hold on much longer. The previous day, he had discreetly moved three hundred troops into H.M.S. *Sea Eagle*, the naval base on the edge of the city. Just after 5 p.m., half an hour after Callaghan gave the order, the first platoons of the Prince of Wales's Own Yorkshire Regiment began to deploy around Londonderry. James Chichester-Clark announced that the measure was being taken because "after three days and two nights of continuous duty, the Royal Ulster Constabulary find it necessary to fall back on their police stations, thus exposing the citizens of Londonderry to the prospect of looting and a danger to life". By evening, more than four hundred soldiers were in Derry, in full battle kit with automatic rifles and light machine guns. As they moved into position, the fighting ceased. The Bogsiders had won.

As the police and the 'B' Specials withdrew from the area, the Catholics rushed from behind the barricades, cheering and singing and yelling "We have overcome!" The troops were not entering the Bogside, only creating a cordon around it and setting up posts across the city. Bernadette Devlin said: "We are ready to negotiate with the British Army." Two London Home Office officials were flying to Belfast to join General Freeland as political advisers at army headquarters, and it appeared that the very "re-evaluation" of Britain's Constitutional relationship with Ulster, which had been discussed so often, might be on the verge of becoming reality. The defence of the Bogside seemed about to become part of the Irish legend—a greater victory for the Catholics than all the months of Civil Rights marches and protests. Catholic exultation was boundless, as the news travelled across Ulster. It was an incredible volte-face. For centuries, the British Army had been bitterly hated and feared among Ulster Catholics. Now, the troops were being greeted as saviours. The struggle in Derry had become headlines across the world, and had triggered the romantic impulses not only of the public, but of many politicians. It would be days and weeks before there was serious analysis of what had happened, and why. Bogside had not been a riot, but a full-scale pitched battle in which it had been miraculous that no one had died. Both police and Catholics had been in an impossible position. The Bogsiders had strong reason to hate and fear the police, perhaps even to be out-raged at their coming; certainly they had been under extreme provocation. But once the riot began, it was equally clear that the police could not simply disengage. The R.U.C. had been miserably under strength for an action of this kind—undoubtedly, they would have moved against the Bogside from the rear, which was almost untouched in the struggle, had they had the men. But they were fully employed containing the situation in Rossville Street and William Street. Their use of C.S. gas became wild in the extreme in the later phases of the battle, as the frustration of stand-ing firm in the face of a hail of petrol bombs and rocks became acute. But gas is not a killer. The Bogsiders made much play in the

next few months of police "brutality" in the use of gas* in an area
where women and children lived, but under the circumstances in
which the police were operating, it was very difficult not to sympathise with the R.U.C. The Catholics joined battle with unpreced-
ented savagery, and they were met in kind. What was more difficult
to accept was the manner in which Protestants were permitted to
join the police line. When the R.U.C. withdrew on Thursday
afternoon, Bogside would not see them again for many months.

Early that Thursday evening, however, the news was still
coming in of the take-over of the troops in Derry and the obvious
confusion of the Government. Across Ulster, real terror was grip-
ping many Protestants, who had seen film and pictures of the
Derry Catholics in action, and could see their co-religionists in
every town bursting with excitement. In Armagh, a riot developed
in which a Catholic mob were engaged with police and 'B' Specials.
Shooting began, and a Catholic was killed—the first death in the
Northern Irish riots. That word, too, soon flashed across the
province. In simmering Belfast, passions were becoming high.

The key areas of sectarian unrest in the Ulster capital began only
a few hundred yards from the central street, Royal Avenue. Three
streets branched out at right angles from Royal Avenue which
disappeared into the hinterland of Catholic and Protestant slums.
The first few yards of the streets were large shops and businesses,
but gradually these trickled away into the pubs, tobacconists,
shops and houses of the sectarian communities. The streets,
although they had other names at either extremity, were generally
known as the Falls Road, the Shankill Road and the Crumlin
Road, running almost parallel out of the city. The Falls Road was
the centre of the Catholic area. At the end nearest to the city
centre stood Hastings Street police barracks, where for weeks the
police had lived in a state of tacit siege, venturing out cautiously,
and then usually in vehicles. Two hundred yards higher up stood a
vast new Catholic housing block, Divis Flats—a tower facing on to
the road, with three other buildings in the complex a little way

* The massive use of C.S. in the Bogside became the central theme in a
violent public argument across Britain about both the morality and possible
harmful effects of its employment. A Home Office Committee was established
to investigate, and reported guardedly that under normal circumstances, there
was no risk. However that may be, the key question seems less about the use of
C.S. than about the alternatives possible in containing a riot. In Bogside, the
police far exceeded reasonable bounds. But elsewhere gas averted several
potentially disastrous confrontations in the next few weeks.

back from the street, each with long concrete terraces on each level. Beyond that, the Falls was just a dirty, unprepossessing ramble of ageing buildings, interspersed occasionally with churches, factories, and one or two new buildings. On either side the whole of its length, side streets of exactly identical decaying terraced houses ran off, on one side leading to the Grosvenor Road, on the other to the perils of the Protestant Shankill, some four hundred yards away. At some almost precisely definable point along each street between the Falls and the Shankill, Catholic territory ended and Protestant ground began. In some unhappy places, spurs of Catholic territory—vulnerable salients—jutted out into Protestant country, where the Union Jacks and obscenely anti-Catholic slogans on the walls began. Catholic slogans advocated "Join your local I.R.A." or, later, "Long live Free Belfast". On the Protestant walls, however, it would be "Fuck the Pope" or "Craig for P.M.". The overwhelming impression on both sides of the battlefield was of dull, unbroken, depressed gloom. The children crawling in the dirty streets, the silence, the few cars parked by the roadsides, and the air of pointless hate ate into one's spirit within an hour or two in the area.

Further out of the city, in the area known as the Ardoyne, there were Catholic enclaves in similar streets, but surrounded by Protestant houses. In every confrontation, it was in the places where the Catholics were at a tactical disadvantage that they suffered most seriously, and by this time, evictions of families who found themselves in the "wrong areas" had reached alarming proportions. Anonymous and semi-illiterate hate letters and threats had been part of life for weeks. But in the entire Catholic area of the city, there cannot have been more than thirty guns available for use, most of them shotguns, and almost all scantily supplied with ammunition. Among the scores of figures who would probably have called themselves I.R.A. men, hardly a dozen guns could be mustered. The incidents on Wednesday night, when the police station had been attacked, had created a restive air among the Catholics, and the urge for action among some of the younger elements, but little more.

On Thursday evening, however, the Belfast police, especially those in the immediate vicinity of the Falls Road, were furiously angry and in some cases, very frightened. Reports of events in the Bogside had infuriated them, knowing only too well what their colleagues had faced. They themselves had been violently engaged a dozen times in recent weeks, and while the latest confrontations had mostly involved the Protestant mob attempting to attack Catholic flats in the Shankill Road, they knew very well that it was the Catholics who were the real enemy. They believed, that night, that in the situation that was developing, the Catholics were capable of anything. In every bar, as the drinking got heavier and the talk wilder, the excitement was mounting. The police felt memories of the 1920's warfare in the streets stir as if it had been yesterday. They knew how few men they could muster if really in desperate straits. They no longer had the appetite for endless baton charges in the face of a mob hurling every missile they could find at their ranks. They were edgy and tense, and they were tired of being the target of both violence and criticism. As they peered cautiously through the fenced windows of the police barracks, they were well aware that the riot the previous evening could only be the beginnings of their troubles.

Then, late on Thursday afternoon, word reached Belfast from Londonderry that horrified the Catholic community—the 'B Men' were out. They heard that 'B' Specials had been in Derry carrying rifles, and that what amounted to a full call-up of the Specials had taken place. It was as if the Government had declared a kind of fearsome Open Season on Catholics. Within hours, every street knew it; they began to build barricades, ineffectively as yet, and in insufficient numbers; but every Catholic child had been reared on tales of the 'B' Specials' doings during the Troubles. More than anything else, this was the news that provoked the younger Catholics to action. As darkness fell, a crowd of youths were gathered in the Falls Road, hurling stones towards the Hastings Street police station and massing in ever increasing numbers. The police began to deploy to meet them. Armoured cars and a line of police formed up between the police barracks and the crowd, and reinforcements were summoned. Towards 10 p.m. forces of police and 'B' Specials were spread round much of the Falls Road area, others were heavily guarding the Shankill Road, and the first skirmishes began in the most devastating battle in the Ulster crisis of 1969.

Near Divis Flats up on the Falls Road, about five hundred Catholic youths were scattered, some lighting fires in the roadway, others working on barricades, others breaking up paving stones to use as missiles, others clutching petrol bombs, of which there were many in evidence. They seemed uncertain what to do. They chatted, sang fragments of songs, marched and counter-marched up and down the street, and threw occasional stones and petrol bombs, most of which fell short, at the police line in front of Hastings Street. Then police armoured personnel carriers began to sprint noisily up and down the street, either reconnoitring or in a futile hope of breaking up the crowd. The carriers provoked storms of petrol bombs and stones, and flames licked the armour plating before being doused by police colleagues on foot. Then the police began to make short charges up the road from their line, batons and riot shields in front of them. Each time, the front ranks of the mob would break and run as they advanced, only to reform when the police drew back. All the time, the crowd was thickening. A bulldozer left on a building site higher up the street was started by two youths, and driven amidst massive cheering down the slight slope in the road towards Divis Flats and the police. But en route, its drivers lost their nerve and crashed it into a telegraph pole beside a factory, where it was immediately set on fire by a petrol bomb. Now, the petrol bombs were starting to fly faster, and the crowd was getting braver. More and more police were moving in, and hand-to-hand actions were beginning. The petrol bombs had started fires in several shops and houses along the streets which were beginning to burn fiercely. Up the side streets, police and 'B' Specials were massing, with Protestants from the Shankill Road also clutching petrol bombs, dustbin lids and sticks, behind and beside them. The chaos grew as some lights were knocked out by stones, the fires grew bigger, and the engagement more and more widely spread out over an area more than a mile square. It will probably never be established for certain who fired the first shot.

The police claim that a man in the mob opened fire on them with an automatic weapon. As at this time the situation in the Falls Road was becoming totally chaotic, and many of the crowd were running for cover, this can never be confirmed. What is certain is that within a few minutes, the entire situation had altered. Gunfire had become general, the streets in the line of fire cleared like magic, and the Falls Road became the centre of a violent guerilla battle that continued until dawn.

The 'B' Specials and the R.U.C. were now in action together. There were on the streets of Belfast four forces, closely engaged and beyond the reach of serious central direction. First, the Catholics; then the 'B' Specials, all armed with revolvers, rifles or sub-machine guns; the R.U.C.; and the Protestants from the Shankill, who began to mount heavy petrol bomb attacks on houses and factories on the fringes of the Falls area. The R.U.C. had by now convinced themselves that they faced something approaching a Catholic revolt. Fantastically, in Great Britain, their senior officers had permitted the calling out of armoured cars mounted with heavy machine guns. Many R.U.C. men also had 9mm Sterling sub-machine guns as personal weapons. There was the absolutely clear feeling among the police that they faced a direct threat. After the first gunfire, every time shots were heard, from whatever direction, the police would loose off burst after burst of sub-machine gunfire at something—or nothing. And the armoured cars began to career the length of the Falls Road emptying belts of heavy calibre ammunition in the direction of any supposed threat.

In the silence and the darkness broken only by gunfire, crackling flames from the fires, and faint shouts, there were a handful of Catholic snipers operating; also, without doubt, some Protestants. But even with field glasses, it was only half a dozen times that one caught a glimpse of a muzzle flash from a rooftop or a figure silhouetted against the skyline. Two police were hit in Dover Street, and carried to the shelter of the personnel carriers behind the police lines. But even with a finely-sighted rifle, it would have been very difficult to make effective return practical against snipers that night. They moved too fast, there were not many of them, and they were small and only occasionally visible targets. The police embarked on a rampage of machine-gun fire that shattered every observer who witnessed it. Shots were believed to have come from Divis Flats: the police replied by hosing fire in the direction of the flats. An armoured car sprayed the buildings with heavy machine-gun fire, sending chips flying off the concrete parapets, and causing havoc within. The gunfire was general, but a few seconds later a yell went up from the first floor: "A child's been hit!" Upstairs, a nine-year-old Catholic boy who had been sheltering in the back room of his family's flat, lay on a bed with half his head blown away by one of a burst of five heavy calibre bullets that had smashed through the frail partition walls. He was plainly dying. The police declined to send an ambulance across the Falls Road under fire, and called to the flats to carry the boy across. With a man waving a white shirt frantically beside them, two men carried the boy across to the police lines to an ambulance, to die a

144

little later. On the roof of the flats, another man lay dead, hit by several shots. In the buildings, everyone crouched beneath the concrete parapets to avoid the fire. Young men with piles of petrol bombs lined up beside them watching for a target. An R.U.C. man was brought across under a flag of truce to tend to the wounded, of whom there were by now several in the flats.

On the street corners, the battle still raged. 'B' Specials with their revolvers shot out the street lights—oblivious to the danger of ricochets—in the hope of making themselves poorer targets, then leaned around the streets with cigarettes dangling from their lips. Senior officers—such as were to be seen—appeared to have neither plan nor will to impose any kind of fire discipline. At intervals, a policeman would lean around a corner to loose off a burst of fire, then duck once more. Still the armoured cars continued their relentless patrols, turrets swivelling and guns elevating and depressing as they sought a target. One car swung round behind the police line, and halted in shelter while the crew jumped down to drink tea supplied by a local Protestant. The gunner, in his shirt-sleeves, harangued a group of police: "You know, of course, Dr. Paisley has been telling us this would happen these nine months, but none of us had the sense to listen. . . ." It was a remark that explained much Catholic feeling towards the police. That night, it was rarely that one saw a policeman be brutal or even discourteous. But worse, perhaps, the police were involved in a battle under utterly false illusions, completely without understanding or direction or even acceptance of basic riot tactics. How could men only half-trained with firearms be allowed to attempt to pick off snipers with machine-gun fire in a crowded city area? How could Protestants be suffered among the police lines for every Catholic to see? How could Protestants wreak so much havoc among Catholic houses and businesses without interference or care from the police?

It was not only in the Falls Road that the battle was in progress. In the Ardoyne, Catholics behind barricades had been under heavy fire from police and from the Protestants. Fires were now blazing in widely scattered areas both there and around the Falls. A big mill was burning fiercely. Still the police were seeking targets, but finding fewer now as everyone but the snipers and a few hardy petrol bombers dug themselves deep into cover. The I.R.A. men, such as there were, the militant Catholics with the guns: they were all out by now—but by any reckoning, there cannot have been more than a dozen snipers working, most of them poor marksmen. So much gunfire was coming down, however, and the police were so uncertain whence it came, that they fired all the more ruthlessly. Many people had been hit, although most mercifully slightly. Only three policemen had been touched by gunfire, while more than fifty civilians were wounded.

This was the battle that need not have been a battle; the police, feeling in serious danger and wild with anger against the Catholics, took drastic action, and the Catholics retaliated to the best of their ability. The Catholics had started it, for sure; but in English terms, when shooting must be done comes the moment at which policemen withdraw.

As dawn came in the early hours of the morning, spasmodic firing was still breaking the silence, and plumes of black smoke drifted skywards from the fires. The police gradually withdrew, taking the Specials with them. Including those who died of wounds, six men had died in Belfast during the night, including one shot down as he crossed his own kitchen; 105 people had been injured by the official count, and many more lay having their wounds dressed at home, reluctant or afraid to appear at a hospital. Even the figure for the dead was uncertain. There was word of others whose bodies lay charred to cinders among the ashes of buildings in which they had been shot. More than one hundred homes had been destroyed, more than a dozen factories, while over three hundred houses had been damaged by petrol bombs. All these counts ignored the endless broken windows and charred shop fronts. The Falls Road looked the battlefield it had been.

As the day lightened, with every traffic light shattered, young Catholics stood directing traffic amidst the rubble. Many buildings were still blazing and the roadway was covered with the litter of rocks and glass. The police had melted away: they stayed tightly shuttered in Hastings Street barracks and the other stations across the city, while between Catholic and Protestant areas the barricades were built up to huge proportions, and intermittent skirmishing continued throughout the daylight hours. Of the dead, only one was Protestant; of the houses burnt, all but a handful were Catholic. At the further end of the Falls Road the scene was incredible, with almost every tree and telegraph pole chopped off at its base to form a barricade. Sixty buses were commandeered by the Catholics on Thursday evening and during Friday, by the simple expedient of telling the drivers to get out or be pulled out.

These too were forced across the streets along with bakery vans, upturned cars and trucks, scaffolding and vast numbers of paving stones to create the mountainous barricades eight or even ten feet high, every one manned. The Protestants had their own barricades, and clustered behind them making occasional forays.

There was no more hesitation: almost every Catholic in a sensitive Protestant area crossed the lines with all speed, leaving home and property behind him. Trucks hastened through the streets carrying what furniture could be shifted, while young Catholics guarded the removers. For several hours, a kind of anarchy prevailed, with Protestants and Catholics confronting each other, but mostly too busy consolidating their own positions to consider immediate action. In the centre of Belfast, untouched by all that had passed, shoppers were noticeably thinner on the ground, but there none the less. Sanity ceased a few hundred yards away, but in Royal Avenue it was as if nothing had happened, with only the smoke from the fires on the horizon to cast a shadow across the city.

Then, that afternoon, came the British Army. In response to Chichester-Clark's urgent pleas, a battalion of the Royal Regiment of Wales and another of the Queen's Regiment were ordered into the Falls Road. They began to deploy along it. But pitifully few in numbers for fighting in the warren of alleys and sideroads around the city, they could not occupy the outlying areas. They set up command posts along the Falls, but they had only the barest knowledge of the geography, far less the positions of Catholic and Protestant front lines. Still the fires were burning in the big factories and warehouses, and the soldiers were openly bewildered by the shambles of the situation they were being called on to face. By the Catholics, they were received as salvation. The sight of armed British soldiers in the streets where the previous night had been the police machine-gunners brought the housewives out plying the troops with food and tea. The Protestants sulked behind their lines, chatting to the police who were still in the Shankill area in strength. The army did not move into the barricaded Catholic area on the Grosvenor Road side of the Falls—only along the Falls line facing the Shankill. Even now, when the British Government answered Chichester-Clark's latest request for aid in Belfast, they hoped that this could be a temporary "fire-fighting" action. Still they prayed that no major troop commitment would become necessary. And the forces sent into the Falls were painfully inadequate.

Thus as night fell, the struggle resumed. And in the Ardoyne, where no troops were disposed, the Protestants stormed into the outlying Catholic streets, hurling petrol bombs as they came. House after house caught fire. An advance army patrol found two Catholics holding off one Protestant mob with shotguns. The soldiers told the Catholics to disappear quickly if they wanted to avoid trouble. But the Protestants, not so easily deterred, kept coming. The troops, under the strictest orders to open fire only if life was threatened, could not bring themselves to do so. Only a handful strong, they fell back and pleaded for reinforcements. It was some time before these could be found; and when a full Company returned to the area, they found two entire streets ablaze from end to end. The Protestants retired once more behind their barricades around the corner as the army took up positions, and a young lieutenant who went to parley with them came back shocked, to report that two policemen had been with the Protestants behind the barricade. At another barricade, Protestants swarmed out when they saw three reporters and cameramen behind the leading platoon, and struggled to get within striking range before being driven back by the soldiers. In half a dozen places, Catholic snipers were unconcealedly holding off the Protestants with gunfire where the troops were not intervening. Protestant snipers were working too, and Catholics set fire to a factory to burn one sharpshooter off the roof.

As the night wore on, the thinly stretched troops began to learn. Another battalion of the Light Infantry arrived as reinforcement, and the lines were extended to cover as many as possible of the trouble spots. At one point along the Falls Road, a young officer and his platoon were firing gas cartridges from behind a barricade to drive off Protestant petrol bombers. The attackers would creep forward in short runs, silhouetted figures only detectable by the quick rattle of feet. As they edged towards the Falls, the officer yelled through a loudhailer to hold off or be gassed. There would be another short rush, a tinkling crash as the petrol bomb landed short, and the succession of dull cracks as the gas cartridges left their trail of smoke across the sky. The bombers came up again and again, but never confronted the troops head on. They were doing more than enough damage without that.

In the street fighting that was taking place, the overall situation was as baffling and fragmented for army headquarters as for those on the spot. Many soldiers stood-to all night, hardly knowing what was happening, not coming under attack, hearing confused reports on the radio net, seeing the blazes a few streets away and hearing only spasmodic shots. A mad situation developed when young volunteers—some of them English tourists—commandeered a fire engine abandoned by its crew when it had come under gunfire. For most of the night, the volunteers raced from blazing house to blazing house, working with manic speed and amazing efficiency. Finally, in the early hours, the regular crew re-appeared once more, and the volunteers were sent packing. But as an army officer remarked: "I can't help feeling those fellows have been tackling some of the fires the regulars would have been happy to leave alone."

As army patrols moved into new areas as the night went on, Catholics stood by their houses calling at them. From some of the women, it was "Thank God for the Military!" But many of the men were too enraged by the army's refusal to fire on petrol bombers: "If you won't use the guns, give them to us who will!" came yells from Catholics who ran alongside the officers, begging them to go into action against the Protestants. Yet the army had been briefed in a manner that left scant discretion—they were to use minimum force. And in that confused and bewildering night, every commander, however junior, knew that his career could be damned for ever by making a mistake in a situation so explosively political. The troops on the ground behaved superbly, almost caricatures of what the British Army is always meant to be, with the throwaway casualness of officers who knew how critical the position was and the easy resignation of the Other Ranks. However hard one tried to remain calmly detached, after watching the previous night's battle, in which it seemed that no sanity was left on any side, it was easy to feel on the verge of tears at the sight of files of British soldiers tramping in, making the wisecracks yet moving with rapid efficiency. Under the conditions in which they entered the battle, and with the numbers of men available, they did their job brilliantly. After Thursday night, there was no shadow of doubt that without the army, the Protestants would have totally over-whelmed the Catholic area given a few more hours, and the police would have done little to stop them. It had been terrifying to chat amiably to police and 'B' Specials in the firing line on Thursday, hearing them no longer in doubt—merely quite certain that now they were at open war. Challenged about the Protestant thugs with them in the line, they'd shrug their shoulders and say: "Well, they've got to protect their homes, haven't they?" Much was said later about the number of Catholic firearms in use on Thursday—but there had been so pitifully few. Perhaps it was merciful that this was so, for with the police firing almost continuously for more than three hours during the main engagement, without doubt had the Catholics had more arms, they would have used them. By Friday night, the Protestant mobs attacking Catholic streets were becoming highly organised, with white armbands on their sleeves to distinguish them from the enemy, and clear plans of attack. Fantastically, at one point a Protestant contingent behind one barricade summoned the army platoon commander nearby to demand protection, as they claimed to be in danger of imminent attack from the Catholics. A few yards away, every Catholic house in Bombay Street was blazing from end to end. The army's guns remained trained in the direction of the Protestant barricades.

Gradually, the sniping fire tailed off, the petrol bombers were driven back. The army were learning very fast how the police were regarded in the Catholic areas. Earlier in the evening, the police had appeared in their armoured cars in many places, and had even told the troops to stay out of certain areas. But now, it was the army who were preventing the police armoured cars from entering Catholic streets, to the frantic relief of the inhabitants. For the first time in many hours, people began to drift home, or hung out of their doorways watching anxiously as army Land-Rovers cruised around the streets, the soldiers with their rifles raised watchfully. The troops had gained command without firing a round of live ammunition. Only one soldier had been slightly wounded by gunfire. All along the fringes of the Catholic area, facing the Protestants behind their barricades, the army began to consolidate. The fire brigade was bringing some of the big blazes under control, although a few burnt on for days. The shattered and smouldering ruins of houses, shops and pubs lay the length of the riot area, from the Falls into no-man's land. Along the Falls Road itself, soldiers lay by the houses wrapped in their ponchoes, trying to snatch some rest, while others strengthened the barbed wire entanglements they were beginning to erect at the key positions. The Protestants were not beaten—they had suffered only a handful of casualties; but they had been held. A line had been established, and was under guard; the police had been driven out of the Catholic area, and sulked among the Protestants. By morning, the city was once more under control.

8

DAMMING THE BREACHES

ON SATURDAY, AUGUST 16th, amidst the shambles of the Falls Road and the Ardoyne, Belfast arose to find itself a war zone. Kniferests and concertina wire blocked off parts of the city. Troops checked vehicles moving in and out of the sensitive areas. Army Land-Rovers, forests of wireless aerials swaying above their body-work, cruised through the city laden with soldiers and stores. Within their own ghettos, Catholics and Protestants worked to strengthen their barricades while the army patrolled between them, creating blockades of its own. Later, middle-class Ulster-men who never dared to venture into the battle area claimed that the extent of the damage had been much exaggerated, since it was confined to only one quarter of the city; but in that quarter, more than a mile square, there seemed to be acre upon acre of wrecked buildings and shattered shopfronts. The debris spilled across the streets as families laboured to save what they could, and still more evacuated their homes either from damage or fear. As in every riot, every war, it was the women who shook their heads and wept in utter dismay, while the men clustered on the street corners, talking only about revenge on the guilty. Every plane into Belfast brought new contingents of reporters and cameramen from half way across the world, as Ulster, to its bewilderment and fury, became the focal point of universal fascination.

From every political group and faction, statements, accusations and counter-accusations poured forth. The Paisleyites and the Protestants damned the Catholics for their "revolt", their un-provoked attack on the police. The Catholics, feeling that they had only narrowly escaped an attempt by the police and the Protestants to exterminate them, cried for justice against those who had assaulted them, and demanded army protection for every Catholic corner of Belfast. From Armagh, Cardinal Conway was making vague noises about fairness and an end to violence, while the Protestant right-wingers called for cast-iron guarantees that the coming of the army would in no way affect the Constitutional relationship of Britain and Ulster. The police were issuing statements justifying their own role in the Belfast battle, including one insisting that it was imperative for Ulster to know that they did not open fire until they themselves "had come under heavy gunfire attack almost simultaneously in various parts of the city".

The British Government at Westminster was already facing the frightful realisation that the army might be in Ulster for a long stay. It was plainly impossible for the police to return to either Falls Road or the Bogside in the immediate future, and somehow peace must be maintained. And so many other vital questions thrust themselves on the politicians in London: what changes, if any, must be sought in the relationship between Westminster and Stormont? What were the prospects of more and worse violence in the streets, and how many troops would be needed to deal with it? What immediate action could be taken to ease the situation? And what long-term steps could be found to ensure that such a tragedy could never occur again? In seeking the answers, a British Government and British minds had to seek very rusty precedent indeed; it was so very many years since anything like this had occurred in the British Isles, so long since any domestic political crisis had dissolved into such nightmarish chaos, requiring such drastic solutions.

The disaster of Northern Ireland had been several hundred years in the making. In all that time, with the benefit of hindsight it is easy to pinpoint scores of opportunities and moments of decision wasted by stupidity or negligence. But now, such a situation having been created and having to be faced in August 1969, the utter impotence of the authorities in seeking a speedy and effective solution was in no way surprising. The tragedies of Belfast and Bogside set the seal on a catastrophe that had been building up for years and months; that those who had to cope with it found themselves in dire trouble shocked only newcomers to Northern Ireland.

In the days after August 12th, Catholics and Protestants, rioters and politicians, drove themselves into a world of insane illusion from which it was weeks before they began to emerge. They approached their grievances with a burning intensity that left them blind to any spark of reality or reason. A few days after the Belfast holocaust, a Catholic hotel barman heard a group of reporters discussing the police actions in facing the Catholic mob in the Falls Road. "What mob?" he suddenly interrupted. "There was never no mob—the boys in blue just came in and tried to murder everyone in their beds!" He didn't care that eye-witnesses saw the facts differently, he didn't even want to listen. He was only sure, like every Catholic in Belfast, that he had been the victim of a Protestant onslaught. Likewise Paisley, a little later, when he was calling fire and brimstone on the Catholics for attacking Protestant property: everyone asked how he could explain that almost every house destroyed in the riots was Catholic. Paisley thought for a moment, then replied with utter outward sincerity that Catholic houses were so jammed with stores of petrol bombs that even a spark would set them alight. His followers, hanging on his every word in this, their hour of trial, trusted him implicitly.

In this atmosphere, reasonable men had to attempt to urge sanity on Ulster. Protestant believed only Protestant, and Catholic only Catholic. In the pubs, on the street corners, in the church halls, in the refugee centres, Ulstermen talked to each other and learnt by heart a personal version of reality from which nothing would shake them. So many bitter feuds between streets, between individuals, between factions had now been opened that no provocation was needed to drive them into warfare on the instant. Forget Civil Rights and Catholic struggles and Protestant demands—from August until well into autumn, violence was sown simply by sectarian loathing. Civil Rights leaders and Protestant militants became only the drum-beaters for factional propaganda. Every man who had seen a rock fly past his head had a grievance now, and looked only for a target on which to revenge himself. Incidents and disturbances were scarcely worth individual analysis: the news of a minor riot meant only that Protestant had met Catholic somewhere where the army had not arrived in time. Both sides were making preposterous demands with all the fervour of injured righteousness. In Derry and Belfast, the police had almost ceased to be a factor in peace-keeping, and had become merely the gloomy furniture of the Protestant areas. Any sense of Ulster as an entity, already slipping before August, had now disappeared completely. Every man spoke for himself and his own cause— Catholics and Catholic church leaders, Protestants, Paisley, the Orange Order, the police, the Falls Road, People's Democracy, John Hume and Ivan Cooper, the Bogside, the I.R.A., the Stormont—each man was his own voice and nothing more. To negotiate with one man or one body meant nothing to the rest; situations could be grasped only as they occurred, at the most trivial tactical level. A state of spiritual anarchy had been created, in which the authorities must do the best they could to weld the fragments back into some kind of manageable entity.

But if at this moment most of Ulster, and of the world, looked to the British Government to begin this process, Stormont could also have a critical role. Now, when so many people were so deeply shaken by all that occurred, James Chichester-Clark might have a slender chance of gaining a new foothold in the province's confidence. But instead of accepting that in the weekend of August 16th, he faced an entirely changed situation in which a totally new approach was needed, the Prime Minister of Northern Ireland, still judging it from the cloudy mists of Stormont Castle, hurled his options to the wind. He chose to fight his next action not only on old and bloody ground, but from a personal standpoint that anywhere else in the world would have sent him hastening towards political oblivion.

Chichester-Clark expressed his opinions and made his decisions, in the days following the riots, on information at best incomplete, at worst disgracefully wrong. He studied the police account of the events of Thursday night, and announced that "well-disciplined and ruthless men working to an evident plan attacked the police at a number of points in the city". Despite the almost total lack of evidence of their effective presence in Belfast, it was being prominently reported in Ulster and in the South that armed I.R.A. men were coming North in large numbers to join battle. This news received wide currency at Stormont. In Dublin, Jack Lynch, in yet another quite vacuous gesture, had further increased the alarm of Northern Protestants by mobilising the Irish Army's reserves and talking of troop concentrations near the Border. With the Protestants in an uproar and the Catholics making violent threats from behind their barricades, Chichester-Clark now lost his head because all around him had lost theirs. He chose to adopt a classic Protestant stance to explain all that had happened, in defiance of massive independent evidence to contradict the police account of the situation. On Sunday, August 17th, he held a press conference to show the people of Ulster and of England where he stood. It was probably one of the most disastrous and ill-handled exercises in public relations ever seen in politics.

At a time when above all, Northern Ireland needed reassurance that the crisis was in firm hands, its Prime Minister came forth to the world like a blind man in a snowstorm. He fended off every question about the manner in which the police had behaved, and about how large areas of Catholic Belfast had been devastated. He said that it was plain that the first shooting had been against the police. He appeared to regard this assertion as blanket justification for all that had followed. Before a crowded audience of the world's press, he threw forth platitude after platitude, inanity after inanity. Finally, after much pressuring, there was the promise that all specific complaints against the police would be investigated. To whom should they be addressed? enquired a journalist. Deadpan, Chichester-Clark's Home Affairs Minister replied: "The police", as the whole room dissolved into helpless and bitter laughter.

Chichester-Clark had already made his quota of disastrous errors; on August 15th and the days following, some twenty Catholics had been arrested and were being detained without trial under the Special Powers Act. These were those regarded as actual or potential I.R.A. men. The Prime Minister had convinced himself that what was happening around him was a serious conspiracy to bring down his Government. At his press conference, he insisted that "Republican elements" were behind all that had happened, men deliberately seeking "to subvert a democratically-elected Government". In this, he missed the essence of the crisis. There were indeed elements—and strong ones—in the Catholic community who would dearly have loved to have done everything of which he accused them. There were very many who wished more than anything else to see Stormont abolished and Northern Ireland brought under direct rule from Westminster or Dublin. But although Bogside had organised to fight off the police, in Belfast much of what happened was plainly spontaneous. Catholics in the Falls Road area had rioted; they had acted illegally, dangerously, and in the end disastrously. But all this could happen only in the climate that already existed, and none of it could excuse the subsequent actions of police and Protestants. The vast majority of the damage to property and injury to persons was against Catholics. Only a very limited proportion had been done by the Catholics themselves. For all the guard dogs and police who were now creeping around the bushes in Stormont Park, there was no evidence of any direct attempt to overthrow the Government. The major charge against the Catholics was that of deliberately seeking to push Chichester-Clark into a position in which Westminster had no choice but to intervene: there were many reasonable Englishmen who felt that there was strong moral justification for the Catholic policy. The Unionists and the Protestants had forced the Catholics into a corner; when they attempted to come out of it, Protestant elements sought to force them remorselessly back. The Catholics had to bear a considerable share of responsibility for the violence that had taken place, direct or otherwise. But it is the duty of Government to keep a sense of proportion, whoever else has lost theirs. Instead, in Ulster, the authorities at every level lost all grip and sense of reality.

Over the weekend following the riots, Catholics and Protestants forgot any semblance of common ground. The Protestant spokesmen, both inside and outside Government, attacked the Catholics bitterly, while the Catholics howled for retribution against their "persecutors". On the streets, stalemate prevailed; spasmodic incidents continued hourly in Belfast, but the troops held the situation in temporary control, although in urgent need of reinforcement. The Bogside was mercifully peaceful, but like the Falls Road area, it now existed in a vacuum. Encircled by protective troops, humming with apprehension and debate, the two pockets were by their own will completely isolated. The writ of Government and law and order had ceased to run, and vigilantes patrolled the streets while others manned the barricades, utterly determined that government would return only when a peace treaty had been granted and ratified. The terms of the Derry Citizens' Defence Committee for a surrender included at this time: the abolition of Stormont; return of all "prisoners" captured by police in the Bogside; amnesty for all who had taken part in the defence; and disbandment of the 'B' Specials.

It was clear to all concerned that to attempt to re-enter either Bogside or the Falls area by force could be disastrous. The troops might, at the beginning, have been able to do it bloodlessly; but there had been neither enough of them available nor clear enough orders. By the time the army had regrouped, it was too late. The Catholics might be grateful to the army and friendly to them. But short of a pitched battle, they would have no representatives of authority inside the barricades until terms had been agreed. For the present, the situation was left in uneasy limbo, the army somehow preserving a semblance of order, while the Governments of Ulster and Britain set to work to shore up the trembling framework of tranquillity.

At this moment, it was abundantly clear that for all his noise-making Chichester-Clark had not a card in his hand; by calling

7a On the afternoon of August 15th, bewildered British soldiers found themselves thrown into the Falls Road, Belfast, to hold the line between Catholics and Protestants.

7b At the end of August, the British Home Secretary, James Callaghan, arrived in Ulster to see the Prime Minister, James Chichester-Clark, and to visit Belfast and Londonderry.

8a On the night of October 11th, following the publication of the Hunt Report, the Protestant Shankill Road engaged the British Army in a head-on clash.

8b The morning after: Sunday, October 12th, the Army moved into the shattered Shankill Road area in overwhelming force, searching Protestant homes for arms and checking every man who showed his face on the street.

for armed support from England, he might not have signed away Stormont's independence, but he had given Westminster the indisputable right to make some decisions of their own. This option, in the next few weeks, the British Government exercised to the full.

On Monday, August 18th, General Sir Ian Freeland, C.-in-C. of the British Army in Ulster, gave a press conference at his headquarters outside Belfast. He announced that by the end of the week, his forces would have been more than doubled to 6,000 men, including two squadrons of armoured cars. Reinforcements were already on their way from England. It was abundantly clear that these men were urgently needed, and with four infantry battalions in Belfast and two in Londonderry, there seemed some chance that the lines could be held. But there was something more important than this. For those seeing Freeland for the first time, it was the feeling of relief in talking to the first man in the Northern Irish crisis who seemed to have the clearest idea of what he was doing and how he would do it. A handsome, white-haired figure of great charm and humour, he made his points firmly and decisively. His men, he said, were under the strictest orders to fire only when life was directly threatened. They had automatic weapons including machine guns, but these were to make a show of force. No one, he said firmly, would be using machine guns in a city area, or he would want to know why. "Automatic weapons," he said, in unquestionable tacit damnation of the events of Thursday night, "are very dangerous things." He declined the idea of a curfew on the grounds that it would probably be quite unenforceable: "What do you do if people disobey it? Shoot them?"

In a province where for years far too many people had had far too many guns with far too much freedom to use them, Freeland's remarks were music to the ears of those who had been in Belfast for long. He made no secret of his fears for the situation, of the risk that the troops would become the targets of popular hatred and even violence if the Government could not accomplish something quickly. He did not pretend that his job was simple. He merely seemed to have a great deal of commonsense, an obvious grasp of the situation, and a merciful sense of proportion. In a word, he was at this moment a godsend to Ulster. When the following evening, after a meeting in London between Harold Wilson and Chichester-Clark, it was announced that he was to become Director of Operations for the province with overall powers over the 'B' Specials and riot police, everyone who had met Freeland went to bed a great deal happier.

Chichester-Clark's London meeting with Wilson on August 19th, following a full meeting of the British Cabinet, marked a turning-point of the Ulster crisis. Now that the army was in, it was clear that there was an absolute limit to how far the Unionists and the Protestants could ever go again. Whatever rampages and rows took place within the Unionist Party, whatever the feelings of the Protestants, the temporary setbacks, there could no longer be any question of total Stormont freedom of manoeuvre. The British Government's problem, at this critical moment, was to re-establish peace and press forward reform with even greater speed; to do this, concessions must be made to the Protestants and Unionists to dissuade them from violent revolt. But there was a clear line beyond which these concessions would not go. Following the London meeting, the British Government offered the firmest public guarantees that the Constitutional relationship was not in doubt, and that Ulster affairs would continue to be in the hands of the Stormont. But when Harold Wilson appeared on nationwide television later that evening, he agreed that the future of the 'B' Specials was being reconsidered. Nor did the joint Stormont-Westminster Declaration following the Chichester-Clark meeting leave London's future influence in much doubt:

"The United Kingdom Government," began the third paragraph, "have ultimate responsibility for the protection of those who live in Northern Ireland when, as in the past week, a breakdown of law and order has occurred. In this spirit, the United Kingdom Government responded to the requests of the Northern Ireland Government for military assistance in Londonderry and Belfast in order to restore law and order. They emphasise again that troops will be withdrawn when law and order has been restored.

"4. The Northern Ireland Government have been informed that troops have been provided on a temporary basis in accordance with the United Kingdom's ultimate responsibility. In the context of the commitment of these troops, the Northern Ireland Government have re-affirmed their intention to take into the fullest account at all times the views of Her Majesty's Government in the United Kingdom, especially in relation to matters affecting the status of citizens of that part of the United Kingdom and their equal rights and protection under the law."

"*The fullest account at all times*" . . . Wilson considered placing one of his own Ministers in Belfast to handle the Stormont Government. This was dropped as being too bitter a pill for Protestant opinion, but two senior English civil servants were dispatched to Belfast. Oliver Wright, a former British Ambassador to Denmark, was sent to Stormont Castle, and Alec Baker to the Ministry of Home Affairs. These two, particularly Wright, were to become London's eyes at Stormont. Henceforth, Chichester-Clark and his Unionists could never make a move without Westminster knowing it. Wright, an extremely shrewd and able man, became the Ulster Prime Minister's polite shadow. The mists around Stormont Castle were dissolving a little. . . .

Beyond this, on August 21st, the setting-up of an inquiry into the structure and organisation of the Ulster police was announced. It was to be headed by Lord Hunt, the leader of the Everest ascent, who had in the past acted as the British Government's official and unofficial envoy on several missions. Hunt set to work immediately to produce the speediest possible report. A Tribunal of Inquiry under Mr Justice Scarman, a prominent and highly reputed English judge, was also established to investigate the riots of July and August and the sabotage in April. They were to begin taking evidence within a matter of weeks. And it was decided that at the earliest moment, the British Home Secretary, James Callaghan, should come to Ulster to see for himself what had happened and what was being done in the name of British government. All this— statement following statement and decision decision—conveyed for the first time in the entire Ulster crisis some sense of urgency in facing the realities of terror.

Northern Ireland, however, remained in a violently jumpy frame of mind, unsurprising when all around alarm was succeeded by alarm in the days following August 14th. Relations with the Irish Republic were still very unhappy indeed. On August 15th, Dr Patrick Hillery, Eire Minister of External Relations, had been making loud noises at the Foreign Office in London, prior to flying to New York, to demand action from the United Nations. It was not, of course, forthcoming. But the demand was heavily reported both in Dublin and Belfast. Still the I.R.A.'s threats and comings and goings were keeping the Border in a state of acute tension. The I.R.A. were highly unpopular in the Catholic areas of Belfast, because it was claimed that having made so many violent promises, they had delivered nothing when the hour for battle came. I.R.A. men from the North had driven frantically South during the riots to beg for guns and ammunition, only to return empty-handed. Now, they had a handful of weapons collected in the Falls Road area, but still little ammunition. The vaunted Irish Army first-aid stations to the South of the Border remained almost empty. The refugee camps that had been set up in the Republic were handling a few hundred Catholic women and children made homeless or merely terrified by the riots, but some of these were already making their way cautiously homewards by the following week. On the night of August 17th, an attempt was made to attack Crossmaglen police station, just North of the Border, in a style that had all the markings of the I.R.A.—including the failure of the explosives to go off. But despite the massive publicity given to the doings of the Republic, the only effective consequences were in a heightening of Protestant feeling.

In Belfast, bulldozers were working to demolish the worst and most dangerous of the wrecked buildings in the Falls Road area. The Government set up a cash payments office to provide immediate succour for small businessmen who had lost everything in the riots and needed urgent replacements of stock or money to re-open their shops. The Civil Rights Association were making loud demands for the release of "political prisoners", those held under the Special Powers Act, while Bernadette Devlin made a melodramatic dash out of Bogside to Shannon Airport, in the Republic. On August 22nd, she flew to New York to begin a heavily publicised tour of America demanding cash and support for those who had suffered in the riots. The manner of her departure from Bogside had been prompted, she claimed, by the certainty of peril from police or Protestants. In fact, at this stage no charges were pending against her. But as has been noted earlier, by this time it was not only the Government's sense of proportion that had suffered a jolt in the riots. In Belfast, Ian Paisley, whose trumpetings were growing in volume and outrageousness with every passing day, was demanding "no comfort or succour or help to the enemy!" By this he meant that the Catholics should gain nothing from the events of the week of August 11th.

As Belfast trudged among the rubble, leaping in its seat at every report of a petrol bomb or a burst of shots in some far corner of Ulster, there was still the utmost confusion about what major new measures could and would follow the holocaust. On the day following Chichester-Clark's London meeting, Brian Faulkner stated categorically that there was no question of the

'B' Specials being disbanded—although on television, Wilson had strongly implied that there was. The issue of the 'B' Specials had become the focal point of feeling among both Catholics and Protestants. The Protestants fixed on them as the symbol of Ulster's domestic independence and of Protestant power; the Catholics saw them as the perpetrators or accomplices in all that had been done to them in the riots. On August 22nd, General Freeland took the first step towards satisfying Catholic feeling, while further infuriating the Protestants: he ordered the handing in of all 'B' Specials' weapons to central armouries, to be issued only for duty, and returned afterwards—there were to be no more Protestant sub-machine-guns under 'B' Special beds.

Paisley's attitude, and that of the Shankill Road Protestants, was characteristic: "No amount of sugar coating will destroy the fact that the Specials are going to be destroyed," he proclaimed. "The Specials have been Ulster's first line of defence—they are the teeth of the Northern Ireland Government. Those who draw its teeth are out to destroy it." The Specials themselves were seething with indignation at the insult of disarmament, following the worldwide abuse that had fallen upon them. At this moment, if the Catholics were still afraid, they could at least feel that the tide was flowing with them at last. The Protestants, on the other hand, saw before them the beginnings of a frightening political landslide—one which could destroy all that they believed in and fought for. So, they heard, a Community Relations Board was to be set up by the Government. So Westminster had its foot in the doors of Stormont Castle. So the police were being damned for their role in the riots while the Catholics were ruling their own corners of Belfast and Derry, protected by the British Army. An official at Stormont, amiable and normally courteous, burst out one morning in the days following the riots, as cuttings from the world's press lay before him and journalists besieged his office: "I'm sick and bloody tired of the way this province gets kicked around! You people seem to be looking for some kind of Utopia here!" His feelings were understandable. What he really meant was that he was tired of the way in which the system which controlled his province was "kicked around". He suffered, like many others around him, from no element of malice or ill-will in his character —but a sluggish and long-established attitude to his society which made the new pace and urgency around him almost intolerable.

The Unionists sent two of their M.P.s to America to attempt, with singular lack of success, to counter-balance the publicity given to Bernadette Devlin's by now admittedly wild speech making. The Party also published a bitter and crude pamphlet for circulation in both England and Northern Ireland entitled "Ulster —The Facts". This compared Bernadette Devlin earning her Parliamentary salary of £60 a week for throwing rocks, with the lot of a policeman injured in the riots. The pamphlet hurled abuse at the Catholics for their efforts during the riots, and adopted the conspiracy and treason theory for all that had happened. It was at best undignified, at worst a disgraceful piece of propaganda, coming from a political party at this moment. It was to be criticised as such by Mr Justice Scarman when he presided over the first sittings of his Tribunal.

The Unionists were also doing their best to enlist the support of the English Conservative Opposition for their efforts to hold back the Westminster influence. Throughout 1969, Unionist M.P.s both individually and collectively had been seeking aid against the British Government from the Tories. Since the Conservatives and Unionists at Westminster allegedly form a single Party, it might have been expected that they would be sympathetically received. But while right-wing English Tories in normal times might be able to make common cause with the Unionists against the Labour Party, on the matter of Northern Ireland, the Conservatives had throughout been polite, officially eager to assist, but in practice determined to remain uninvolved. They would not openly oppose the Unionists, but their Shadow Cabinet were almost throughout in tacit sympathy with the British Labour Government. Tory M.P.s acted as channels of communication for the Unionists with the Government; but beyond that, they did little. Edward Heath, their Leader, kept in close touch with Chichester-Clark. Their Shadow Home Secretary, Quintin Hogg, watched the situation closely and discussed it with James Callaghan. But beyond supporting the principle of Ulster and Britain's unchangeable Constitutional relationship, the Tories seemed entirely happy to leave the British Government to hold the hot potato. They were the instruments of various unofficial approaches, and discussions between London and Belfast. But the Tory leaders made a long series of wholly non-commital speeches about the Northern Irish situation—deploring violence and pleading for sanity in a manner that would have suited the Pope or Calvin equally well. Throughout the summer and autumn, the Tories sat on the fence. "Self-discipline, responsibility and respect for your neighbour have always been words of high value in the Conservative vocabulary," said Sir Alec Douglas-Home in a September speech. "We must make sure that the nation recaptures their meaning." The Report on the Ulster riots "showed conclusively how the anarchist will take advantage of any opportunity to promote chaos". Edward Heath expressed Tory policy on Ulster in four points:

"1. We support whatever fair and reasonable measures are necessary to preserve security, law and order within Northern Ireland.

"2. We support those measures required to deal with trouble-makers from outside.

"3. We renew our support for the speedy implementation of the reforms announced by the Northern Ireland Government.

"4. We reaffirm our pledge that the constitutional position of the Province as part of the United Kingdom shall not be changed other than at the wish of Northern Ireland itself."

At the Annual Party Conference a few weeks later, Quintin Hogg made an emotional and lengthy speech following a brief visit to Ulster: "You can imagine," he said towards his conclusion, "the searing experience it is to go to part of the United Kingdom, part of our own country, and to find a situation which is little better than that in Nicosia or Jerusalem. We must help bring it to an end, and bring it to an end because we must see a wholly just society in our time. If the disaffected are sometimes disloyal, we must make them love the Union Jack as we love the Union Jack, and respect the Queen as we respect the Queen, because the Union Jack is the loyal symbol of liberty and justice and law. . . ."

The Conference passed a five point motion supporting the Constitutional relationship, the "use of British troops as a temporary measure", the Stormont reform programme, an end to discrimination of any kind, an early return to law and order, and a solution based on "the ability of the two communities to live side by side". All entirely unobjectionable, but the Unionists could expect little active help from the Tories in a situation in which most Englishmen achieved a remarkable degree of agreement about their feelings.

Ulster Protestants had long ago sacrificed any chance of presenting a sympathetic case to the British public. Throughout the entire crisis, most of all in the latest riots, whatever crimes the

Catholics had committed the Protestants had surpassed by immeasurable lengths. And in their personalities, the Catholics were far more fortunate. The bumbling Chichester-Clark made only a laughable impression on the British public, while Paisley seemed a figure of monstrous dimensions to anyone outside Ulster. To the "foreign" public all Protestants tended to be grouped together, Paisleyites and moderates. And the moderate Protestant politicians' chance of public success was destroyed by their own reluctance to say anything that might upset the right-wingers. They were afraid to speak their minds even to say the very things that might have assisted their cause in the eyes of the world. They thus lost any chance of popular sympathy outside Ulster. And as in America, there were many "moderates" who thought success for their society meant a few quiet nights: this to be achieved merely by bludgeoning the Catholics back into silence.

By the closing week of August, much was being done, but the total emotional log-jam that had existed since August 17th seemed unshakeable. The troops still stood on every street corner; the pronouncements of the opposing factions were as wild as ever; and peace appeared not an inch nearer. The question of the reforms had almost been forgotten. In the morass of bloody grievances that had been created by the riots, every principle for which the original battles had been fought was set aside. For the moment Catholics cared far more about disarming "the enemy" than about housing allocation and discrimination. What point in worrying about discrimination when you are looking at the discriminators only across the top of a barricade? The Government at Stormont were taking a score of minor tactical initiatives, but it was clear to Ulster that the handling of strategy now lay firmly at Westminster. For days, the issue had been only that of keeping peace on the streets and reinforcing the troops to do it, together with handling the worst physical problems of the disaster areas. Now, when it was being accepted that the army's guns would be in Ulster for many weeks to come, and that it would be months before there was any chance of dispelling tension and acute unease from the air, some steps had to be taken to find a path out of the wreckage. On August 27th, the British Home Secretary arrived in Belfast.

On the day he came to Ulster, James Callaghan had been at the Home Office for one year and seven months. Prior to that, he had been the Labour Government's Chancellor of the Exchequer at one of the unhappiest periods in British economic history. Having been Chancellor at the time of the devaluation of the pound and having been responsible for a long series of bitterly unpopular domestic economic measures, Callaghan's reputation—at least outside the Labour Party—had taken a hard battering. Beyond this, for some observers in Ulster in the months leading up to August, it had been difficult to keep patience with the attitude of the British Government in London. While understanding all the endless dilemmas and problems facing Westminster in dealing with Stormont, London sometimes seemed to lack any conception of how rapidly and irrevocably the situation in Northern Ireland was declining. Inevitably, the Labour Government had to accept much of their information from the Ulster Government itself, supplemented by newspaper reports of English correspondents on the spot. But as the province neared the brink of disaster and then trembled, it was impossible to avoid the feeling that London's reluctance to intervene until the final trump had been sadly misguided.

But at Belfast Airport that Thursday afternoon as Callaghan landed, the past was forgotten. He stepped from his aircraft to be greeted by Chichester-Clark and General Freeland. And after all that had passed in recent days there could be only an overwhelming and self-astonishing feeling of relief: Thank God, here comes a professional. However easy it may be to think and write cynically about politicians and their motives and actions, the coming of James Callaghan introduced a new and wholly welcome element into the Ulster crisis. Large, amiable, tough and, to the public, wholly sure of himself, Callaghan during his first three day trip to Northern Ireland cast Chichester-Clark and his colleagues into the shadows where they belonged. In Callaghan, striding around Belfast and Londonderry, head hunched on his shoulders as he gazed intently around him, was revealed the contrast between a major political leader and the parish-pump amateurs who had hitherto been left in control of a chaotic nightmare.

When he arrived in Belfast, Callaghan was under no illusions that he could accomplish any magical conjuring trick to restore peace to Northern Ireland. "But," he said, "I would hope that I can help to reduce tension and perhaps even be a catalyst towards some solutions. I come in a spirit of looking forward, not back." During the succeeding three days, he talked to almost every major personality in Ulster, from Cardinal Conway to Ian Paisley. For many of those involved, it was important merely to have someone of influence to whom they could talk, unfettered by past alliances or hatreds. Callaghan listened patiently to them all, learning as he did so for the first time what staggers every newcomer to Ulster: the incredible depth of fear and suspicion that underlies every speech and action, incomprehensible to anyone who has not seen it for themselves. He was much moved, and not a little shaken. He saw the Falls Road, and the Bogside, the Cabinet at Stormont Castle and Ian Paisley at his hotel. Paisley, with whom he tried hard to reason logically, brushed him aside; his worst fears of the preacher's total intractability were realised. In Chichester-Clark he found a remarkably receptive audience, but a sadly depressed one. Chichester-Clark would listen to Callaghan, agreeing completely with much of what he said. But he would then admit himself at a loss as to what to do next. It was the Home Secretary's urgent task to push some spine—and a new kind of spine—into a Government that had lost all urge to initiative and forward movement. Callaghan had to propose what Chichester-Clark must dispose; the reforms already agreed must be pushed into law, new changes must be instituted, and the means be found to implement them speedily. With the leaders of the Catholic factions, Callaghan could only urge moderation and patience, trying to convince them that he both understood their interests and was determined to safeguard them. Nothing would remove the Unionist right-wingers' suspicions of Westminster, so the Home Secretary could only try to impress on them that whether they liked it or not certain changes were coming. It was their decision whether they came amicably or painfully.

For three days, the Home Secretary dominated Ulster, with Chichester-Clark one pace behind and to the left. He carried an impression of certainty and forcefulness which may have concealed many inner doubts of his own, but was vital to creating a new kind of climate across the province. When he left, steps had been agreed which advanced the cause of sanity a few inches more: the setting up of working parties on housing, jobs, and community relations; an immediate British Government grant of £250,000 towards relieving distress caused by the riots, and the establishment of Government machinery to investigate citizens' grievances. And much more important than these, Callaghan had given many people of every faction in the crisis "a shove in the right direction", which had been sadly lacking for far too long. Later, as new problems forced Ulster into new fears, it was tempting to say that

Callaghan had failed in his efforts to get the province moving. Certainly, he had not been wholly successful. But without him, Northern Ireland's miserable autumn would have been even less directed and probably much bloodier. On his August visit, the Home Secretary inspired a beginning which could not have been achieved without him.

But during the weeks after Callaghan's visit, while Stormont Castle hesitantly prodded its way towards reforms and changes, in the streets of Belfast and Londonderry the wretched and bitter stalemate continued. It defied all reason in its misery and stupidity. In Derry, despite spasmodic minor exchanges, the Bogside remained barricaded but moderately peaceful, surrounded by its army cordon. But in Belfast, a state of guerilla warfare persisted which kept the entire city on its nerve ends, and was without parallel in British history.

Behind the barricades of the Falls Road area, the Catholics continued their daily life amidst wall slogans proclaiming: "No R.U.C. HERE"; "Chichester-Clark The Mad Major"; "Chichester-Clark and R.U.C. child-killers"; the community was ruled by the Belfast Citizens' Defence Committee, led by the dour hard-bitten figure of Jim Sullivan, who had in the past served several years detention for suspected I.R.A. activities under the Special Powers Act. It was the Defence Committee, composed of representatives of almost every street in the barricaded zone, who organised the vigilante force to man the barricades at night, and negotiated with the army about patrols and protection. For the Catholics, after so many years of miserably drab and dull lives in their mean streets, there was no doubt that at night, they found a weird romance in their extraordinary situation. Braziers burned by the checkpoints on the fringes of the Falls as they searched incoming visitors—such as could get through. Guitar or banjo-players, or just little groups of singers, clustered around the fires in their improvised shelters while the children played on the burnt-out cars and trucks, or studied the machine guns of the soldiers patrolling outside. Few cars moved, since the army only permitted those with special permits to travel in the danger zones at night. And the troops wearied of their squalid existence holding the line.

Still they were on duty eighteen or even twenty hours a day. And even after this there were only a few snatched hours of rest in some abandoned factory or warehouse. The Catholic women brought them tea at their posts by the barbed wire. But from the other side, Protestants hurled abuse and stones; or merely sulked in furious silence. Even with 6,000 men in the province, the army was still over-extended. Now, every Catholic area including those on the fringes of the city had to be protected, and it was an unenviable job for the bewildered soldiers. Every night, there were reports of a burst of shooting from some anonymous sniper who would fade away long before he could be pinned down; or a petrol bomb, or an outbreak of stone throwing in some winding street between the Catholic and Protestant strongholds. The troops carried their weapons loaded at all times, and as the weeks wore on, there were several embarrassing cases of careless soldiers shooting each other or themselves in accidents.

The frustrations of the situation began to tell. Four "pirate" radio stations were broadcasting constant propaganda from locations beyond the reach of the law without a fight. The Catholics had Radio Free Belfast in a room above the Long Bar, a seedy pub in the midst of the "liberated" area, where the Citizens' Defence Committee had their headquarters. The Protestants had Radio Orange, Radio Loyalist and Radio Shankill. Their efforts at propaganda were both more savage and more ruthlessly directed. Protestant teenagers would taunt the army by tuning into Radio Shankill's dreary viciousness on their transistors, just across the barbed wire from the army outposts. The Protestants, chatting on street corners with equally disgruntled police on weekend evenings when the pubs closed, rumbled angrily at every twist of Stormont reform, and above all about the Catholic strongholds' total freedom from authority and control. Not that much law prevailed in the Shankill Road area; the police were there, certainly, and investigated every report of shooting or petrol bombing. But on the frontiers, the Protestants gathered to taunt the army with complete impunity. The supreme irony of the situation was that the Protestants, allegedly more British than the British, now detested the British Government and the British Army as the allies of the Catholics. Paisley preached his sermons and screamed his abuse; the Shankill Road Defence Association, a violently aggressive Protestant counterpart of the Catholic Defence Committee, demanded instant action to break down the Catholic barricades; and in the streets the Protestants became weekly more daring in their efforts to test the mettle of the army at the barricades.

The authorities' policy in Belfast was dominated by their horror of provoking some new outbreak of bloody rioting. The army's aim throughout September was "peace at any price". To this end, imbued with the doctrine of "minimum force", the soldiers sought to keep the peace by the threat of their presence alone to break up the crowds, and the length of their patience to withstand endless provocation. For more than three weeks after their arrival in the city, the military blanket around the Catholic areas maintained a kind of truce with notable success. Day after day, army officers negotiated with the Catholics gently and usually unofficially about the barricaded zones. Army protection was now, they argued, more than adequate to protect them from Protestant attack. In the Shankill area—where there was less reason to fear violent assaults—most of the Protestant barricades were already down.

Then, on September 7th, a Sunday, Protestant and Catholic mobs gathered in force in the streets with only the army between them. Amidst Protestant screams of "brutality", the tactical commander ordered his men to fire C.S. gas to disperse them. Catholic faith in the troops was marginally increased, but Protestant hatred was doubled. Early in the morning of September 9th, a Protestant was shot dead in a fracas in a mixed Protestant-Catholic street in Belfast. On the evening of September 9th Chichester-Clark appeared on television in Ulster to insist that if the barricades in the Bogside and Belfast were not taken down voluntarily, they would have to be removed: the joke had gone on long enough. But while it seemed unlikely that the Catholics would resist forcibly if their barricades were torn down by the army, there was still lingering doubt as to whether without the barricades, the army could keep the warring factions apart. This concern, on the following day, General Freeland took steps to dispel.

In the face of a grotesque situation, Freeland decided on a grotesque answer. If Protestants and Catholics could not be kept from violence as long as they could reach each other, the Army would prevent them from reaching each other, and provide the guarantee of security the Catholics sought before dismantling their own defences. On the evening of September 10th, army engineers began the construction of a vast iron-staked and barbed wire entanglement "Peace Line", rigidly enforcing the frontier between the Catholic Falls and Protestant Shankill areas. As the locals quarrelled bitterly over precisely which houses should be on which side of the line—one of the Mayor of Belfast's properties on the border caused much dissention—it was impossible to know whether to weep or laugh. In the end, those correspondents who now knew Belfast well laughed hysterically, with the feeling that black comedy could go no further. It was incredible: a Berlin Wall in a British city to keep British citizens from each other. The line, once completed, became a kind of nightmare tourist attraction, with the animals in their own self-appointed zoos peering defiantly across at each other through the wire. And even now, the Peace Line saga was by no means ended.

On September 15th, the army moved into the Falls area in force to dismantle the Catholic barricades. That afternoon, accompanied by army bulldozers and massive crowds of spectators and senior officers, they were beginning operations when Catholic men began to return from work. Angry groups gathered at each barricade, shouting at the soldiers and in some cases hurling back the paving stones and scaffolding on to the barriers as fast as the army could remove them. Desperate to avoid a head-on confrontation, the troops somewhat sheepishly withdrew, riot shields and all. It had been a farcical performance which was only redeemed by good fortune a few hours later: the Belfast Citizens' Defence Committee, which had been making angry noises all the past week, suddenly did an about-turn and agreed to the removal of the barricades. In the following days, to the immense relief of all concerned, the barricades came down. The troops, the Peace Line and the army checkpoints were, everyone agreed, enough.

But on September 28th, another Sunday, all that had been done seemed set at naught. A Protestant mob gathered by the Peace Line in a side-street a hundred yards off the Falls Road. They hurled rocks and petrol bombs as a platoon of troops stood in line on the Catholic side, doing nothing. Then the Protestants, clambering across the Peace Line, nearby roof-tops and rubble, swarmed into the Catholic street. They set five Catholic houses ablaze and began a barrage of missiles on the soldiers. Only after what seemed an eternity of idleness did the troops make a move: they fired C.S. gas and drove the Protestants back across the line, leaving a ruin behind them.

The army's credibility had suffered a shattering blow. The troops themselves were becoming enraged, sick to death of standing by while the Protestants came out for battle, prevented by the politicians from taking firm action of any kind. Day after day, farcical exchanges continued at the barricades, with the troops impotent. Only on October 2nd was it announced that groups of men in every infantry company were to be equipped with flak-jackets and batons and detailed as riot squads, to advance on mobs to close quarters while their armed colleagues covered them from the rear. For the men, still over-tired, underfed and short of sleep—for in street fighting a full Brigade is swallowed up in a few acres of alleys and houses—it was a step forward, but as yet they were to have no chance to use the new tactics. All that could be achieved was a drastic strengthening of the Peace Line at key points. Now, the zoo effect was to be complete: corrugated iron fences were built ten feet high to keep Protestants and Catholics out of sight of each other. Seeing the enemy was alone enough to provoke battle, it appeared. On these terms Belfast went about its daily life. The nightly minor incidents to keep tension alive; the troops everywhere, their determination and effectiveness in question; and the Protestants ever more eager for a confrontation, little matter with whom.

Up at Stormont, meanwhile, the Government was still struggling to stem the tide. Early in September, the establishment of a Public Protection Authority was announced. Intimidation and threats had become a critical factor in Belfast. At the P.P.A., teams of Military Police and R.U.C. men stood by to investigate complaints that were telephoned in. In the first week, six hundred calls were received. Ignoring even those only loosely concerned with protection, there were still several hundred people in Belfast who had found the notes under their doors, the illiterate scrawls through the post, that left them in fear for their property and their lives. It was almost impossible to find the sender, in many cases. The authorities could only make a show of force in the hope that this would deter the petrol-bombers or the snipers. The level of sectarian hatred aroused by the riots had brought to life all the latent horrors of Ulster. Now, in the city ghettos, social segregation had become a reality. Even in the country, every issue was being debated across the religious border with passion and fear. When, on September 12th, a key document in the Civil Rights struggle was published, it seemed almost an irrelevance in the face of the Belfast of the autumn.

Lord Cameron's Commission delivered its report on the causes and course of the Civil Rights struggle and the early riots up to April at the very moment at which Civil Rights seemed forgotten. The battle for reform had been utterly obscured by the struggles of men who seemed to ignore the reasons for their enmities, and were only determined on collision. Yet the Cameron Report was, and will remain, the textbook of the Ulster crisis. Brilliantly constructed, articulately written, forcefully expressed, it clarified almost every criticism of the Protestants and the Unionist Party made since time immemorial.

The Report examined, and found proved, all the Catholic grievances about discrimination in housing allocation, the questionable moral status of the Special Powers Act, the unfairness of local electoral boundaries. It damned Paisley, Bunting, and William Craig (all of whom had declined to give evidence to the Commission). It found many of the accusations against the police in October 1968 and January 1969 proven. And despite scepticism about the People's Democracy and certain of its leaders, it vindicated the Civil Rights movement, and especially John Hume, in almost all that they had done. In effect, the Report was a devastating condemnation of the policy of successive Unionist governments since Ulster was created. At a press conference following its publication, Chichester-Clark and his deputies tried to brush aside the criticisms, saying they were more interested in the present than in the past. Instead, they sought to focus on those passages of the Report criticising certain specific actions of the Civil Rights leaders. "We all expected a certain amount of criticism," said the Prime Minister almost indifferently, reviewing Cameron's comments on the Unionists. Inevitably, however, it was not only the Unionists who sought to pick their own passages of the Report for attention: the Civil Rights leaders glossed over the less complimentary remarks about themselves, and trumpeted gleefully about Cameron's allusions to the Government.

The Ulster Government could indeed, when Cameron appeared, boast that many of the imjustices the report highlighted were now being set to rights. Only the Special Powers Act and the 'B' Specials, of the major Catholic grievances, were as yet untouched. But almost all those detained under the Special Powers Act following the August riots had been released, and the future of the 'B' Specials was under review. Action as distinct from legislative promises might take longer, but this must be the case in any Parliamentary system. In September, most of the reforms were slipping quietly along the governmental pipeline. On the 26th, Dr Robert Simpson was appointed as Ulster's first Minister of Community Relations, and immediately resigned from the Orange Order as a gesture of good faith in his new job. The Unionist

Parliamentary Party met to discuss the Cameron Report, and amidst considerable surprise accepted its findings with little public demur. With Westminster's influence overshadowing every action of Stormont, with opinion in London overwhelmingly sympathetic to the Catholic cause, the battle for Civil Rights—as they had been expressed in the autumn of 1968—seemed almost won.

Yet in the chaos that followed August, so much seemed to count for so little. Civil Rights, irrespective of Government promises, could become a reality only when a majority of Ulstermen willed them to. Now, with the army only holding Catholics and Protestants apart by sheer force of arms, such a day seemed very far off. The Catholics were worrying about self-preservation first—the civil rights could come back later. It has already been seen how Catholics and Protestants in Belfast were at each others throats with scarce a thought for formal demands except—from the Catholics—those concerning the police, the Special Powers Act, and their own freedom from punishment for crimes committed during the riots.

But whenever the Catholics glanced over their shoulders to see what the Government was doing and Chichester-Clark was promising, they saw very little to justify any emotional confidence; nor, for that matter, did many independent observers studying the scene. Even after all these months of strife, with so much time to learn, the Unionist Government seemed still to be ignoring the greatest lesson of 1969: reform without matching goodwill was meaningless.

In September, when the Cameron Report was published, the Government brought out an accompanying commentary, listing the reforms that were already in train, and remarking on the efforts they had made and were making to vindicate themselves. Yet in the last paragraphs of the commentary, they tossed away every point they might otherwise have made: "The Government of Northern Ireland . . . now ask for the active support and co-operation of every member of the community and for the rejection by every responsible body and every responsible person of the hostile, revolutionary and subversive elements which have been seeking to destroy the constitutional structure of the State—as has now been amply demonstrated by the Cameron Report." These words were the most thinly-veined stab at the Catholic militants—partly justified, perhaps. But at a moment when it was so vital to show and to seek good-will, this endless petty pin-pricking—almost childish bitchiness—from the Stormont Government was not only undignified, but it also kept open the very wounds they might have been seeking to heal.

Every new reform that was announced, every concession that was made, appeared in its presentation to be the most grudging concession to intolerable pressure. If only once, just once, the Government had extended the hand looking as if it meant it, much might have been accomplished.

This was perhaps yet another key moment: it was futile to seek any longer to mollify the Protestant extremists—they had long ago stepped outside the pale. But the Catholics, while united in their tribulations, were no longer as organised within the Civil Rights hierarchy as they had been a few months before. They were uncertain where they were going, still bewildered by the course of events. The Government might now have begun the moves to gather them back into the fold. But whether by a failure of public relations or of purpose, the Chichester-Clark Administration did not do so. The Prime Minister himself was by now deeply suspicious and resentful of the press, and by treating the media with desperate caution and obvious lack of trust, he lost any chance to see his policy and his ideas passed on to the people. That is, assuming that he was merely hiding them, rather than accepting that they did not exist. Once again, a chance was lost through the disastrous lack of communication that has been remarked on before.

On September 24th, Catholics and Protestants clashed again briefly in Derry. A Protestant died before the army could restore control. In Belfast, every night and every weekend brought its quota of incidents and miniature demonstrations. There were 67,000 guns on licence in Northern Ireland, and despite increasingly rigorous army checks in the trouble areas, some of them were finding their way into the ghettos. It was also unfortunate that even at this stage, the army's "velvet glove" policy left many loopholes for tragedy. The authorities still feared the consequences of house searches for arms; as a result, even when a sub-machine gun burst was fired from a Catholic block of flats under siege by a Protestant mob, when order had been restored the army declined to enter the building to look for the gun. They had searchlights and machine-gun posts on high buildings, patrols constantly working through the streets—except in Derry, where the Bogside barricades had been replaced by painted white lines on the perimeter, beyond which no soldier could go. They had a vast communications network reporting constantly on incidents throughout Belfast. They had been reinforced to a total strength across the province of 7,500 men, of whom more than 3,000 were in Belfast. And yet still, with no really decisive steps having been taken to deal with them, hooligans and fanatics petrol-bombed, sniped, conducted their street feuds and indulged their recriminations almost with impunity. Superficially, a walk through the silent streets of Belfast at night revealed nothing except the massive army presence. Yet the constant stir of isolated incidents maintained the fear and the tension the length of the Peace Line.

Above all, while the Catholics still licked their wounds, nagging and needling the Government ever more now that they were winning, the Protestants seethed. In the streets of the Shankill and the Crumlin, English journalists went at night at their peril, the army ventured only on cautious patrols around the fringes, and the Union Jacks still fluttered at every window. Chichester-Clark visited the Protestant areas one afternoon (they thought it might cause a riot if he showed his face in the Falls). Women harangued him from their front doors about keeping the 'B' Specials: "They was all there was to save us that night when the Catholics went mad, sir." They told him about how frightened they were of what the Catholics might do next, and about the importance of standing up for the Constitution and of getting the army out: "We want our police back. . . ." Chichester-Clark, embarrassingly embarrassed amid this flood of fluent conversation, tried to find the right thing to say: "Well, the British Army couldn't begin to understand a situation like this. . . ." Down the street, Protestant territory ended at an army barricade. A police officer shouted to the Prime Minister's detective "Don't let him get past the line of the last Union Jack". Among the bunting and the flags that decked the road in defiance of the Papists beyond, Chichester-Clark was safe. For the Protestants, he was not only Prime Minister, but the only Prime Minister they had. He was still, they prayed, the best hope of salvation for their Protestant society.

Yet with Callaghan's visit, the Reform programme, and the army with its bayonets protecting the Catholic line, the Protestants were not at peace. They believed themselves the victims of a colossal sell-out; the British Government was dominating *their* leaders, the Bogside had beaten back *their* police, *their* 'B' Specials were in jeopardy, and the Catholics were crowing in triumph at the political victories. The 'B' Specials were not just "the police"—they were locals, men well-known in each street and respected for what they sought to do. The Specials had come home after their nights in action around the Falls saying that the Catholics had nearly murdered them. Now, the British officer commanding the British Army had removed all 'B' Specials from sensitive areas, gave them their guns for a few hours a week only as a carrot to salve their pride, and plainly trusted them as one might a herd of hungry jackals.

Protestant fanatics, the men of the Ulster Volunteer Force and the Shankill Defence Committee, played on these emotions and this anger with little difficulty. Paisley, ever the genius at finding grievance and bellowing it to life, aroused feeling to fever pitch. His new church opened in Ravenhill Road with a capacity congregation, and an overflow in a marquee in the courtyard. It was the setting for a Sunday clash between the army and Protestants who sought to march down Ravenhill Road when all processions and assemblies were banned. The army used gas to break up the crowd, and provoked further Protestant fury.

They felt isolated, cornered. They had been savagely criticised, consigned to social oblivion by the world's press and by many English politicians. The Catholics had rioted, and were now being handed every bouquet England could lavish upon them. They themselves were the schoolchildren sent out of the classroom; instead of repenting past error, they only sought future violent satisfaction.

In the second week of October, James Callaghan returned to Northern Ireland. "It is important that the citizens of Northern Ireland should realise," he said, calling for an end to "this nonsense" in the streets, "that there is no going back in the interest Westminster has shown in the affairs of this country." He came to review the progress of reform and to hold further talks with the Stormont Government. Most especially, he came to deal with the latest and one of the most critical reforms in the Ulster programme: that of the police. The Hunt Committee had produced its report on the future of the Royal Ulster Constabulary and the Special Constabulary. It was obvious before its publication that some dramatic re-establishment would be in order, and it was abundantly clear that the 'B' Specials, the shining white knights of the Protestant ghettos, ghettos could never be the same again. On Friday, October 10th, Callaghan waited diplomatically outside while James Chichester-Clark introduced the Hunt Committee's Report to a crowded press conference in the Committee room at Stormont Castle. Hunt, to the surprise of no one but the politicians, was to be the final straw for the Protestants of the Shankill.

9

THE SHANKILL

In the light of all that followed, many observers remained utterly at a loss to decide why the authorities chose a Friday to publish the Hunt Report. Throughout a year of turbulence in Ulster, it had been the weekends that invariably brought chaos. When the men had been paid, could get drunk at their leisure, and had time to gather in their anger, they took to the streets. Nor was there any doubt about the Protestant mood: two weeks earlier, on September 30th, Ian Paisley had led a mob of 6,000 of his supporters to demonstrate outside the Stormont building while the Cameron Report was being debated. There had been ugly scenes in the lobbies, a yelling horde screaming outside while the police looked on indifferently, and fantastic cheers only for William Craig when he appeared to wave to them from the balcony. It had been one of the nastiest crowds Ulster had seen, far past reason, bent only on action. Its behaviour might have been warning that Hunt would have to be handled with kid gloves.

Yet the Government determined—perhaps to fit in with Callaghan's schedule—to introduce Hunt on a Friday, leaving the Protestants the whole weekend before them in which to think about it. And the proposals of the Committee, while all that the Catholics might have sought, were every inch as radical as the Protestants had feared. One may summarise the main points of the Report as introduced by Chichester-Clark on October 10th:

1. The practice of police carrying firearms for routine duties should cease.
2. Armoured cars and machine guns should cease to be part of the R.U.C.'s armoury.
3. The reserve force should be reconstituted on a different basis, in two parts—one, unarmed, as an ordinary police reserve; the second, no more than 4,000 strong, *under the command of the British Army Commander in Northern*

Ireland, for emergency security duty—*its character and functions to be determined by Westminster.*

4. The chief officer of police to be vicariously liable for wrongful acts committed by members of the force.
5. Efforts to be made to increase the level of Catholic recruitment, and expand the entire force.
6. An independent public prosecutor, rather than the police themselves, to determine whether indictments should be brought against citizens.
7. The R.U.C.'s uniform to be changed.

Beyond these, there were a mass of other proposals for the detailed reorganisation of the force. It was suggested, for instance, that certain police stations near the Irish Border served no real purpose, but only "induce a defensive or 'blockhouse' attitude". There were recommendations for closer links with the English police, and for improved training and promotion procedures. Cameron had already cast doubts on the moral status of the Special Powers Act—now Hunt said:

"Some of the Regulations made under the (Special Powers) Acts . . . may well be necessary, but could be covered by ordinary legislation. We consider that the task of the police would be made easier if the few essential provisions were provided for under ordinary legislation, and the Acts were repealed." Also: "A number of police officers told us that they considered . . . that the relationship between police and public would be improved if the Acts were repealed."

Hunt, in his introduction to the Report, concluded by saying: "It is our conviction that nothing less than the full implementation of the proposals it contains, within the shortest time possible, can suffice to lay a sound foundation for the good order and security of the province." In one devastating paragraph, he concluded that membership of the Orange Order was incompatible with "the task of demonstrating impartiality at all times". And at the end of the Report, the Committee decided: "As regards those tasks of a military character which have hitherto been carried out by the Royal Ulster Constabulary and the Ulster Special Constabulary and which are concerned with the protection of the province from armed attacks from within or outside its borders, we consider that in principle and in practice this responsibility should properly rest with Her Majesty's Government at Westminster."

The clear aim of the Hunt Report was so to reshape the R.U.C. that it would re-emerge as a new force with a new chance. With a new uniform, a new structure, a new role, it could have the opportunity once more to make its peace with the community. The 'B' Specials, for all practical purposes, were to be castrated. They could have a uniform, a structure, and some training, but under the control of a British Commanding Officer and a British government, they could never again make mischief in the ghettos. The R.U.C. and the U.S.C. were to cease to be the military arm of the Unionist Party and the defenders of Ulster, and revert to their proper role as enforcers of the law. Commenting on the Report, Chichester-Clark said: "In particular, we accept the principle of a civilianised and normally unarmed Royal Ulster Constabulary. . . . We agree that the Ulster Special Constabulary should be replaced." Asked what reaction he expected from the Province, he added: "The first impact will be that these are very sweeping and radical changes. Nobody ever likes change, and the people of Northern Ireland are very reluctant to accept change." Optimistically, however, he said that in the end he was sure the people of Northern Ireland would realise that these reforms meant more, and not less security.

Then the authorities produced their rabbit from the hat. The Inspector-General of the R.U.C., the ageing, amiable, but wholly forceless Anthony Peacocke had decided to resign, said Chichester-Clark politely, on the grounds that "the far-reaching changes which will now take place in the force could best be carried out under the command of a police officer who has practical experience of police operations in Great Britain". With that, Callaghan and Chichester-Clark introduced to the gathering the new Inspector-General, arrived hot-foot from London: Sir Arthur Young, Commissioner of the City of London police. Young, large and impressive, had spent years organising colonial forces and handling terrorist situations, before taking over the City. One of the ablest policemen in Britain, he had been personally recommended for the job by Callaghan. He had a reputation for brains and toughness, and most important of all, he was not an Ulsterman. To cope with the complex problems of persuading the Catholics to accept the police back in their midst once more, there could be no better officer. Diplomatically, and for the long-term future of Ulster, Young's appointment was Callaghan's shrewdest stroke. With no family to worry about, Young simply moved into an hotel near police headquarters as soon as he arrived, and set to work to make what he could of the confused, bitter, and considerably demoralised force he inherited.

When a final analysis is made of the struggle for Civil Rights in Northern Ireland, Hunt may come to be judged as the last major initiative in the Government's moves to meet the Catholic grievances. Much more remained to be done in fulfilling the scores of promises made in the months since October 1968. It would be years before any real foundation of mutual Protestant and Catholic trust had any hope of success. There were setbacks and changes and amendments and disputes. There will be time a little later to examine some of these. But of the great Catholic demands of the autumn of 1968, almost all had at least been acknowledged. The climate was overwhelmingly favourable to the Catholics where key influence now lay—at Westminster. And Chichester-Clark's Government, despite much hesitation and fumbling, was none the less being prodded along the right road. The major initiative had already shifted from the Catholics to the authorities; now, if only for a brief space, it was seized by the Protestants. The task of government for weeks and months, while bringing the reforms into reality, was to persuade the Protestants to accept them either by choice or force. It is also important to see that on the weekend of October 10th, following the Hunt Report, the Protestants were as yet unhumbled. They had been abused, certainly; but for many months, they had almost literally been getting away with murder. Their forays against the army had gone unpunished; the excesses of their extremists had in many cases been undiscovered, while the outrageous demands of their leaders had continued unabated. The Stormont Government had, since October 1968, wasted much energy on attempting to pacify Protestant feeling. Certain Stormont politicians had given countenance to the view that the Protestants were being unreasonably treated. And such damage as had been done to Protestant property had almost all been the result of their own outbursts. In the Shankill, during shopping hours, it was still business as usual, with only a handful of gutted buildings to compare with the desolation of the Falls. No one, either in England or in Ulster, by October 10th had had the nerve to show the Protestants of the Shankill that the time had come to call a halt. In the ghettos, there were many very tough men indeed, for whom a razor fight or the sight of a jagged bottle held no terrors. For weeks, it had been clear that they would consider suffering in silence only when they met forces tougher than themselves—and this, to date, had simply not happened.

On Saturday, October 11th, the Shankill Protestants were in an uproar at the news of the Hunt Report. Their beloved 'B' Specials were to be taken from them—no amount of sugar coating, as Paisley would have said, could conceal that from them. The police were to lose their guns and change their uniforms. An Englishman, a Callaghan man, was to command the R.U.C. They saw that for the future, the very existence of Ulster would depend solely on the whims and will of the very men they mistrusted above all—the British Government at Westminster. They felt stripped of their armour, naked to the invasion of the Catholics, the Irish Republic, every menace they had fought for three hundred years.

They demonstrated in streets in a dozen scattered corners of Belfast, while troops stood by in full riot gear. On Friday night, swarms of angry Protestants had roamed the streets in a rage, now others began to gather in the Shankill. Towards Saturday evening, with militants haranguing them as they came out of the pubs, and with beer and whisky flowing freely, they were massing in force. Towards 10 p.m. some 3,000 strong, they began to move down the Shankill towards the City Centre.

But anyone who knew Belfast knew that the City Centre was not their target. Some two hundred yards short of the Royal Avenue intersection stood a new apartment complex called Unity Flats. In a moment of wild optimism, some city planner had attempted to break Belfast's traditional housing pattern by establishing this Catholic community in the centre of the Protestant ghetto. Already that year, Unity Flats had been the target of previous Protestant onslaughts: its ground floor shop windows were boarded and sealed. As the mob started down the road towards it, the police—who were, after all, supposed to be the men who could handle the Protestants—lined up across the road to hold them. Troops were standing by behind them; an arc of soldiers already stretched much of the way around the Shankill area, and as nervous Catholics clustered in the Falls, the Army manned the Peace Line in strength. But this was not to be a general riot. The Protestants had chosen the Shankill as their battleground, and it was there and only there that they fought that Saturday night. The police sought to face them on a road perhaps twenty yards across.

As they surged up to the police line, seeking to break through, rioters pushed cars in front of them to batter a path. Hand to hand combat began: Protestants, enraged by the recommendations for the reform of the police, were engaging the police themselves. Then, suddenly, shots rang out. On the Shankill Road, two policemen fell—one wounded. The other was dying. Within minutes, the police had drawn back; the army, the 3rd Battalion the Light Infantry, moved in to fight it out with the mob.

For weeks, they had stood by and watched while the Protestants abused them and fought around them with impunity. For weeks, they had stood in the streets for hours on end, unable to make a move. Now, as a rain of rocks and missiles descended, the riot squads, in flak jackets and helmets with batons in their hands, moved in. Driving into the mob in wedges, they seized man after man and dragged them out, back to the police tenders at the rear. They were not gentle with them. Yet everyone who knew Belfast knew by now that the battle for sanity had gone too far to be dealt with gently. No one, English reporters, officers, onlookers, police, turned a hair as rioters were dragged down the street and thrown into the wagons. Soldiers wear large boots.

Yet still, as the army brought up armoured personnel carriers to the front line, the mob was only slowly being moved back. And as the first tear gas was hurled over into the crowd, the sniping began. Not only with rifles now; there were automatic weapons up on the rooftops. The army riot squads pulled back. Instead, the army began an advance up the Shankill that took most of the night to move a quarter of a mile. With their armoured personnel carriers in front of them, every headlight blazing to dazzle the mob, and with infantry behind them hurling gas and firing back at the snipers only when a clear target showed itself, the battle moved painfully up the Shankill, the Protestants fighting every inch of the way. They were contained: there were troops and police ringing the whole area to prevent the struggle spreading, and the Shankill was the only battleground. But in that street, the scene was incredible.

The Protestants stood thirty yards in front of the advancing army line hurling petrol bombs and rocks in a continuous storm. Up on the rooftops, snipers were blazing away with apparently limitless ammunition. That whole night, the army fired only twenty-six shots—when marksmen picked their targets. But the Protestants, although they could hardly see the soldiers behind the dazzling army floodlights, emptied burst after burst towards the

3rd Light Infantry line. Behind a barricade of wrecked cars alongside a shop belonging to the Mayor of Belfast, one man was emptying Sten gun magazines as fast as he could reload. The army could not fire at him—he was surrounded by a mob of Protestants, including women; had they hit one of the crowd, the political fuss would have been appalling. A petrol bomber could be seen crouching with another man just behind the corner of a side-street by the army line. One man would light the inflammable rag, then the other would make a sudden dart to hurl the blazing bottle under the front line of armoured cars. In the end, the army shot him, as they also shot one of the snipers. They may have killed more, but as in August, it was easy for the men on the roofs to carry away any embarrassing bodies. It was incredible to see men, women and children all fighting it out together, despite the bursts of gunfire that sent them ducking for cover until they were sure they were not aimed at them. As gas canisters burst in the street, there would be a momentary pause while men pulled water-soaked handkerchiefs round their faces, or dashed down a side-street until the smoke blew away. But if you are determined enough, even gas holds no terrors. By midnight, many of the rioters were not even running as the gas cartridges exploded. And they sang. There on the street corners with the gunfire in the background from the men on the rooftops, and the rocks and petrol bombs crashing and shattering, they sang. They have good songs, the Protestants—"Derry Walls" sung by a thousand voices in the shambles of the Shankill would have graced a Hollywood spectacular: "With heart and hand, and sword and shield, we'll guard old Derry Walls!"

The army, with twenty-two men wounded, sixteen of them by gunfire from the snipers, were winning, but winning the hard way. In the early hours of the morning, as the fire slackened and the mob began to melt away, they were holding most of the Shankill, but unless they were willing to open fire indiscrimately against the mob, they had to suffer several hours of ruthless punishment. In their rear, the police were holding some of the "captured" streets, in far different mood from that of many months. It had been a Protestant—one of their own people—who had killed a policeman and tried to murder another. It had been the Protestants who sought to batter through the police line, and were now engaged in head-on battle with the British Army. That night, there was no more question of the police resenting the army presence. They just thanked God it was not they who had to face the maniacs whose continuous screaming and songs could be heard interspersed with the rattle of gunfire.

When daylight came, to reveal the Shankill Road at last emptied of rioters, the army had stopped playing games. Armoured cars, some mounted with heavy guns, cruised the length of the Shankill. Troops were on every rooftop, searching every car, clustered in dozens around their trucks and Land-Rovers, standing beside every street corner, and shop. The Protestants, emerging from their homes with their eternal looks of injured innocence, were appalled by the treatment that awaited them. Every man who passed an army picket was ordered to face the wall, hands against it, while he was searched from head to foot for weapons. This, no matter whether he had already been searched a dozen times that day. Overhead, a helicopter hovered, broadcasting from loudspeakers to the Protestant streets: their homes were to be searched for arms; anyone resisting would be fired on. The troops were everywhere, backing up the police who conducted the searchs, which revealed a handful of weapons and a radio transmitter. The army had now, at last, lost their sense of humour. They were sick of being targets for the venom of every Protestant who found a grievance; they had been infuriated by their own casualties the previous night; now, they were exasperated by the attitude of the Protestants on the Sunday morning. They had fought in Aden and Cyprus, Borneo and Malaya—but to have to go through this nightmare among the British . . .

On Sunday night, for some bizarre strategical reason, the army determined to hold the Shankill only as far up as Northumberland Avenue, a cross-street more than three hundred yards from the end of the ghetto. Here, the line of armoured cars and sandbagged emplacements was once more under spasmodic petrol bomb and sniper fire from the Protestant mob beyond. This time, however, tear gas and the strength of the army positions persuaded the Protestants to keep their distance. Like savages in the jungle, out there in the darkness they beat drums and dustbins in a frenzied tattoo. They built up a barricade, and set fire to a bus in the street. But the army declined to charge. They left the Protestants until boredom or exhaustion sent them drifting to their homes. The next day, a battalion of the Parachute Regiment flew into Ulster and immediately took up position to secure the full length of the Shankill. There were now 8,000 troops in Northern Ireland.

In its incredible intensity, the battle of the Shankill had surpassed anything that had taken place in August. Fewer people had
been killed and wounded—because of the superhuman restraint of
the army; far less damage had been done, because of the limited
scope of the struggle. But the manner in which the Protestants,
with an insane fury, had sought to take on the British army face to
face, and had fought it out with them all night before capitulating,
defied the imagination. Yet at last, the Protestants had found that
the army meant business. On Monday morning, eighty battered
men appeared in court on charges arising out of the riot. Two men,
well known to many Protestants in the Shankill, lay dead, and the
army stated quite freely that they had been shot deliberately by
their marksmen. James Callaghan, while he returned to London
much subdued by personal acquaintance with Ulster in battle,
knew also that a critical point had been made. The Protestants, at
last, had met opposition that was too tough for them. The Shankill
might still be in a fury, but it had learnt the price of excess.
Among those across Belfast holding grim post-mortems on the
events of Saturday night, there were many who felt that Constable
Arbuckle, the dead policeman, had not died completely in vain.
While Ulster autumn turned to winter, there might be minor
incidents and outbursts, but never again was there violence on the
scale of October 11th. Symbolically, the Province had learnt the
hard way that the Hunt Report was going to be accepted.

Minor protests and demonstrations continued. A Protestant
was killed in an attempt to blow up Ballyshannon power station,
just across the Border in the Republic, on October 22nd. A gas-
works explosion on November 5th on the edge of Belfast caused
fears of a new outbreak of sabotage. But several Protestants had
already been charged with the blasts in the spring; many other
extremists preferred to lie low—at least for a time. It was not
until early 1970 that nerve-racking sabotage commenced
once more. Even Paisley, undoubtedly alarmed by the
very close scrutiny of certain of his actions during the year
by the authorities, dropped from sight. The army continued its
vigil, and the Peace Line stayed. Reports persisted that arms were
being brought into Ulster in quantity by both Catholics and
Protestants but if this was true, the weapons were not yet visible.
The I.R.A., it was known, were split within their own ranks about
whether to take a more violent stance in Ulster. Yet while no
precaution could be relaxed, and normality could hardly exist

amidst barbed wire and massive security precautions, a kind of peace prevailed. Fear continued: too much had happened now for anyone to feel safe against repetition. But once again, as during spring, attention shifted from the depressing pallor of the streets to the political struggle. From October 12th onwards, the massive work of consolidation had to begin, hampered by the unending suspicions and scuttling actions of the Unionist right-wingers. It is easier to draw this date line with the benefit of hindsight, because for weeks following the Shankill riot, many people in Ulster paid less attention to politics than to their horror of a renewal of full-scale battle. Each weekend, police, army, politicians, and Belfast citizens watched with bated breath for the black smoke in the sky, the sound of shots, the reports of massing crowds. But these never came. With a Government order making the pubs close early on the weekend evenings, the Government ban on all processions and meetings that had been imposed on September 26th, and the troops now able to enforce it, on the streets the breathing space came at last. There was a chance to pick up the tangled threads stretching back through all the months of change and confusion.

IO

CLEARING THE DEBRIS

THE AUTUMN AND winter in Northern Ireland highlighted the divisions in both the Unionist Party and the Civil Rights movement in the aftermath of the bloody summer. While the British army stood in the streets of Belfast and Londonderry through the rain and the fog and the snow, the Catholics argued over the future direction and aims of their policies, and the Chichester-Clark Government suffered from the increasing disillusionment of the Unionist grass roots.

By the introduction of Military Police into the Bogside and the Falls Road area in October, the authorities paved the way for the return of R.U.C. patrols in concert with the Military Police—although initially, there was great R.U.C. reluctance to volunteer for unarmed duty in the Catholic strongholds. Within days of the Hunt Report's publication, many of the R.U.C. were on duty without weapons. Attempts to introduce the new uniform speedily were frustrated when the police declined to accept second-hand English police uniforms rushed over from Britain, but Sir Arthur Young scored an early success in his negotiations with the Catholics about accepting the return of the police. The re-structuring of the force went ahead rapidly, despite considerable misgivings from some officers. And considering the state of feeling about the police in the Catholic community in August, by winter much had been achieved.

But far more trouble revolved around the reshaping of the Special Constabulary. It was determined to call the force to replace the 'B' Specials the Ulster Defence Regiment, and much effort was put into persuading the Specials to join the new force—to be, it was decided, 6,000 strong. But the battle around the future of the Specials had gone too far. The Protestants maintained a constant barrage of criticism around the new proposals. Initially, there had been talk of having English officers to command the units of the new force. This idea was now set aside in deference to Protestant feeling. Several bodies of Specials resigned *en bloc* to show their disgust with the plans for their future, although most were later induced to relent: the last thing the Government wanted now was a mass of disenchanted ex-Specials roaming the streets. The Catholics, on the other hand, grew increasingly angry as the suspicion grew that the new force was coming to sound far too like the Specials under another name, with the pressure being put upon the members of the old force to enlist in the new. When the proposals for the U.D.R. were debated in the House of Commons at Westminster, both Bernadette Devlin and Gerry Fitt, together with several English M.P.s, made determined if unsuccessful efforts to get changes made in the constitution of the Defence Regiment—and in its name. In the end, the plan went through. The Defence Regiment begins its formal existence, and the 'B' Specials end theirs, on April 1st 1970. But the seeds of much future misgiving had been sown among the Catholics, while the Protestants still remained angrily dissatisfied. The U.D.R. was a compromise that pleased no one. At Stormont, William Craig expressed loud dissatisfaction at its creation, and several other Unionist M.P.s, while declining to challenge the Government openly, indicated the strongest misgivings about the disbandment of the Specials.

Throughout the winter of 1969, however, every other reform agreed by the Government since the beginning of the Civil Rights campaign either passed into law or became the subject of action. When the Stormont had promised an Ombudsman—a Commissioner for Complaints—they had originally borrowed the services of Sir Edmund Compton, the English Ombudsman, as an interim measure. On November 27th, however, a permanent Ombudsman was appointed—John Benn, formerly a senior civil servant at the Northern Ireland Ministry of Education. During Sir Edmund Compton's brief period of office, embarrassingly few matters had been referred to him for investigation, largely, perhaps, because rather more pressing problems were occupying Ulstermen's minds. Whether Mr. Benn will find the job a more fruitful opportunity for keeping the community's sense of justice satisfied is unlikely to emerge for some time. However, in December 1969, a Commission to investigate complaints against local authorities in Ulster was also established. And the legislation permitting a universal franchise "One man, one vote", passed into law, and will apply at the next local election in 1970.

7—U1969 * *

Housing allocation was also largely removed from the power of the local authorities, and placed in the hands of a new Central Housing Authority, in the fervent hope that justice would thus not only be done, but be seen to be done. And although the reform of the local authorities themselves will take rather longer, without housing allocation powers, most Councils lost much of their potential for mischief.

The reorganisation of the local authorities, and with them the re-drawing of the local electoral boundaries to end the grotesque bias against many Catholic areas, had been the subject of Brian Faulkner's White Paper in July 1969. But by autumn, when there came the breathing space for reconsideration, Faulkner largely superseded his own White Paper by setting up a new Commission to review the local authority structure during 1970. There was some Catholic clamour about delays thus entailed, but Faulkner has been applying all his considerable abilities to making the best of the opportunities that are now presented. The original White Paper could only have been at best an interim measure to cool the immediate Catholic clamour.

The Community Relations Board and the Minister of Community Relations were in existence and operation. The Crowther Commission on the British Constitution held hearings in Belfast early in the New Year of 1970, and its report may yet prove to have some influence in reconsidering the basis of political power in Ulster, and the relationships between Stormont and Westminster. Yet there has been no review of the Special Powers Act; in the wake of all that had passed, the Government refused to sign away any power concerned with the maintenance of the law and order. One considerable disappointment had been a Firearms Amnesty held during September: from the 2nd to the 21st, anyone holding weapons illegally had been permitted to hand them in to the police without liability to prosecution. In England, similar efforts produced massive results a few years ago; in the Ulster of 1969, only a ridiculous handful of arms were turned in. Those who held them were keeping them.

But the most energetic efforts were being made, with considerable help from Westminster, to boost the industrial and economic situation in the Province. Roy Bradford, the Minister of Commerce, had been travelling extensively abroad in efforts to convince potential foreign investors that the Ulster crisis need be no deterrent to creating plant—and thus jobs. Faulkner, in his own sphere, was making similar attempts. For while in the ghettos much damage had been done, outside the cities in the industrial areas, production had been barely affected. The vast Harland and Woolf shipyard, scene of desperate trouble in the 1920's, remained uncannily peaceful even during the worst of 1969's upheavals— partly thanks to the efforts of Trades Unions officials to keep the men's minds on their livelihood rather than the sectarian battle. While Northern Ireland's economic prospects took a serious knock in 1969—and the press incurred much Ulster fury for its reports, spreading so much alarm in England and on the continent—a major economic drive was now in progress. The Londonderry Development Commission announced a series of plans for vast housing projects and industrial developments to improve the housing and jobs situation in the 1970's.

All this, then, had been accomplished in the space of a year. Much of it had been done only after devastating pressure had been exerted on the Government of Northern Ireland; some of it had been directly inspired by the Westminster Government, all of it had been the subject of bitter struggles among the Protestant hierarchy. But by the winter of 1969, every legislative step towards Catholic equality had been taken. The Government could reasonably look itself in the face without embarrassment for the first time since the creation of the Province. In the steps that had been taken, the framework of an equitable and civilised society had been laid. What was now needed, and seemed as far off as ever, was the flesh and blood of sanity and good will.

In the eyes of many Unionist back-benchers, the Chichester-Clark Administration had become no more than the mouthpiece of Westminster. With the formidable and serene figure of Oliver Wright stalking the corridors of Stormont Castle, Sir Arthur Young at police headquarters, and James Callaghan now making no secret of his strong personal commitment to knocking some sense into Northern Ireland, James Chichester-Clark's personal acceptability to the Unionist rank-and-file had waned very seriously indeed. Through the autumn ran the continuing thread of Unionist unrest, with the Government seeming increasingly isolated from those on whom it had to rely for power. On October 7th, a young liberal Unionist M.P., Richard Ferguson, announced that he was resigning his South Antrim seat. He had had a nervous breakdown, and some of his family were near to collapse. Ferguson's constituency party, who had earlier passed a vote of no confidence in him, had hounded him literally to the point of breakdown for his support of liberal policies. Telephone calls and letters from local Protestant extremists, unrelenting pressure on every side, had crushed his will to resist. And while Ferguson's decision provoked an outcry among the moderates, across the Province more and more local constituency parties were forcing the pressure on Unionist M.P.s not only to fight the encroachments of Westminster and the proposals of the Hunt Report, but to join battle with the Chichester-Clark Government. At the time of the spring election, a liberal Unionist organisation named the New Ulster Movement had been formed, to support Terence O'Neill and his policies. In November, a right-wing Unionist group led by John Taylor demanded that members of the New Ulster Movement be ineligible for membership of the Unionist Party. The issue itself became only the spearhead of a long series of right-wing struggles. William Craig, as his public pronouncements became wilder, only gained popularity with the Party rank-and-file.

During the autumn, there seemed serious question as to whether Chichester-Clark could survive the growing right-wing storm. Beyond that, there was the critical dilemma of whether the Government at Westminster would accept the premiership of a right-winger—certainly, at no price could they afford to tolerate Craig, although his chance of gaining the Leadership were still mercifully slender. Chichester-Clark indeed weathered the tide, but while the right-wingers became temporarily more subdued, the feelings remained. If the Catholics, still relatively silent, took to the streets once more, there could be little doubt that Chichester-Clark's personal position within his Party would be shattered. Against a background of simmering Unionist feeling and deep division within the Party, Chichester-Clark's Government was struggling on with a dangerously narrow base of support.

Meanwhile the Civil Rights movement, however, was even more deeply divided, and fraught with personal clashes of will between every element in its political make-up. The Catholics, with their wagon rolling on a surge of triumph, were at least as uncertain as the Unionists in which direction their future should lie. The demands of the militants for more and faster reform and action from the Government became on the one hand, less heeded by the mass of the Catholic community, now preoccupied with recovering some sense of normality out of the chaos—and on the other the cause of increasing internal dissention. The wheel had come full circle: Dr Conn McCluskey, whose Campaign for Social Justice in Dungannon had done so much to set the Civil Rights movement in motion, was now warning that the extremist elements in the Civil Rights Association Executive were threatening the very fibre of Catholic protest. John Hume and Ivan Cooper still had the respect of many of the Catholic community, but increasingly little real power. Cooper, however, was making a name for himself within the framework of Stormont politics. With Bernadette Devlin's local constituency association in Mid-Ulster more than a little disenchanted by her excesses, Cooper's name was already being mentioned as her possible successor at Westminster.

Miss Devlin herself had suffered a disastrous loss of prestige following her excesses in the Bogside, her wild speech-making both in America and in Britain, and her public contempt for the Westminster House of Commons as an institution. But in late autumn, well aware of this and alarmed at the possibility of losing such a critically useful instrument of propaganda, certain of her advisers urged her to change her tactics somewhat. She began once more to appear in the Commons when Ulster issues arose; she seemed to have accepted the need to play the game of conventional politics for at least some of the people some of the time. Her popularity among Ulster Catholics also gained one much-needed boost in December. By an extraordinarily ill-judged exercise in selective justice, Miss Devlin was charged on a number of counts for offences arising out of the Bogside riot, and appeared at Londonderry Magistrates' Court, where she was sentenced to six months' imprisonment, subject to appeal. Sir Dingle Foot, Q.C., conducted her defence, seeking less to contradict the evidence about her activities than to show that in the circumstances then prevailing, it was justified. The trial received massive publicity in Northern Ireland, and at a moment when her fortunes were seriously in decline, Miss Devlin's prestige was considerably redeemed. In the witness box, she gave nothing away. At her wittiest and most defiant, she parried every thrust from the somewhat pedantic prosecuting counsel to the unsuppressed amusement of the packed Catholic audience. Miss Devlin, while seemingly down, is certainly not yet out.

And while in their meetings and private councils, the Civil Rights leaders argued about policy—for when so many specific grievances had been answered, it became so much harder to crystallise the less clearly-defined ones—in the streets it was still the Protestants whom Ulster watched with apprehension. As new troops arrived to replace units being relieved, it was difficult for the recent arrivals to understand the alarm and fears as shoppers and workers went about their business every day. The army aimed gradually to reduce its visible presence, while still keeping strong reserves available. But if Ulstermen still treat 1688 as if it were yesterday, the events of August and October were only hours ago. Bitter memories remained. The Protestants raged when members of the militant organisations were given drastic sentences for their part in the riots, and others were jailed for the pipeline explosions of the spring. They were further incensed by renewed Catholic pressure for the Unionist Party to break its links with the Orange Order. With the astonishing silence of Ian Paisley, their most formidable spokesman was lost. With only spasmodic minor Catholic demonstrations and meetings, the most direct provocations were reduced. With the battles over the major reforms ended, the issues around which they had joined battle were lost. But they had established a fund of deep-seated resentment and fear which would not disappear in a matter of weeks and months. While every passing day of peace was time won, it would be a very long time indeed before Ulster could go to bed at night certain that all would still be well in the morning.

For those who had to count the cost of what had passed, the bill was frightening. When every claim had been met and every debt paid, the Government would be liable for up to £12 million. Ironically, one of the most sizeable items on the account was that for the call-up of the 'B' Specials, who were paid for their duty. Mobilising the Specials had cost nearly £480,000. After frantic efforts, many of those who had lost their homes in the riots were now being rehoused, although some were condemned to months in trailer-homes, and others had been forced to spend weeks in the hastily improvised refugee centres in schools and church halls. The army, in the interests of good relations with the local people, had set their engineers to work building Adventure Playgrounds and amenities on wasteland in parts of Belfast. The burnt skeletons of the factories and houses had now been removed from the streets, and plans were in train for rebuilding. One hundred and seventy homes had been destroyed in Belfast, and 370 damaged. Sixteen factories were gone, and throughout the riots some 2,000 people had been injured. Eight hundred police had been wounded. Even these figures are only part of the tale, since many more civilians, even some of those seriously injured, declined to be treated in hospitals.

Nor was Ulster easily to be able to forget what had passed; as the Scarman Tribunal sat in Londonderry, every day the papers carried details of the evidence being given by police, Catholics and reporters as to events in the Bogside in April; and Belfast was still to come. When Scarman originally set out to conduct his inquiries, it was assumed that he would be reporting by the end of the year. But as the Tribunal became bogged down in the incredible weight of evidence, accusation and counter-accusation, so the predictions lengthened. It now appears unlikely that any report can appear much before the end of 1970; by then, it will be too late to take much useful action on his conclusions. To some observers, it would have been agreeable to see more definite and speedier analysis of the behaviour of certain policemen in Belfast in August.

Yet once again, the question arose of the value of pursuing "justice" beyond a certain point. In the tragedy of Ulster, so many of those engaged on every side committed incredible crimes that it became almost meaningless to attempt to sort the guilty from the innocent. The morale of the R.U.C. had been weakened to danger point by the massive criticism heaped upon its officers. There may even now be those serving in their ranks who by rights could be convicted on charges of manslaughter. Yet to have indicted every man who committed an offence during 1969 might have shattered the remains of the force beyond recovery. This may prove a case in which the ultimate interests of Ulster have been served by passing over some of the unhappier incidents at moments of violent stress. The province had to be policed, and at moments in August, the situation seemed to be approaching at which even this would become quite impossible. Now, with the aid of Lord Hunt, James Callaghan, and Sir Arthur Young, some kind of basis for operation has been salvaged and is being strengthened.

In the autumn of 1969, observers studying the progress of Ulster after the battle of the Shankill looked for, and expected, some further dramatic punctuation marks in a climacteric year. But none came. It would be tempting to say that the battle for Civil Rights in Northern Ireland ended not with a bang, but with an endless series of pops. In one sense, perhaps this is true. Catholics may yet suffer months and years of problems and set-backs before all the legislative action turns to reality and the hatreds and bitterness of 1969 can be forgotten. But while the militants still clamour for renewed pressure and action, it is difficult to see what at present the Government could do, save press ahead with the policies already in operation; and above all, seek some means of finding the communication and showing the goodwill they still seem so hesitant in handling. During the autumn, there was great pressure from both London and the Protestants for the Catholics to show some reciprocal feeling for the concessions and efforts that have been made. There might be more public pledges of loyalty to the Constitution; less of the perpetual needling of Government and Protestants; a truce in spirit as well as in action. Certainly, the Catholics have been slow to accept the need for this as part of the price of victory. But having been forced to fight so hard for what they have won, having struggled through so much anger and violence and bitterness, it is inevitably a slow process to agree that peace must arrive. For fifty years, and more, they had suffered the enemy. From October 1968, they had fought him to a standstill, and by resort to the most drastic tactics and after the most bitter struggle, they had won. It is only on the playing fields of boys' clubs that men are urged to accept victory gracefully. The Catholics were spoiled by triumph, and indeed lacked a real appreciation of what they had gained. But in the climate of Ulster in 1969, this is not to be wondered at. Too much blood had been spilled for either side to find it easy to kiss and make up. The surprise was not that relative tranquillity was marred by continuing anger and petty recrimination, but that peace of any kind was restored at all.

Ulster will have to wait to discover the full effect of all that has been set in motion and promised towards reform. The army will be the only effective guarantee of peace for many months to come. Catholics and Protestants may yet seek to renew the battle around their mutual loathing. But while before October 1968, Ulster was by law, decree, and custom a society disgracefully in-equitable to one-third of its citizens, by the conclusion of 1969, the opportunity for a new society had been created.

II

CONCLUSION

W HEN I FIRST went to Ulster to begin the painful journey towards understanding what created the events and personalities of
1969, I not only knew nothing about the province, I had no sympathies or loyalties of any description—only, possibly, a strong
dislike for the principles of the Catholic religion. But as the
weeks went by and personal experience broadened, a detectable
feeling for the Catholics crept more and more prominently into
everything I wrote, coupled with a dislike for the Protestants, the
Unionists, and much of which they stood for. Perhaps the turning
point came in September, when in the hotel where the correspondents were staying, we heard that a Protestant mob had
gathered to petrol-bomb a Catholic pub in the Donegal Road of
Belfast. Half a dozen of us leapt into a car, parked near by, and
strolled singly into the crowd, who were standing around survey-
ing their handiwork, watched from a safe distance by a dozen or
so police. Suddenly, two Protestants grabbed me by the arm and
asked if I was a reporter. I tried to mumble an answer and slip
away, but they knew they had me cornered. One moment, there
were two men yelling at me about the Pope-loving English press,
the next moment there were sixty, pushing and shoving and
shouting around me. I was more frightened than I had ever been
in the worst of the riots and shooting battles. Then, two policemen forced their way through and with some difficulty hauled me
out, and told me to lose myself quickly. Shaken and furious, I
went back to the hotel.

It had been a trivial incident, far less serious than those around
several colleagues, some of whom were badly damaged. But from
that day, I found it impossible to regard the Protestants with anything resembling dispassion. I watched them hammering at the
British Army, petrol-bombing Catholic houses. I heard Protestant
"moderates" in the country areas expressing their fear and unconcealed dislike of the Catholics and their demands. I saw

Chichester-Clark in the moments of crisis talking like an irritated schoolmaster at a cricket match. And on the other hand, I went into the Catholic bars in the Falls Road area to be treated only with cheerful friendliness. I was in Divis Flats during the August riot, watching the police lines across the road as the Catholics could see them. And I never found it possible to sympathise with the Unionist Government's attitude to most Catholic demands.

In all this, I am merely seeking to admit a bias. I hope it did not extend too far. Catholics and Civil Rights leaders became, as 1969 went on, at least as proficient liars and masters of deception as their opponents. Catholic accounts of many of the major events simply ignore and omit any inconvenient facts about a situation. And while it will be years before anything like the full facts are known about many of the events and personalities, I have tried hard in this book to do reasonable justice to everyone. Only the evidence of my own eyes may sometimes have obscured aspects of the broader picture.

At the outset of the struggle for Civil Rights in Northern Ireland, the Catholic demands were blatantly reasonable, and could only be resisted in a society dedicated to the principle of living in history. In their methods of expressing their feelings, the Catholics sometimes exceeded the bounds of order. But the Protestants and the Unionists, in their perpetual heel-dragging and outright opposition, dwarfed any shortcomings in the Catholic camp. Terence O'Neill,* while an extremely able man, was very slow in adjusting his own pace to that of the situation so suddenly created. But it is probably fair to say that even had he made a sounder appreciation of the strength of the Catholic forces, his end would have been the same: the Unionists had condemned him from the moment he began to inch towards acceptance of reform.

In the end, it had to be the Government at Westminster who turned the tide; without their influence, it is difficult to see how the Protestants could ever have been induced to accept the kind of radical reform so desperately needed in Ulster. And the moderate Unionists' judgement proved accurate in one respect: James Chichester-Clark, while lacking any qualities of leadership or initiative, proved in the end the least objectionable instrument for Westminster policy that could be found within the Party's ranks. Given his "shove in the right direction", and kept under

* He became Lord O'Neill of the Maine in the New Year Honours.

constant surveillance and pressure, Chichester-Clark was conscientious, hard-working, and reasonable. As the months went on, there were signs that he was growing into the job. Hampered by a traditional Ulster Protestant upbringing and an innate conservatism, he would never be a great leader. But his speeches became markedly less Protestant-orientated and his confidence in public increased considerably. No one—except the Catholics—could ever hate Chichester-Clark: he is plainly much too decent a man—honourable, courteous, self-effacing, bluffly gentle. Had he become anything but an Ulster Unionist politician, he would probably have enjoyed a peaceful, amiable, quietly popular country life. But having put himself in the forefront of the battle line, he had to suffer the consequences of being judged not as a pleasant country squire, but as a politician. The ideal circumstances for meeting Chichester-Clark would be at drinks before Sunday lunch at his house in County Derry—for a chat about the pheasant shooting. It was less propitious to have to see him only for a discussion about slaughter and destruction in the streets of Belfast.

In the centre of the fray throughout 1968 and 1969 stood the Royal Ulster Constabulary. They became increasingly a part of the battle between Protestants and Catholics, a continuous source of grievance to the Civil Rights leaders and the ghettos. The greatest problem of the police, of course, was that while the sudden dart of a Protestant petrol-bomber remained sunk in vague anonymity and obscurity, the misbehaviour of a policeman was an immediately memorable and definable act. Throughout the riots, there was a hard core of police who without question behaved disgracefully. And while their colleagues might not be guilty of the same misdemeanours, they were equally reluctant to interfere with those who were. R.U.C. men, on a number of well-documented occasions, also showed a clear lack of determination in preventing Protestant onslaughts on the Catholics.

Yet having said all this, one must remark again that the great majority of police were plainly reasonable, responsible, and decent men. They showed, when properly led and organised, outstanding courage, restraint, and sense of duty. Their tragedy was that very often, they were atrociously led and quite undirected. Their senior officers seemed to lack powers of leadership and even more, any conception of what riot control was all about, a lesson easily learnt in part from a study of the American Riot Report. The issuing of machine guns to police in Belfast in

August will remain a disgraceful blot on the senior hierarchy of the R.U.C. Many of the police who were engaged were neither malicious nor vicious, only ill-led and entirely wrongly controlled. Thus far, it has been the policemen who were seen to kick Catholics or break windows who have incurred censure. It is probably more appropriate to look higher up the ladder for those really responsible for the worst police disasters of 1969. But now, with Sir Arthur Young at the head of them and the Hunt Report behind them, there is no reason why in the future they should not become a police force as good as any in Britain.

Then there are the vast majority of the people of Ulster—the "moderates". Perhaps it is important now to re-emphasise one key aspect of the Ulster crisis that was easily lost in 1969: that throughout, only a small fraction of the population were ever directly engaged in the politics or on the streets. Only Belfast and a handful of other towns saw serious unrest and violence. Only, at most, 30,000 people ever had direct personal experience of the battles, although many more were passive spectators. This left the remainder of Ulster's $1\frac{1}{2}$ million people sitting on the sidelines. Many of them raised their voices at one time or another pleading for peace and sanity. But very, very few of them ever did the slightest thing to bring it closer. Among the Protestants, there was never the social pressure that should have existed to drive Paisley and his kind into the wilderness where they belonged. Among the Catholics, there was never any attempt to sooth the most alarming Protestant fears. When Bernadette Devlin said: "I realised the task was not to free the Six Counties, but to start all over again the national revolution," she was allowed to remain uncontradicted, as one of the most prominently publicised Catholic spokesmen.

During the Northern Irish crisis, the press and television came in for the most violent criticism from the politicians and many of the "leaders of the community" in Ulster. Partially, this was because in an age when exploitation of the media is a key political weapon, the Catholics became adept at it, while the Protestants never began to understand its uses. But it was also true that on a number of occasions, the very presence of television cameras helped to create incidents that might otherwise have died away, while the reports of violence thrown daily in the faces of Ulstermen provoked many to thoughts of participation. Jack Lynch's August television speech was directly responsible for the Wednesday night Catholic riot in Belfast.

Television, by its very character, can only fit a tiny fraction of reality on to its screen, and yet make that fraction appear to be the whole. In this, television in 1969 did a disservice to Ulster by giving massive coverage to the riots, far less to the less dramatic aspects of the situation; similarly, the newspapers. But without the media, there is no shadow of doubt that the Catholic cause could never have triumphed either as speedily or as completely as it did. Many Ulstermen who raged about the press did so merely because the newspapers' sympathies lay pretty clearly with the Catholics and in favour of reform. The media gave short shrift to the failings of the Stormont Government and the excesses of the Protestants. In contrast with many of Ulster's other papers, admittedly smaller and less influential, the *Telegraph* in 1969 pressed constantly for reform, peace and reason, in that order. Every English correspondent in Ulster relied heavily on its columns for information and background; and any Ulsterman who read it throughout the year would have been left with the most accurate available account of everything happening around him. It was only Ulster's tragedy that by summer, truth as such had ceased to exist. Every man had his own unshakeable truth, and was guided by it.

When the final accounting is done for 1969, it is likely that much emphasis will be attached not only to the isolation of the men in government from those whom they ruled, but to the failure of the politicians to make use of such assets as they had. In other words, when a measure was adopted to meet a specific Catholic demand, it was allowed merely to become submerged in the welter of debate already surrounding the next point at issue. There was never any concerted effort to present Government action in a positive way; the Cabinet's decisions emerged merely as belated responses to Catholic initiatives; it was always the Government's efforts to pick up the pieces after the glass shattered that made the headlines, conveying an impression of an even greater infirmity of will than in fact existed. To some extent, this was inevitable when until October 1968, Ulster politics had been conducted at the level of an English County Council. When the crisis came, neither the men nor the machinery were fitted or geared to cope with disaster on such a scale. Of all the men in the Stormont, only Terence O'Neill, Brian Faulkner, and possibly Roy Bradford understood the scale of the situation, and possessed the political sophistication to deal with it. Faulkner, of them all, allowed himself to be misled into thinking that an understanding of the nature of the position enabled him to control it.

Faulkner made several serious attempts to gain power from October 1968 through 1969. On each occasion, his sense of timing and judgement failed him. He incurred widespread dislike and contempt for his manoeuvrings to outflank his rivals—and especially for his apparent indifference to which flank he approached them from. The tragedy was that had he avoided the temptation of personal bids for power, his prestige by the end of 1969 could have been unclouded. His evident top-rate ability as an administrator and planner both at the Ministries of Commerce and Development won the grudging admiration even of many Catholics. When he applied his mind to a problem, he usually emerged with a concise and comprehensive plan to deal with it. This skill alone, priceless in the sparsely-populated field of able Ulster politicians, could have made him the most useful single figure in the Stormont. Instead, by insisting on playing political games, he left a bitter taste of suspicion and mistrust among both politicians and observers.

But the very structure and tradition of Stormont made it unfitted to cope with a situation on the scale of 1969, and indeed when the British Government gave the province internal self-government, they can never have intended that Stormont should have to take decisions of such moment. Many of the difficulties of 1969 could never have come about had Westminster and the Unionists agreed sooner to a more liberal interpretation of the Government of Ireland Act. It seemed farcical that if Northern Ireland was to be the beneficiary of every advantage of being a part of the United Kingdom, the United Kingdom Government none the less had to hold its hand at the critical moments. Never has there been such a damning case against regional self-government as was presented by Stormont's conduct in 1969. At least, with luck, that lesson has been learnt, however painfully. Stormont was given powers out of all proportion to its proper importance, and beyond the responsibility of the kind of men available to exercise it. Ulster, 5,000 square miles of it, was allowed to become a major national problem because the Government of Britain could not step in and "put a stop to all this nonsense". One million Protestants were able to run their God's Little Acre in such a manner as to threaten a civil disaster; in England, Councils responsible for the welfare of far greater numbers of citizens can be obliged to accept Government policy on, say, education whether they like it or not.

All this, then, was the fruit of historical circumstance and lack of comprehension and decision on a fantastic scale. Somehow, the British Government managed to pull the chestnuts out of the fire. Perhaps in a few years it will be possible to look back on the Ulster crisis in a fresh and less magnified perspective. It was brought to life by the human issues and lives at stake, rather than by the real size of the personalities and population involved. Peace now is a very frail thing. Irrespective of the future of the Catholic leadership and the Civil Rights movement, the hate of Protestants and Catholics can break out once more at any time. The Catholics, in all this, can only have been reinforced in an emotional gaze towards the Irish Republic. And the Protestants, who know it and sense it, feel also the other irony of their own battle throughout 1969: that the British, whatever their politicians may say publicly, will shed very few tears indeed when that distant but inevitable day arrives, and Ulster and the Irish Republic are reunited as logic dictates.